BEA, BOAC & BALLOONS
A lifetime in aviation

by
Alec Jenkinson

By the same author:

BALLOONS AROUND THE WORLD–
A Register of Hot Air and Gas Balloons.
May 1975.

BALLOONS AROUND NEWBURY–
Twenty Adventurous Years.
December 1992.

Copyright © 1999 by Alec Jenkinson.

All rights reserved. Apart from any fair dealing for the purpose of private study, research, criticism or review, as permitted under the Copyright, Design and Patents Act 1988, no part of this publication may be reproduced, stored in a retrieval system, or transmitted in any form or by any means, electronic, electrical, chemical, mechanical, optical, photocopying, recording or otherwise, without prior written permission. All enquiries should be directed to the publisher.

British Library Cataloguing in Publication Data

ISBN   0 9503756 3 2

Published by:
Alec Jenkinson,
9 Orchard Court,
Malmesbury,
Wiltshire,
SN16 0ED,
England.

Design Consultant:
Barry Ketley

Printed by:
Hillman Printers (Frome) Ltd,
Frome,
Somerset,
BA11 4RW,
England.

Available through:
Midland Publishing Ltd,
24 The Hollow,
Earl Shilton,
Leicester,
LE9 7NA,
England.
Tel: 01455 847 815
Fax: 01455 841 805

Acknowledgements

This book has taken almost two years to assemble. It took this time to wade through all my diaries, notes and log books. To confirm the details were accurate I made contact with friends and acquaintances from years ago. As many lived overseas it was necessary to make some long-distance telephone calls. A joy for me was to hear again voices from the past and to learn how they had fared in life.

For their help and advice I am grateful to many people. My special thanks must go to: Roger Barrett, Kim Cameron, Rene Chong, Gill Eaton née Whiting, Chris Hall, Karren Hall, Barry Ketley, Anthony Robinson, Anthony Smith and Reggie Tristani née Le Geyt. Many others have given me encouragement to persevere and to them I am also indebted.

CONTENTS

Chapter 1	The years Nought to Thirteen	5
Chapter 2	School days in Bermuda	8
Chapter 3	My family	10
Chapter 4	The uncertain five years	11
Chapter 5	Training to be a BEA Flight Clerk	13
Chapter 6	Some log book entries from Jersey	17
Chapter 7	A winter flying around Scotland	21
Chapter 8	Life as a Flight Clerk at London Airport	25
Chapter 9	The year of expansion then cessation	32
Chapter 10	The BEA Ground Duty years	34
Chapter 11	Joining BOAC - and overseas postings	42
Chapter 12	On the ground but in the air	51
Chapter 13	Getting a licence to fly hot air balloons	53
Chapter 14	A lot of 'Firsts' crowded into 1973	61
Chapter 15	More home and away - for work or ballooning	68
Chapter 16	Still many activities despite some health problems	74
Chapter 17	A highly charged year and with speed - Concorde	79
Chapter 18	Australia and Yugoslavia - plus many others	84
Chapter 19	Eleven overseas trips plus the Bristol Balloon Fiesta	88
Chapter 20	Uganda and 12 countries yet fewer flying hours	93
Chapter 21	Visits to Eastern Europe plus USA World Championships	113
Chapter 22	Seventeen trips to Europe	117
Chapter 23	Transferred to Ground Duties within British Airways	121
Chapter 24	New house, new workplace and BA computer at home	126
Chapter 25	The years 1986 to 1999	130
Appendixes	Extracts from my logbooks	138
Index		157

1
THE YEARS NOUGHT TO THIRTEEN

Shakespeare was wrong. He wrote "There is a tide in the affairs of men ...". In my life there were three (high) tides and one low water. The peak times centre around aviation; flying with BEA in the 1950s, overseas postings and travel with BOAC and British Airways plus adventures with hot air ballooning in the 1970s. The 'low' years exist now as I have a slow decline with multiple sclerosis. Another saying goes "Thursday's child has far to go". For me this has been true. I visited 86 countries around the world. My log books show I crossed the Atlantic 85 times and flew across the Equator on 36 occasions. I can account for 2,944 flights and at least 5,410 flying hours, which means the total distance travelled as being more than two and a half million miles by land, sea and air.

This book recounts some of the highlights of my life.

It all began around tea-time on Thursday 24 August 1933 when I was born at 39 Kelly Street, Greenock, Renfrewshire, Scotland. A year later my parents, Alex and Eileen, moved to Brougham Street, Greenock where my brother Gordon Craig was born on 3 June 1935. I was baptised Alexander Kenneth but used a Scottish nickname, Sandy, to avoid confusion with my father's name. Seemingly I went to a convent school in Greenock for a year in 1937/38 but have no recollection of this.

My father who was an armaments officer with the Admiralty was posted to Gosport near Portsmouth in the summer of 1938 and we moved to 21 Fayre Road, Fareham, Hampshire. I attended Redlands Lane Junior School, which was less than a quarter of a mile from home (or 100 yards if we crawled through the broken fence). The only real memories are of the quarter pint bottle of milk we got at mid-morning, and later gas mask practice every Monday and the air-raid drills to the shelters in the school grounds.

In November 1941 my father was again posted but this time to Gibraltar. His passport shows him as a Government official and he embarked at Liverpool and presumably travelled in a convoy through the Bay of Biscay. During his stay on the Rock he sent us regular airmail type letters which were all read and passed by a censor.

In January 1942 my mother, grandmother, brother and I evacuated ourselves to the Isle of Arran in Scotland to avoid wartime air-raids. The journey north took more than 24 hours. It was a train from Fareham to Portsmouth, changed to another for London, Waterloo, taxi across London presumably to Kings Cross for an overnight Glasgow train. This steam engine had at least 2 enforced en route stops due to air-raid warnings. At Glasgow there was another change of rail station for a train to Ardrossan. Then on to a paddle steamer for the journey across the Firth of Clyde to Brodick on the Isle of Arran. Finally a taxi for the last 10 miles to Kilmorie.

Our home was a cottage attached to Ivy Bank farm. The accommodation was basic with no gas, no electricity and an indoor water tap although the main supply was an outdoor spigot. Some 25 yards away was the outside loo not far from a midden. Paraffin lamps gave us light and a coal fire provided heat for the rooms and cooking. We took regular walks to the beach to collect drift wood and coke to supplement our coal stock which if not rationed by supply was restricted by cost. There was very severe weather soon after our arrival and photos from a Brownie box camera show snow drifts up to window sill height.

It was an arable farm with fields of wheat, potatoes, kale and turnips. There were a dozen cows and scores of free-roaming chickens. With war-time double British Summer Time there was more than ample light for harvesting to continue on Arran until well after 11.00pm. The farmer let me drive the horse and cart between fields and barn. During the ploughing season I followed for days before asking if I could try my hand. Luckily the 2 Clydesdale horses knew how to walk in a straight line but my skill improved and I was only 9 years old. Could this have been the start of a character-trait to try anything and have a go ?

Apart from the tradition of 'First-Footing' on Ne'er Day (New Year's Day) there was a local custom that neighbours would visit each other in the morning and be greeted with a glass of ginger wine and shortbread biscuits. Although only youngsters Gordon and I followed this ritual and were given a few thimblefuls of the drink at a few nearby farmhouses.

A few other memories from the farm include turning the milk churn to make butter which was tedious but worthwhile. The gathering of potatoes was boring, dirty, cold and often wet. The type of potatoes grown were called Arran Pilot and Arran Banner presumably because they thrived in the local soil. Happiness for me was at a nearby farm at lambing time, seeing a foal stagger to its feet just minutes after birth or watching calves being born.

Lagg was a small nearby village which had only an hotel and a combined post office/general store. Half a mile away was the beach which was basically pebble with little sand. A few hardy holiday makers visited in summer but the water was never very warm. At nesting time I collected from the pebbles oystercatchers' eggs and had them fried for breakfast and if lucky, sometimes for a change also lapwings' eggs. Kilmorie was a sparsely populated rural area and the school had 2 classrooms with at most 15 pupils. My mother used to deliver the post 3 days a week and had to walk between 6 and 10 miles on each round. Weekly a mobile shop visited each cluster of farms where goods could be bought against the ration card.

My father left Gibraltar on 25 January 1944 but the ship had to wait off the Azores for a convoy escort back to British waters. When he landed at Port Glasgow a fortnight later he brought with him bunches of bananas. This was the first time I had seen or tasted bananas since before the war.

In March 1944 we returned to the same house in Fareham. The nearby cities of Portsmouth and Southampton had been badly damaged by air-raids but Fareham was relatively unscathed. However one lunch-time that summer I can recall seeing a single rogue German bomber drop two bombs on a nearby naval training base, HMS *Collingwood*.

My brother and I went back to Redlands Lane School. Memories from this era include being made a prefect and getting caned with a ruler across the palm of my hand for some innocent misdemeanour (talking in class was considered naughty at that time). The BBC introduced schools broadcasts and these lessons by wireless (radio) were interesting when reception allowed. A year later I was accepted as a day student at St. John's College, Southsea (Portsmouth). This involved a bus journey of about 30 minutes. I was bold enough to persuade one regular bus conductor to let me ring the bell at the en route stops.

The College was run by the de la Salle Brothers and took 200 students of whom about a quarter were boarders. To avoid the refectory lunch (I still hate sago pudding) a friend and I used to sneak out to a 'British restaurant' for soup and pudding which cost just a few pennies. As this was near Southsea Pier we either played dare-devil with the waves on the beach –wet feet were common– or went to the amusement arcade to see if we could find out what the butler really saw!

In Fareham the now disused air-raid shelters (where we had often spent uncomfortable nights during the blitz) became play areas after school. To celebrate the end of the war there were street parties to commemorate VE and VJ days and I can still clearly remember the tables laden with delicious goodies.

Habits and hobbies: Probably the most consistent aspect in life has been my strong desire to keep lists, records and statistics. The information in these pages has come mainly from 42 diaries, 7 passports, 3 published balloon books, 4 personal flying logs, countless reports and articles printed mostly in balloon journals plus umpteen files of correspondence, newspaper cuttings and unsorted miscellanea.

The habit started in 1940 when I kept a daily list of the names of the BBC Home Service news readers of the one and six o'clock news bulletins. Names included Stuart Hibbert, Alvar Liddell and others. The diaries and log books record details (dates/ times/ routings/ aircraft registrations) of 90% of the numerous aircraft flights I made.

Stamp collecting has been an interest on and off through life. It started with a sixpenny mixed pack from Woolworths when I was 11 years old and stopped a few years ago. I carried many different British and overseas commemorative first flight covers in aircraft and balloons.

Across the street there was a girl with a bicycle. I was keen to learn how to ride it and had lessons in the corner of a field, in return for which we played 'Doctors and Nurses'. A few months later for my 12th birthday my parents bought me a second-hand bike.

Train spotting for a penny platform ticket was fun with my 'Ian Allan' numbers book. After many polite requests one train driver allowed me to ride on the footplate of his tanker-class engine on the 7 mile Fareham to Gosport line. To pull the chain for the steam whistle gave me a feeling of exhilaration on several journeys I made.

For a few years some school friends and I collected birds eggs–from memory my total was 20 different varieties. During at least one season we exchanged duplicates but then decided 'finders would be keepers'. Collecting butterflies and 'mounting' them with a pin to a board was another fascination. There was a plague of the Cabbage White variety and these were caught and killed to protect their grubs from eating our garden greens.

My father was a dedicated vegetable grower and from his allotments we had a constant supply of truly fresh organic produce during and after the war years. To keep 2 manure pits in active use Gordon and I would collect horse droppings from the street or cowpats from nearby fields and earn 3d a bucketful. At times I enjoyed helping my father spread and dig in the compost, then water the plants from a nearby well. Dad grew many rows of excellent runner beans and any surplus was used as barter with other growers.

Dorothy our milk delivery girl used a horse and cart which I was allowed to drive on non-main roads. Halfway through the 6 hour round a fresh supply was obtained from the farm. On the cart some milk was distributed by the gill measure direct from a churn. Although a rationed product my reward for helping was an extra pint for our house and sixpence for me.

Two other memories of those post-war years include the annual August Bank Holiday gymkhana staged in nearby fields when a group of us had a pre-burrowed trench in a hedge to gain entry and avoid paying. The excitement of free entrance made the show more enjoyable. The other was travelling by train with my father to Fratton Park football ground on some Saturday afternoons to see First Division Portsmouth. My brother, although more active in sports, preferred to play at the local recreation ground rather than attend the professional matches.

For nearly a year I was a member of a scout group before joining the local junior Red Cross. The main attraction of this was to learn to play the bugle. Thinking I might have musical talent my parents bought a violin and I had 2 tedious lessons a week. Within 12 months we had moved to Bermuda.

Fareham, Hampshire. Me on my father's bike, Summer 1940. Note my father's tin helmet and square case containing his gas mask.

Isle of Arran, Scotland, February 1942. My brother (right) and I during severe snowy weather with drifts up to window-sill height. We had no school for more than 3 weeks as the classrooms were without heat.

2
SCHOOL DAYS IN BERMUDA

Life was to change dramatically when my father secured a much sought after posting to the British Dockyard in Bermuda and he left England in November 1946. The winter months that followed brought severe weather conditions in Britain with weeks of sub zero temperatures and many blizzards. It was therefore a double delight for my mother, brother and I to leave Southampton on 13 April 1947 on the aged Cunard liner Aquitania for Bermuda via Halifax, Nova Scotia. This was the last Atlantic round trip by the Aquitania, before the breakers yard. The ship was still in its wartime troop carrying configuration and the accomodation was cramped and most uncomfortable.

Ten days later the Aquitania anchored off Bermuda and we were taken ashore by tender to a new life in the aptly named Sandy's Parish of Bermuda. Our first home was called Scaur Lodge which had been the garrison headquarters for a now obsolete fort emplacement. The two storey building was dilapidated but we stayed there for about three months before moving to a bungalow nearer the dockyard. The address was 'Anstruther' West Side, Somerset where we spent the next three years. Built on the edge of a small cluster of buildings it was only a hundred yards from a delightful beach and only a mile from the village of Mangrove Bay.

Within weeks of arriving my brother and I were enrolled at Saltus Grammar School located just outside the capital, Hamilton. This was the only truly recognised learning place for boys on the island. In order to get there we had to cycle 3 miles to the dockyard and then board a ferry for a 30 minute crossing to Hamilton harbour. There were about 20 boys and girls from dockyard families who used this ferry (the girls went to a convent school). The boat ride was a chance to do our homework, to crib or even get up to mischief - but I think that is best forgotten.

Bermuda was a British colony and as recently as 1995 the inhabitants voted by referendum to continue their colonial status. During our period there about 40 families exercised major control over most aspects of life on the islands. Their sons attended Saltus before going to American or British universities. At morning assembly we sometimes sang 'Jerusalem' and the words "on England's green and pleasant land" seemed odd to me, but maybe not in a colonial setting. I usually achieved above average results in most subjects but a favourite was the debating society club. Here I learnt to speak in public without fear. This confidence has remained with me throughout life and I can still talk too much even today!

On 20 October 1947 a fairly major hurricane hit Bermuda with the eye of the storm passing almost overhead and causing tens of thousands of pounds worth of damage. Most of the local cedar trees were uprooted and destroyed. Our house was unscathed. During the hour long lull in the centre of the storm my father, Gordon and I went to the nearby bay. The sea looked

My brother, Grandmother and I pictured near Fareham in the Autumn of 1945. This derelict site had been used by the US Army as a base for their smoke-making machines. The foul-smelling smog covered the area to conceal targets from enemy aircraft.

Bermuda. Taken with my mother outside St Joseph's Church in early 1948 where Gordon and I were altar servers.

vicious as the waves crashed against the rocks, but there was no wind. The trees were almost stationary yet overhead the low clouds were moving very fast. When the wind started to pick up from another direction we ran for home.

Gordon and I became altar servers at St. Joseph's Catholic Church. The Canadian parish priest was Father Donald McPherson. He probably had more influence in developing and moulding my character than anyone else. I persuaded him to introduce High Mass with all its Latin trimmings once a month and I started writing short articles for the monthly parish newsletter. This involvement with the church and its liturgy almost certainly led to my entering a seminary for the priesthood two years after returning to England.

Father McPherson was a keen drummer and sometimes had jam-sessions with personnel from the nearby US air base. This was interesting as I used his wire-recorder (tape recorders were not available then) to mix the input of sounds. As a sixteen year old the assertive side of my character was starting to show as I helped organise several church bazaars and other functions. Was I maybe becoming too outgoing and bossy?

Apart from a variable indoor and outdoor cinema in Somerset there was very little local entertainment. Father decided to stage a Black and White Minstrel Show mixing a series of well-worn jokes with traditional Al Jolsen songs. There were 9 of us in the cast and my role was in the chorus and exchanging banter. It was a great success and repeated a year later in October 1949. The rehearsals at the church rectory together with other musical evenings annoyed my parents and maybe reduced my school study. But to me they were happy times.

Other interests in Bermuda, apart from swimming and messing about in boats included helping my father make colour transparency photos for mail order sale to Americans. Radio fascinated me and I took part in quiz programmes on the local station, ZBM Radio Bermuda. I spent hours listening to American radio stations and listing their identification call signs such as WWVA Wheeling, West Virginia.

Private cars for personal use were only just being imported to Bermuda the year we arrived. The favoured model was the Austin Devon. One of my school friends had illegally learnt to drive. This was a challenge for me and I secretly started to drive a small pick-up van. When my father found out he decided to let me (unofficially) drive his Francis-Barnett moped on quiet lanes.

Aviation, which was later to dominate my life held no interest in those days. However in 1948 my father and I went to Kindley Field (then an American air base) to say goodbye to a school teacher. We walked across the tarmac to the aircraft steps (airport security had not yet been invented!). We were then moved away whilst the 4 engines spluttered into life. From memory it was a Pan American Grace aircraft and therefore probably a DC4. This was my first contact with an aeroplane. During the period 1948-49 two Tudor aircraft flying the London-Azores-Bermuda-South America route vanished without trace in the Bermuda area. British South American Airways (BSAA) soon ceased operations and was merged with BOAC in July 1949.

By 1950 the British Government decided to run down and then close the Bermuda dockyard. After three and a half years on the island we boarded the liner Georgic bound for Liverpool via Cork Harbour, Ireland. The date was 14 September 1950.

3
MY FAMILY

My father was the 4th born in a family of 6 children. Until his marriage he lived at the family home at 92 Dunlop Street, Greenock. His early ambition to become a school teacher was dashed at interviews when his nervous speech impediment, a slight stammer, became evident. Instead he joined the government naval torpedo factory as a civilian on the clerical side. That decision had far reaching and long term affects not only for him but for all of us.

Quick promotion eluded my father but he was happy, easy-going although somewhat introvert (probably the stammer) with a love of the outdoor life. He played soccer and golf and enjoyed family walks, seaside picnics, long bicycle rides plus his gardening. With excellent handwriting he kept meticulous lists and records - a habit I obviously inherited. On 31 October 1958 my father had a major operation at the Dunfermline and West Fife Hospital to remove a canccrous growth from his stomach. He appeared to recover completely but the condition recurred about 18 months later. After a further operation he suffered much pain and distress before dying on 05 October 1960. Today I harbour a deep regret that I never got to know my father better.

My mother and her brother were born at Wigan in Lancashire. The family moved to Gourock, Scotland and my mother admits to being a bit of a "tom-boy" at school. This strong and often forceful characteristic is still there now (in 1999) and she is aged 91. A recent medical report described her as "fiercely independent" but I think the word "stubborn" also applies. My mother was more sociable than my father and for many years enjoyed working - mostly in the nursing profession.

As brothers Gordon and I were and still are very different. During our growing years we were given a lot of latitiude partly attributable to a semi-nomadic life. Gordon was scolded more than I and Mum tried to keep a rein on his love to play football at every opportunity. We rarely played together, almost never argued or had fights and whilst I accepted and tried to achieve at school he was a bit of a rebel. His career was in the dockyards at Portsmouth and Rosyth (Fife) until enforced early retirement a few years ago.

"Ga-ga" was the baby name I used for my maternal grandmother. She favoured and spoilt me. Inevitably there was a family row and Gran moved out to stay with relatives and friends. I was 17 years old but kept contact with and frequently saw her until she died in Southport Hospital in July 1976, aged 95 years.

Above: A family group taken in the summer of 1940 in the front garden of our home at Fareham, Hampshire.

Left: My Grandmother and I in a studio portrait during a visit to London in August 1961.

4
THE UNCERTAIN FIVE YEARS

After Bermuda the priority for me was "what to do with my life ?". Partly because of my love for writing and drawing my parents chose architecture. A small firm in Southampton agreed to accept me as an articled apprentice for 2 years. It was early October 1950 when I started to commute by train from Fareham to Southampton using a weekly season ticket in a third class carriage. For a short time train numbers were again a hobby. Within a year my interest in architecture started to wane and evening lectures on Doric columns and the like became boring. Finally in August 1952 by mutual agreement I left the firm.

During those 2 years the Church had a strong influence on me - both spiritually and socially. With more than 20 teenagers in the Fareham parish there seemed a need to have an active youth club. By the summer of 1951 the church hall was renovated and became the social centre on 4 evenings a week. Initially there was just a tea and biscuit stall with a ping-pong table and a darts board. Later some parishioners donated a gramophone and some 78 rpm records. Most of us took part in dancing lessons which consisted mostly of the old fashioned ballroom dances.

Next I helped organise a football team to play in a junior league based in the area. Our church team never did very well but the away games by charabanc were popular and well supported.

A newly ordained curate Father Patrick Murphy-O'Connor came to the parish in 1951 and we had long discussions over a 12 month period on whether I should dedicate my life to the priesthood. Bishop John Henry King of Portsmouth was approached and agreed to accept me as a candidate for his diocese. It was necessary for me to study at the late vocations theological college at Campion House, Osterley, Middlesex.

In September 1952 I set off to begin a new life. Father Clement Tigar, a Jesuit who ran the College, greeted nearly 60 new students. The 2 or 3 year course consisted primarily of theology, philosophy, English, Latin and Greek. The regime was fairly strict with basic dormitory style accommodation spread over 5 houses.

The ages of the students ranged from early 20s to mid 50s. Their former occupations included policemen, van drivers, teachers, ex-military and even ex-non Catholic church ministers.

A typical day would be:

0605:	Rise, wash and shave in cold water
0640:	Meditation and Mass
0745:	Breakfast in the refectory
0815:	Making beds and cleaning rooms
0845-1250:	Studies in various class rooms with a mid-morning collective cocoa break
1300:	Lunch followed by free period
1430:	Working in the vegetable garden or other selected chores
1630:	Tea
1700:	Revision and homework in the community hall
1830:	Supper - some free time
2000:	More studies or on one night a week, half an hour was allocated for a bath
2110:	To the chapel for evening prayers until 2145
2215:	Lights out

There was a 'Magnum Silencium' (i.e. a total ban on talking) between 2110 and after breakfast the following morning.

There was a voluntary rota to go to Speakers Corner at Hyde Park on Sunday afternoons to recite on our knees the 15 decades of the Rosary. Some passing Catholics would join in. It was rare for us to be heckled by anyone in the crowd yet we were often within hailing distance of some of the 'fringe speakers'.

One Sunday afternoon a group of us went to a London cinema to see the film 'War of the Worlds'. I was one of several who suffered short term distress, which may have been caused by our singular way of living and thinking.

Once a year Father Tigar had an open-day to which students' relatives and friends and especially the college benefactors were invited. Lunch and afternoon tea were provided with tours of the grounds, study rooms, dormitories, in fact everywhere. My contribution was to produce a watered-down version of the Bermuda style Black and White Minstrel show.

My organising trait led me to arrange a special Mass at the Greek Orthodox Church in London with approval of course. The purpose was to let us experience the differences between the Greek and Roman Catholic services and to receive Holy Communion under both kinds i.e. both the Host and the Wine. (This was not allowed to the laity in our church at that time).

About one third of the students failed to finish the course for various reasons, usually the realisation that they did not have a vocation. I was in this category during my 3rd year after the Easter retreat.

In early May 1955 I left Campion House. With a cool homecoming at Fareham I realised future decisions were mine–it was my life. During previous summer holidays I had trained and qualified as a waiter, in full silver service, at the 5 star Linden Hall Hydro Hotel at Boscombe, Bournemouth. Therefore I left home and went to the hotel which was hard work with long hours. I used my one rest day to take local tourist excursions. One such was a day cruise from Weymouth to Guernsey. During the 2 hours ashore the island looked beautiful and the tourist bureau gave us some literature. An advertisement extolling 'The Old Government House Hotel' in St Peter Port attracted me and I telephoned to see if there was a vacancy. With no guarantee of work I took the mail boat to Guernsey in mid June and got an immediate interview and was accepted as a waiter at the hotel. The standards were very high and I was very happy there.

After a month, however, nearby Jersey appeared to be a more lively Channel island. My first ever flight was therefore a 15 minute inter-island hop on a British European Airways (BEA) DC3-Dakota aircraft on Monday 18 July 1955. The registration was probably G-AMDB (based on a scruffy piece of paper I found years later with a baggage label). Flight number was almost certainly BE 774 (as it was an afternoon departure). The St Brelades Bay Hotel on Jersey had a good reputation and the next day I joined as a waiter. Unlike the decorum at Guernsey this hotel had a frenetic atmosphere especially in the kitchen area where many of the staff were excitable Italians. Not surprisingly by August I had moved to the smaller serene and luxury 'Links Hotel' at Grouville. When the main tourist season was over I was retained as a waiter for the off-season golfing visitors.

It was 7 years earlier, when in Bermuda that I had become a self taught car driver. Now I wanted to take official driving lessons and I passed the test with an All Groups Licence in September 1955.

Denis Troy who was a former student at Osterley lived on the island. I made contact with him and we became friends. He had an aunt and uncle with a house on the outskirts of Paris and we travelled there to stay for a week from 29 September. We visited the main tourist attractions including of course the Folies Bergere. Almost everything we did and saw was so strangely exciting that I can still clearly recall the events. This was my first real foreign holiday and was all the more memorable for that.

Two days before Christmas I was in church helping the local priest with Denis and family to prepare the crib and overhead lights. The next event is like a Charlie Chaplin film script. I climbed to the third rung of a stepladder. The connecting rope broke. The ladder collapsed outwards. I fell inwards. There was a crash. To protect my face I lifted my left arm upwards. My face was undamaged. My left arm was fractured. It was a painful Christmas.

Four months earlier the Admiralty had posted my father to Rosyth dockyard in Fife. To recuperate from my fracture I flew on a BEA DC3 from Jersey to Edinburgh via London and Birmingham. The date was 27 December 1955. At Dunfermline Hospital the next day an x-ray showed the fracture of the radius had been wrongly set by Jersey Hospital. Dunfermline re-set and re-plastered the arm. Luckily my right arm was in good fettle to lift many glasses to celebrate the Scottish New Year.

In early March 1956 I said good-bye to my parents and headed south. Using trains I travelled to Southampton and boarded a BEA Dakota for the one hour flight to Jersey. I soon had a temporary job driving a van delivering bread and rolls to hotels in the St Helier area. On 11 April there was an advertisement in the Jersey Evening Post seeking staff to work for BEA at Jersey airport on a summer only basis. The advert listed vacancies for staff on ground duties or as cabin attendants. I phoned immediately and was given an interview time for the following day.

5
TRAINING TO BE A BEA FLIGHT CLERK

Thursday 12 April 1956 at 1115 was the start of the first 'high tide' in my life. Shortly after an interview I was accepted as a cabin attendant, called a Flight Clerk, to fly to and from the mainland until October. The salary was £5.17.6d a week plus £2.0.0. a week flying pay. On Sunday 29 April eight of us flew on BE701 an Elizabethan aircraft from Jersey to London Airport to start a 3 week induction and training course.

BEA had pre-booked our accommodation at two private houses in Ruislip on a dinner, bed and breakfast basis. Both landladies had a similar frugal outlook and identical house rules: no beer, no girls, no television. There was the sitting room with a radio or we could read, study or even play cards. If we went out the night curfew began at 2230 when the front door was locked. I thought it was perhaps typical of a suburban B & B place.

We travelled by bus to Hatton Cross at the south-east corner of the London Airport (LAP) engineering base. There was a short walk passing the 'Green Man' pub to get to the Viking Centre which was the principal training unit for all staff in BEA. The centre was a cluster of at least ten Nissen huts divided into classrooms or other training functions such as flight simulators. The complex had one major drawback. The buildings were less than 300 feet directly below the glide path to Runway 28 Left which was barely a mile away. Many propeller aircraft made more than enough noise to disrupt lessons and concentration.

Our course emphasised safety and survival. Nearby there were mock aircraft frames for us to try the emergency exits on the DC3, Elizabethan and Viscount aircraft. Other parts of the training included a first-aid course plus practising how to extinguish fires. Additionally we had lessons and an exam on how to prepare a DC3 load sheet and balance chart.

On the second weekend we were given a familiarisation flight. It was Saturday 12 May when I chose to go to Madrid on a Viscount 701 and for me an added joy was a lengthy visit to the cockpit.

As flying staff we were issued with lightweight gabardine uniforms for summer use in addition to the regular dark blue ones. At an informal end of course ceremony, we were presented with our "wings" - a metal brevet. (Stewards and stewardesses wore an embroidered half-wing identification.) We also received a multi-page certificate showing the endorsements allowing us to fly as cabin crew on DC3 and Elizabethan aircraft. (BEA used the friendlier name of 'Pionair' for its DC3-Dakota fleet and each plane was given the name of a British aviation pioneer). Later that day, 18 May, we returned to Jersey elated with our new status as a qualified Flight Clerk.

Other items learned from the course together with some historical notes to give a feel of aviation during those evolutionary years were:

Before departure the last item to be loaded onto a Pionair was a canvas bag from the ground engineer. The bag had to contain 5 wooden locks (used to protect the wing and tailplane flying control surfaces) and 2 metal pins from the under-carriage. Sometimes the 2 pitot-head covers (from the air speed indicators) were included. Before take-off the Flight Clerk had to report to the Captain saying "There are 5 locks, 2 pins, 2 pitot-head covers, 32 passengers strapped in, ships papers on board, all checks carried out and correct Sir". (Ships papers were the load sheet / balance chart / passenger lists / cargo manifests and a General Declaration–for customs / health / immigration).

Civil aviation air law states that any craft of the air, whether aeroplane or hot air balloon, able to carry more than 19 passengers must have a cabin attendant for basic safety and emergency purposes.

During the Pionair training course 2 new words came into our vocabulary. Both were short lived. Antimacassar was soon replaced by seat head rest cover. Punkah-louvre had a lovely aura about it and was a good description of the passenger seat air vent on the Pionair. A low powered fan pushed a weak supply of air to the vents but only during flight. 2 fans with rubber blades were fitted to the overhead luggage racks above Row 3 by the summer of 1958. This helped to give a feeling of cool air in the cabin in hot weather.

Flight Clerks were members of the traffic department and in theory did not serve food or drink. In practice on Pionair flights longer than 1 hour 45 minutes a 'flight pack' was given out. The cardboard box typically contained: 1 ham and 1 cheese sandwich, a piece of cake or packet of biscuits, an apple and a carton of orange juice. Before take off on all flights passengers were offered a barley sugar - later to include mixed fruit flavoured sweets. These were totally withdrawn by BEA in 1959.

The name 'Flight Clerk' is rarely mentioned in any history of BEA. This is regrettable. The information below explains why. Flight Clerks operated on all non-catered UK domestic routes from 1955 until 1961. Within Scotland Flight Clerks continued for a further 3 years.

In 1954 / 55 Jersey was the second busiest passenger route on the BEA network with 126,000 passengers (Paris was number one). By the summer of 1957 more than 90% of all Pionair flights were crewed by Flight Clerks. All BEA flights to and from the Channel Islands, the Isle of Man, Belfast (except the non-stop ones to London) and internal Scottish services were manned by Flight Clerks. At different bases, and at different times, Flight Clerks held official cabin crew licences for the following aircraft: Viking, Pionair, Airspeed Ambassador (Elizabethan), Viscount 701, the leased Fred Olsen 700 variants, Viscount 802 and 806, Vanguard 951 and 953 plus the Herald.

Names and numbers supplied by former Flight Clerk Gill Whiting suggest there were almost 350 staff over the years with very few misfits or failures. The control structure was simple. The Senior Flight Clerk was Francis Van de Velde at Ruislip head office. At the 5 main bases there was a Control Flight Clerk responsible for admin, rostering, check flights and general quality control plus routine line flying. Local station superintendents and/or operations controllers could and would adjust ground or flying duties in times of disruption.

Charter flights with inclusive holidays to Europe did not exist in the 1950s. But adventurous Britons liked the idea of taking an aeroplane ride for their holiday to Jersey, Guernsey or the Isle of Man. Crowded steamers, with the possibility of sea sickness, were going out of fashion.

This meant a strong demand for airline seats especially in the summer peak. Many passengers were first-time flyers. A great many were nervous–some even frightened. All Flight Clerks had stories on how they managed to comfort the distressed. We carried aromatic ammonia capsules. The broken phial–with its strong smell–when put into a passengers hand would often distract from the fear. The capsule was also good to ward off air sickness or help recovery afterwards.

The unpressurised Pionairs usually flew below 6000 feet. This unstable part of the atmosphere resulted in many 'bumpy' flights. On fine sunny days the lovely looking white blobby (cumulus) clouds concealed the hot thermal currents rising from the ground. Windy conditions brought their own type of turbulence.

BEA had 38 Pionair aircraft and 8 Pionair-Leopards. The latter was the freighter version though not always used as such. When converted to the 32 seat passenger version there was no airstair just the wide cargo door. The radio officer's position remained in the cockpit on the Leopards with the consequent loss of up to 200 kilos of baggage stowage space.

The maximum take off weight for a Pionair was 12.8 tonnes which today looks minuscule when compared to that of a modern Boeing 747-400. As an example of a 13 and a half hour non-stop flight from Singapore to LHR in the Spring of 1999 these figures show a comparison:

227.3 tonnes is the weight of the aircraft without fuel.
169.5 tonnes of fuel required (including reserves) for the 6375 mile journey.
396.8 tonnes as the aircraft take-off weight.

Top: This plane had an chequered life. Built in December 1943, delivered to BOAC, briefly transferred to BEA, had a few months with Iraqi Airways in 1946, returned to BOAC, then back to BEA for 6 years. Later flew for Cambrian Airways before going to Cyprus Airways and then finally in 1980 left to corrode at Beirut Airport. (BA)

Centre: Passengers embark on the first Pionair Service from LAP to Jersey on 31 October 1954. The wet tarmac suggests why it was rare for a coach from West London Air Terminal to be at the aircraft side. The engineer at the back of the plane has just removed the rudder lock, which I often had to do at the end of the runway in very windy weather. (BA)

Below: This photo of G-AMKE was taken in the early 1950's. For me this plane has a special significance. I operated on it as a Flight Clerk from Jersey to London on 16 April 1961. This may have been the last scheduled passenger flight of a Pionair anywhere within Britain. (BA)

Left: This Pionair/Leopard was photographed in August 1955. (BA)

Below: Elizabethan G-ALZS flying one of the trunk routes of BEA sometime in 1953. (BA)

A close-up view of the Pionair airstair. It was light enough for male Flight Clerks to lift and close the door easily but some of the girls had more difficulty. (BA)

6
SOME LOGBOOK ENTRIES FROM JERSEY

My first under training flight was on BE 673 a Pionair G-AJHY with Flight Clerk Gerry Le Feuvre from Jersey to LAP–London Airport. (The name Heathrow was not yet in use). Captain Simm and First Officer Hind were the flight crew. BE 708, an Elizabethan aircraft registered G-ALZZ, was the return flight flown by Captain Baker. The date was 22 May 1956.

Two days later it was another return trip to LAP but on different Elizabethan aircraft. Northbound the aircraft was G-ALZY with Captain Deacon and southbound it was G-AMAG flown by Captain Baker. During our London turnaround time a warm (weather) front passed through Jersey and in the subsequent warm sector there was 'fast-fog'–a slang term for low cloud–over the airfield. The Captain made 3 approaches to Runway 27. I was fascinated because within moments of overshoot-power being applied to the engines there was a brief view through the ragged cloud base of the runway lights below. I don't think the first such experience of multiple overshoots is ever forgotten and I enjoyed it.

Dinard in France, just 20 minutes away, was the diversion airport. After two and a half hours we returned to and landed at Jersey in clear weather. Roy Lewis was the Flight Clerk teaching me the procedures.

After more flights under supervision I made my first flight as a solo Flight Clerk on 31 May on a Pionair aircraft G-AJDE to LAP. There were 32 passengers on BE 651 with Jersey crew Captain Ballands and First Officer Ward.

Many of the rostered duty days included a 'double' return to LAP or a 'double' return to Manchester or even a 'triple' return to Southampton In most cases we had the same aircraft and flight deck crew for all sectors. This would involve up to 8 flying hours a day with almost 12 hours on duty.

On 15 July I flew on the once weekly trip to Edinburgh. My mother and father had never been on an aircraft before and with customs approval I was able to show them the inside of the Pionair during the turnaround time.

Many of us stayed after work on 6 September to see a little local aviation history being made. Just after nightfall the first ever Viscount aircraft landed at Jersey. An Aer Lingus flight en route from Lourdes to Dublin was diverted to uplift passengers delayed by an unserviceable DC3 aircraft.

In September two vacancies for permanent staff became available at Renfrew Airport, Glasgow. I was offered and happily accepted one of the Flight Clerk posts. During the four months based in Jersey my log book shows: 362.30 flying hours carrying 6,712 passengers on 253 flights of which 16 sectors were on Elizabethan aircraft. I calculated the flown mileage to be 57,000.

Some outstanding memories from Jersey: Talking with many passengers I noted how different were the 'Northerners' from those boarding at London or Southampton. For ex-

A view looking aft at the interior of an Elizabethan. The seats in the front half of the cabin faced backwards. As a Flight Clerk I made 45 flights on 15 of the aircraft on the London-Jersey route. I liked the spaciousness and it had a public address system!

ample some girls on the two and a quarter flight from Manchester would talk freely and without inhibition. Maybe partly attracted by a uniform some girls volunteered the name of their Jersey hotel and virtually propositioned me in flight. Maybe I shouldn't, but I will confess that I did follow through some of the invitations.

But work was not all fun. Some duty days were up to 12 hours long after weather or aircraft technical delays. Little heed was paid to the legal minimum rest period we, as air crew, required overnight. The laws were often broken–but that is history now. In Jersey the word 'season' was a hallowed word and planes flew throughout the night if need be. Tourism had

An Airspeed Ambassador photographed in 1952. BEA called this fleet 'Elizabethans'. The high wing allowed passengers a good view which was popular. This fleet was the mainstay of BEA until the arrival of the Viscount. (BA)

The standard cabin layout of the Pionair fleet was 32 all leather seats. (BA)

Below: A good photo of one of the 38 Pionair (modified DC3 aircraft) used by BEA in the mid to late 1950's. 8 Leopard aircraft were also often converted from freighters to carry passengers. (BA)

leapt ahead to become the number one revenue income for the island–helped by its duty free and no purchase tax products.

Our £2 per week flying pay was probably to compensate for unsociable working hours, the lack of overtime pay and maybe even a legacy from the old 'danger money'. When away from base we could claim meal allowances. These were: Breakfast or Lunch 5/-, Dinner 7/- and for overnight accommodation £1 plus 3 shillings for incidental expenses.

Although there was no great spirit of 'togetherness' some Flight Clerks did have a mischievous sense of humour. Seconds before the aircraft door was shut a colleague might shout "Have a good trip to Glasgow". The plane was only going to Southampton. The passengers would panic, stand up and try to get out saying "We're on the wrong plane". It would take the Flight Clerk on board several minutes to pacify and reassure the passengers that it was a silly joke and the flight *was* the Southampton one. (There was no Public Address system on Pionair aircraft).

ICAO (International Civil Aviation Organisation) changed the phonetic alphabet code. The new words had world-wide enforcement. To me the old aircraft registration words of 'George, Able, Love, Zebra, Nan' were friendlier but it was easy enough to change.

When sea fog or low cloud covered the airfield to give visibility often below 50 yards the state of the airport was referred to as 'clamped'. This I was told was an ex-RAF word from World War 2. But it remained in common use for another 8 years or more, at least within BEA and the Channel Islands.

To understate the situation my summer had been 'wonderful'–or in modern parlance 'brilliant'. Ahead was a winter of flying around the Scottish Highlands and Islands. I remember being happy with a permanent job and doing what I enjoyed most i.e. flying. Of course I could not foresee how quickly aviation was to grow and keep me employed for the rest of my working life.

The colour scheme on the first Viscounts followed the traditional design of previous aircraft with the Union Jack on the tail. By December 1959 a new livery was being introduced with the red 'square' BEA on the tail unit. (BA)

Above: This Dakota was used as a test bed by Rolls Royce and is seen here in 1951 flying with prototype Dart engines. The experience gained helped in the development of the Dart engine for the Viscount aircraft. BEA later used G-AMDB as a dual purpose freighter/passenger plane. (BA)

Below: All aircraft had a new livery by 1961, seen here at LHR as a Viscount 800 taxies past a Vanguard in the foreground and another Viscount in the background. (BA)

7
A WINTER FLYING AROUND SCOTLAND

On 6 October 1956 along with three bulging suitcases I flew by Viscount aircraft from London to Renfrew Airport, Glasgow. The local Personnel Manager had arranged 'digs' for me in nearby Paisley. The accommodation was on the second floor of a small tenement block in Smithhills Street. Inside it was clean, neat, tidy, homely and usually warm.

Mrs Cartmell and her mother were friendly, helpful and meal times were flexible to suit my working hours. My room was comfortable but - and it was a big but - outside, some 50 yards to the right, there was a railway viaduct carrying multitrack lines on the main busy Glasgow-Paisley-Greenock train routes. Underneath the arches were two double width cobble stoned roads. Cars used the outer lane and ancient trams trundled and screeched along their lines which were just below my bedroom window. It took more than a wee while to get used to the noises.

There were two days of airport familiarisation and meeting the staff before my first flight on 10 October. Renfrew Airport (RFW) was spacious, well staffed and with many fewer flights was in stark contrast to the congested conditions at Jersey.

Rostering was easy for Control Flight Clerk Don Campbell as there were just 4 regular duty cycles:

No. 1 was an 8 sector day from Renfrew to Shetland and back.
No. 2 was a 6 sector day to the Outer Hebrides (Benbecula and Stornoway) then to Inverness for lunch and return.
No. 3 was a double return trip to Belfast (Nutts Corner).
No. 4 was split over 2 days. After a Belfast return it was onto Aberdeen for a short night-stop The next morning it was back to Renfrew before a Campbeltown and Islay round trip.

An airport stand-by Flight Clerk was on duty from 0700, with another to cover the afternoon. When not needed to fly this meant working on traffic (ground services) duties.

BE952 / BE953 were the flight numbers on Duty 1. The schedule was:

Northbound			Southbound	
Arr.	Dep.		Arr.	Dep.
	0720	RFW. Glasgow Renfrew	1645	
0825	0845	INV. Inverness Dalcross	1510	1545
0930	0940	WIC. Wick	1415	1425
1005	1100	KOI. Kirkwall Orkney	1250	1350
	1140	LSI. Sumburgh Shetland		1205

At Wick it was a 'one engine turnround' i.e. the starboard engine was kept running during the brief stop. My log book shows the on/off chocks times were usually between 4 and 11 minutes.

Monday morning northbound on this flight was not popular with Flight Clerks. The first 3 or 4 rows of the Pionair were 'cabin loaded'. This meant that the front seats each had up to 60 kilos of Sunday newspapers plus GPO mail bags, all securely tied down, and destined for Wick, Orkney or Shetland. The Flight Clerk helped unload the items, with extra care needed when carrying them over the passengers' heads at Wick.

Benbecula, Stornoway, Campbeltown, Islay, Kirkwall and Wick airports were closed on Sundays. (Likewise were Tiree and Barra served by the Heron aircraft). Aberdeen had no scheduled flights that day. Edinburgh and Renfrew had a few flights, mostly to London. Prestwick, however, was open all hours.

Usually there were 14 crews in Scotland 3 of whom were based in Aberdeen. Most of the Captains were very experienced Scotsmen who knew the Islands well. The others were recently promoted and most had converted from Viking aircraft in London. There were many Junior Second Officers.

In October I bought my first £1 premium bonds. I still have them. I am still waiting for a win.

My father had major surgery for cancer of the stomach on 31 October. It was at the Dunfermline and West Fife Hospital. The operation appeared successful for a while but the condition re-appeared and he died on 5 October 1960.

With a colleague I went to see the Paisley soccer team, named St. Mirren, one Saturday. But the less than orderly behaviour of the crowd entering the ground caused us to go to the cinema instead. Licensing hours were restrictive in Scotland at that time. It was not a good idea to be in a pub at the 2100 hours closing time as some customers were quickly gulping chasers and pints of heavy (beer).

Renfrew was prone to an unpleasant mixture of industrial and household smoke which together with the nearby River Clyde led to radiation fog and or smog which at times caused delays and diversions. Cross-winds were a challenge at airports on the Hebrides and in Orkney and Shetland. This also led to some diversions, cancellations and interesting journeys. My log shows that in October and November I had to place the rudder lock in position on the runway after landing and or remove it before takeoff on 12 occasions.

Multi-directional runways had been built for the RAF during the war, but the Ministry of Civil Aviation had allowed many of them to fall into disrepair. From memory the BEA Pionair had a maximum cross wind component of 18 knots. By early 1999 the length of runway 11/29 at Machrihanish-Campbeltown was still 3048 metres which is longer than any at Birmingham but identical in length to the runways at Stansted and Manchester.

On 26 November the wind was strengthening as we flew north to Kirkwall. During lunch gusts started to rock the empty aircraft. With no tow-bar at Orkney Captain George Childs and Second Officer Moore carefully taxied G-AHCV nose into wind. The 3 duty fire crew plus the rest of us on station helped tie the wings securely to concrete blocks placed beneath. The purpose was to lessen the risk of gusts lifting and overturning the plane. The mini-met office recorded a gust of 84 mph that afternoon. It was dark by 1530 when we were taken to our Kirkwall hotel for the night.

Soon after 0830 next day we were airborne direct to Renfrew. To avoid possible mountain-wave or other nasty met conditions we flew at 12,500 feet - a record for me in a DC-3. Flying around Scotland in winter was adventurous.

'Aircraft struck by lightning over Irish Sea' might have made an eye-catching newspaper headline. It didn't. But the incident did happen to us aboard BE928 on 28 November. G-AGIU was gently bumping along just south of the Mull of Kintyre when there was a brilliant blue flash in the cabin together with a loud tin-like bang. I was mid-ship talking to one of the 12 passengers when the lightning hit. During the turn-round at Belfast the engineers found part of an aerial missing with a small burn mark on the roof. During the morning the same aircraft and I flew 3 more sectors over the same route.

Probably my most memorable flight was on 13 December when the rostered Captain decided it was outside the limits to fly the Campbeltown and Islay sectors due to gale force winds. The Flight Manager, Captain Eric Starling, decided he would take the flight with Ian Turner as Second Officer. BE974, G-AJHZ bumped its way erratically passed Aisla Craig and the Isle of Arran and below the cloud base to make a positive yet very wobbly touchdown on the grass, parallel to a hedge in the corner of Campbeltown airfield. It was too windy for the aircraft to taxi anywhere so with both engines running the airport vehicles came out to meet us. The fire tender parked in front of the aircraft to act as a wind-break while the 8 Campbeltown passengers got off and boarded a little bus.

The Captain left the cockpit to supervise the minimum departure procedures When everyone was clear of the aircraft full throttle was applied to the engines and as far as I can remember we seemed to get airborne in less than 100 yards. The aircraft jolted and staggered back towards Renfrew, still with the 12 Islay passengers on board. Most were air sick, including me, for the first and only time.

Soon afterwards the aircraft flew into clear stable air and I went to the cockpit to find out what was happening. The Captain explained that we were circling the Ayrshire coast because Renfrew was closed with a thunderstorm. He pointed out the towering cunimb cloud. I pleaded with him to land at Prestwick but he said that Renfrew would be clear in 10 minutes. Apart from being memorable it was a nauseating experience. As a gesture of my annoyance and defiance I told the Duty Officer on arrival that I intended to go 'sick' the next day.

Christmas Day was a partial shut-down. Trains, planes, ferries and most of the buses stopped. Some shops were open but the dustbin men worked normally. At New Year the country went into paralysis–together with most of the population. January 2nd was also a holiday.

By 31 December I had flown 179.05 hours on 197 Pionair flights whilst based in Scotland.

My total BEA duty flying in 1956 was 541.35 hours on 449 flights carrying 10,004 passengers and flying approximately 75,000 miles. The total time on duty (including standby) was 1354 hours. Not too bad for just over 7 months !

BE952 on 04 January 1957 to Orkney and back was my first flight of the New Year. During the early part of the month most of the flights were full or almost so. Normally the passenger seat factor on internal Scottish routes was between 35-60% according to my log book.

Businessmen and local officials formed the main core of passengers, although a few tourists travelled to some of the islands in summer or at holiday times. Joe Grimmond, the then Leader of the Liberal Party was a fairly frequent commuter as he was the Member of Parliament for Orkney and Shetland.

During the routine check of life jacket stowage on 12 January at Belfast I discovered that all of them on G-AMJX were shown as being out of date. The Captain agreed to fly to Renfrew where the life jackets were replaced. A voyage report was sent to London maintenance control by the Captain. The reply from my point of view was not reassuring. So my checks continued and I found the same problem on G-ALXL on 08 February.

Hold Number 5 was a small narrow area at the very rear of the Pionair. When used it had a great influence on the balance chart and trim of the aircraft. For speed and easy loading some Wick airport staff twice put bags there. They refused my request to move them. When told of this the Captain came to the back and ordered the items be stowed correctly. The other incident was settled when I refused to shut the airstair-door.

The Royal Hotel in Aberdeen was where we stayed on our scheduled night-stop. The room was basic, not always very warm, but just about adequate for the seven hours there. Breakfast was always good - usually porridge and a full greasy fry-up. We needed it since we had come on duty at 1700 the previous day and we had five more flights to do before finishing at 1300. The pilots did the same duty but used a different hotel.

At the weekend it was a double night-stop which gave me the chance to see something of the Granite City when weather permitted. Scottish drinking laws required that only bonafide travellers could use a pub or hotel on Sundays if they had travelled four or more miles. A local Flight Clerk John McDonald and I sometimes took a bus ride to enjoy the scenery whilst also enjoying a glass or two.

Weather conditions were the most critical part of the flying operation. Fuel was available at only a few stations and the pilots had to ensure there was sufficient for a long diversion should the planned or alternate airfield be closed. It was truly a joy to fly around the Hebrides on a bright, sunny and almost windless morning. But the weather from the Atlantic could change very quickly and by mid-afternoon it might be windy enough to need the use of the rudder locks.

On Saturday 23 February about 3 inches of snow fell at Renfrew airport. There was a delay to the evening Belfast flight until Captain Starling arrived. G-AJIC slithered to the engine run-up point and after several skids we reached the runway and took off. On our return some of the snow had turned to slush but even that proved a hazardous task for taxiing to the ramp.

Viscount 701 G-ALWE crashed at Ringway Manchester on 14 March. This was the first fatal accident of a Viscount and caused some distress to the staff at Renfrew. All the passengers and crew were killed, some of whom were known at Glasgow airport.

During my first 12 months with BEA the statistics are:

727.26 Flying hours carrying 13,867 passengers on 629 flights flying approximately 96,200 miles with 1,714.30 duty hours.
Other flights, familiarisation/positioning, total 32 with 48.45 flying hours.

St. Kilda on the western edge of the Hebrides was chosen by the British Government to site a rocket range. The local people launched a huge protest which resulted in an Official Enquiry. This was held at Benbecula and the BEA Superintendent was one of the main opponents. A relief was required for traffic duties at the airport and I volunteered for the weeks posting. I travelled out on 04 April and returned on the 11th. Accommodation was at a premium because of the press coverage and I was housed in an RAF camp. The regular BEA flights came and went with me preparing the flight documents. There were some rowdy parties which I tried to avoid but I did see something of the area including Lochboisdale. For me it was a very interesting week. Months later the Government greatly modified its plans with costs and access to such a remote area given as the reasons.

The only airborne technical problem was on 04 May when the undercarriage failed to retract on G-AMJY after leaving Renfrew. We returned and 25 minutes later all 30 passengers were on the standby aircraft bound for Belfast.

Captain McDowell flew with Captain Taylor who was ICUS (In Command Under Supervision) for 7 sectors on 27 and 28 May. We made a detour to fly low over Fair Isle, for my one and only view of the island, between Aberdeen and Shetland. At Sumburgh airport during a long turn-round, the Captain suggested we took a walk to the seaside (the airport is just 19ft above sea level). With ATC permission we strolled across a runway and had a paddle in the cold water of the Atlantic.

To satisfy my love of statistics: Sumburgh at Latitude 60.90 N was the most northerly point I ever had a paddle and Capetown at Latitude 33.56 S was the most southerly part of the Atlantic in which I swam.

It was farewell Scotland on 31 May 1957 when I positioned to London Airport on Viscount G-A0HP. This move led to greater changes; within weeks I got job promotion.

Trainee Flight Clerk, Sally Holloman, being shown how to 'dress' a Pionair by Cecelia Boyce. Note in the top right-hand corner the 3 bladed rubber fan used on hot days to circulate the cabin air.

8
LIFE AS A FLIGHT CLERK AT LONDON AIRPORT

Less than 24 hours after my arrival in London, it was 01 June, when I operated an early morning Pionair flight from LAP to Manchester. During the next four and a half years many Flight Clerks (including me) were qualified and flew 6 other aircraft types on this route. The list includes Viscount 701 / 701X / Fred Olsen variants / Viscount 802 / 806 and Vanguard 951.

My first Viscount flight, operating as a Flight Clerk, was on G-AMOG on 16 June. It was also the first time I had been to the Isle of Man.

Sunday newspapers for Jersey left LAP at 0455 cabin loaded on a Pionair. On 23 June I was rostered for this duty which turned out to be an exciting experience. For aircraft trim purposes I travelled on the 'jump seat' of G-AKJH. Jersey airport was shrouded in low cloud. A standard approach to Runway 27 resulted in an overshoot. The very experienced Captain knew the island well and steered the aircraft to get below cloud base over St. Ouen's Bay. We were below the runway height of 276 ft but using familiar landmarks the Captain lined up with the approach lights for Runway 09. Using extra power the plane climbed to avoid approaching high ground. Soon the green threshold lights were visible and we made a perfect landing. I was impressed but listening on the radio headset the Junior Second Officer did not sound so enthusiastic.

Personnel Office gave me a letter on 09 July. It said congratulations on my appointment as Control Flight Clerk London Airport to take immediate effect. In fact I had been acting in that capacity for the previous two or three weeks. My diary shows the interview was on 08 July but gives no other details which show that I did not hanker for the job. It was my first promotion and gave me a prestigious stripe on my uniform. Aged just 23 years when I got the job I was by far the youngest of the Control Flight Clerks and for a short time there was some irritation that someone with so little experience should occupy the top job at London Airport. By late summer our unit needed more space and the section moved from a basement area to the second floor of the west wing of Terminal 1. There were two adjacent rooms, one a rest area with storage space for staff lockers. The other was an office with a name-plate on the door "Control Flight Clerk A K Jenkinson". Windows in the office overlooked the attractive Roof Gardens and we could hear commentary for the public detailing the flight arrivals, and see part of the runway and tarmac stands.

For the record the first BEA Viscount service from LAP to Jersey was on 14 July. G-AMNY was flown by Captains Lowden and Priest with Radio Officer Adams plus myself and Hazel Thorpe as Flight Clerks. The flight was a planned substitute for a Pionair and Sunday was chosen to gain maximum publicity. There were 34 passengers on BE 670 and 46 passengers on the return BE 671.

My notebook shows the main BEA fleet in mid-summer 1957 as:

Number	Aircraft Type	Seats	Notes
27	Viscount 701	47	
19	Elizabethan	47	(49 on Jersey route)
38	Pionair	32	
8	Pioneer-Leopard	(32)	Freighter or passenger use

Plus 3 Heron 1B, 3 Rapide aircraft and 4 King Arthur helicopters plus 2 Bristol Freighters.

In comparison the BA fleet as of early August 1999 was:

Number	Aircraft Type	Usual Seating Layout
7	Concorde	100R
6	B747-136	14F 76J 266M being withdrawn by Nov 99
16	B747-236	14F 64J 298M
55	B747-400	14F 55J 332M
5	B777-236A	17F 70J 148M
19	B777-236B	14F 56J 197M
3	B777-236B	27J 355M-AML Aircraft
6	B767-336ER	30J 183M
23	B767-336	252C/M
54	B757	180C/M
10	Airbus A320	149C/M
17	B737-236	108-116C/M
34	B737-400	141-147C/M
7	B737-300	126C/M

Wholly Owned Subsidiaries
British Asia Airways-based at LHR
| 2 | B747-400 | 14F 55J 332M |

Brymon Aviation-based at Plymouth / Bristol
| 17 | Dash 8 50M |

Codes Used for Cabin Class Seating
F: First, J: Club World, C: Club Europe, M: Economy

Engine failures in flight were rare. Sometimes though a precautionary shut-down was made. The first experience for me was on G-AMOF operating BE 571 Birmingham to LAP on 29 July . Number 3 engine was feathered just south of Daventry due to low oil pressure.

Rostering was broadly based on the aircraft schedules and crew integration. As an example: on Saturdays in August an Elizabethan was allocated for 8 sectors to and from Jersey. BE 652 left LAP at 0555 and BE 699 was due back at 0120 on Sunday. One crew and one Flight Clerk operated 4 flights and another crew the last 4 - which gave good utilisation. Passenger fares were the same, day or night, and there was no weekend surcharge. 'No-show' passengers (i.e. failure to turn up) were rare and most seats were filled.

Probably some European aviation history was made on 27 August when 2 BEA Viscounts were chartered to carry a group of Russian athletes behind the Iron Curtain. The flights from LAP to Prague were the first recorded post-war air services to Czechoslovakia from the West. (At least there are no other known British civil planes to have operated the route.)

G-AMOJ left LAP at 0947 and arrived at Prague airport at 1210. The crew were Captain Sandison, Captain Openshaw, Radio Officer Gay with a Ground Engineer and me (to do the ship's papers / flight documents). Cabin staff served refreshments to the 31 Russians on board. After 30 minutes on the ground the aircraft left for Frankfurt to refuel and return to London. The round trip flight number was BEA 398 for the first service..

For the second flight, G-ALWF, BEA 399, was crewed by Captain Dunford, First Officer Mulcaster, Radio Officer Thompson with the Ground Engineer and myself listed as extra crew. We left Prague at 1501 (all times are BST) also via Frankfurt for LAP.

For an unknown reason there were no cabin staff available to operate an evening charter flight to Geneva on 09 September. It was to be a Viscount 802 and there was no Flight Clerk with a licence to operate this aircraft type. Hazel Thorpe and I had an afternoon survival check to validate our certificates and thereby became the first Flight Clerks with this endorsement. G-AOHI flew empty to Geneva and returned with 47 delayed Air India passengers. For Hazel and I it had been a long day when we landed at LAP at 0316.

Kenneth Moore and a film company chartered a Pionair from Cherbourg to Southampton on 30 September. I rostered myself for the flight to prepare the ship's papers and see something of Cherbourg. Time on the ground did not allow more than a brief tour of the area, but I enjoyed it.

Blackbushe Airport in Hampshire was a recognised diversion airport for LAP. It used 'Fido' - goose-necked oil burning lamps packed closely together at the edge of and for the length of the runway. Apart from illuminating the landing area 'Fido' apparently gave enough heat to disperse and burn off some of the radiation type fog. BE 589 from Manchester was my 4th flight on 10 September when we diverted to Blackbushe to find a tarmac full of aircraft. Even without the need for Customs or Immigration clearance it was 90 minutes before a coach left with us and our 26 passengers. It was a slow foggy journey to LAP arriving at 0100.

The last Elizabethan flights for me were made on G-AMAA on 29 December. To Jersey the flight number was BE 652E with just one passenger and the return flight was BE 661D with a full load of 49 passengers.

My log book statistics from April 1956 to 31 December 1957 show:

Flights: 946
Flying Hours: 1,131.31
Passengers: 20,484
Approximate mileage flown: 158,350

During this time I had flown in 81 different BEA aircraft made up of 38 Pionairs, 8 Leopards, 15 Elizabethans, 19 Viscount 701 and 1 Viscount 802 as an operating Flight Clerk.

1958

Malta was a rostered 3 day duty trip for some crews. Brenda, a stewardess friend, was allocated to one of these and I went along as a passenger. The Phoenicia Hotel was the most luxurious in which I had ever stayed and our tour of the island has happy memories. The return Elizabethan aircraft was G-AMAA on 24 February via Rome. As we approached the Alps the plane met severe turbulence and the Captain decided to turn around and divert to Nice. It was my first visit to the Cote d'Azur and we spent a pleasant evening strolling along the Promenade.

On 6 February an Elizabethan aircraft crashed at Munich Airport and some of the famous Manchester United football team 'The Busby Babes' were killed. As a tribute to the skills and care given to the survivors BEA carried many of the Munich Hospital staff to Manchester about a month after the disaster. I was the Flight Clerk on a chartered Pionair aircraft which flew 32 of the hospital staff from LAP to Manchester on 09 March.

Starting in early April the summer intake of temporary Flight Clerks finished their training courses and I was kept busy with check flights on the less confident people. By mid-summer we had 26 Flight Clerks at London Airport. (In the summer of 1957 there were 32 Flight Clerks at LAP, the greatest number anywhere).

It was May Day when I operated on a Viscount 802 from Manchester to London with Gill Whiting. Then three days later I flew on my first Viscount 806 G-AOYH on a round trip to Manchester.

Gatwick Airport opened in June with the code LGW. London Airport had a name change to Heathrow (to reflect its ancient description) and LAP became LHR. Reluctantly I attended an interview for the post of Control Flight Clerk at Gatwick. I did not want the job because with only 4 Pionair aircraft based there the variety of activities seemed limited. Paddy O'Connor from Manchester was selected and Norman Stott was promoted to his position. It may be of interest to note that my gross weekly pay at that time was £12.17 shillings.

When Viscount aircraft took over more Pionair routes my job on rostering became easier. After Gatwick opened two LHR Flight Clerks were assigned to a weekend crew tour. Sometimes this involved a road journey between the two airports or an overnight stay at Ye Olde Felbridge Hotel. Many duty days were between 9 and 11 hours and all Flight Clerks worked more than their contract 37 and a half hour week - with no extra pay. But nobody complained. On a few occasions after flight delays there were naturally some grumbles when social engagements were disrupted. But there was a great spirit of camaraderie especially at LHR. Staff would help each other and very rarely did I refuse a roster change. A roster request book was introduced.

On 09 July I had my first training flight on a Fred Olsen Viscount V.745 G-APNG to Amsterdam. During the next two years BEA leased a number of Fred Olsen Viscounts of various models and this required London Flight Clerks to have training on many of the types. My log book is peppered with receiving and giving training on them plus operational flights on 5 versions.

London based Pionairs, crews and Flight Clerks operated weekend flights in the Irish Sea area (mainly Manchester and or Liverpool to the Isle of Man) with a Manx nightstop. All the year round there were two scheduled night-stops. One was at Manchester (The Grand Hotel) and the other was at Birmingham staying at the Leofric Hotel, Coventry.

Editor Cheeseman in the *BEA MAGAZINE* of September 1958 wrote:

"Saturday August 9 began badly in both Islands. The clouds were still 'on the deck' but the weather began to clear during the morning. We now come to the story of the spectacular BEA airlift of August 9 and 10 when over 12,500 BEA passengers were handled by Jersey and Guernsey in 442 aircraft movement.

After lunch things began to improve further and from 3 o'clock onwards aircraft began to pour in and the great evacuation began. Flying continued until 0530 on Sunday morning, during which time 204 movements took place and 6,108 passengers were carried. The 57 seater Viscount 802s from London Airport shuttled back and forth continuously, flown in many cases by volunteer crews from the mainland flights.

These included Flight Managers McLannahan, Preston and Greenhalgh, and the latter is credited with doing no less than four consecutive return flights to Jersey. A noticeable feature of the BEA operation was the fine work done by the young Flight Clerks. These keen young people were quite tireless and deeply interested in their responsible duties, and some worked voluntarily up to 20 hours at a stretch during this difficult period."

Gill Whiting and I flew with Captain Greenhaugh and First Officer Laver on G-AOYO for the 8 sectors mentioned above. We departed LHR at 1406 and returned at 0420 on Sunday morning. Our duty day was 19 hours. So crowded were the terminal buildings that the Captain had to organise sandwiches and coffee on board in lieu of proper meals.

To complete a dramatic weekend Gill and I were back at LHR on Sunday 10 August for the scheduled afternoon Viscount to the Isle of Man. The weather there was below landing limits and we diverted to Liverpool and off-loaded the 22 passengers. Operations Control told Captain Scott to return empty to London. We left Liverpool at 1700 and met a series of violent thunderstorms en route. While the Captain was trying to avoid the towering cunimb clouds extreme turbulence forced the plane to drop 4,000 ft. Lightning had struck Manchester radar and the Daventry beacon was also affected. Both Gill and I had pains in the stomach area where our seatbelt held us in position. G-AOHG was tossed about like a bouncing ball on a hillside. This was the worst turbulence I ever experienced on any flight in my life.

August had just one other noteworthy item. On the 23rd I decided to do a check flight on Pam Farrant operating Viscount 701 G-AMOC. During the evening flight I noticed sparks coming from Number 3 engine and immediately went to the cockpit and told the Captain. For a few seconds I think he doubted my description of 'Fire' as the instrument panel showed all was normal. But I insisted and the Radio Officer came to the cabin to check. The engine was then shut down. The problem came from the de-icing ring around the cowling. As the 47 passengers disembarked at Manchester the nose wheel leg partially collapsed. From that day forward London Flight Clerks labelled aircraft 'Oscar Charlie' as a jinx plane.

My only visit to the Lake District was on 09-10 October when the United Steel Company chartered a Pionair from Lindholme (Doncaster) to Silloth airfield. I was on board to prepare the flight documents and there was a stewardess to serve the refreshments. We stayed at Keswick and toured the area with the group of executives on first class excursions.

BEA developed a Viscount 701 with a forward door airstair and high density seating. G-AMOK was the prototype V701X and on 01 November I operated on its first flight which was to Jersey piloted by Captains Barker and Kirkland. The flight numbers were BE L62 and BE L07. To differentiate between LGW and LHR flights the latter services had the prefix 'L' added before the flight number.

Gibraltar had an attraction for me since my father was there during part of the war. With a colleague we flew on a Viscount on 25 November for a visit to the Rock with an overnight stay in Tangier. On 27 November we crossed the Straits of Gibraltar on the local ferry 'Mons Calpe' but used an on-loan Pionair G-AJIC to return before connecting with the overnight Viscount 701 to London.

On arrival at LHR on 29 November I boarded G-AOJE to continue my leave in Scotland. The aircraft had to overfly Edinburgh due to fog and then had a missed approach at Glasgow, also in fog, so we returned to LHR. The 3 hour 20 minutes flying was my longest ever flight to nowhere.

Some memories of London Airport in the 1956 to 1959 era include: a tall revolving beacon with a green and white light. A ground level green light flashing a two-letter Morse code identification. (Both were dismantled by 1958). Using runways which were withdrawn from use for building and pier expansions by 1959. Cross wind examples I remember: landing in a Pionair on Runway 33 Left, a Viscount passing over the Bath Road for 15 Right and a Pionair take-off on 05 Left - which caused a minor upset with Air Traffic Control. The man in the caravan did not like my quick 20 second dash onto the hallowed runway to remove the Pionair's rudder lock. But by the time he had contacted the control tower we were airborne.

1958 was another year of happiness for me.

1959

New Years Day was not yet a public holiday in England and with most flights operating normally my duty trips were an Isle of Man return and Birmingham nightstop. With south westerly gales the 3 flights were boringly bumpy and with passenger numbers of 7, 5 and 5 it seemed like a wasted day. The strong winds meant I had to remove the rudder lock on the runways at both Ronaldsway (IOM) and Heathrow.

Sickness and staff leave gave a shortage of Flight Clerks in Scotland and I volunteered for the temporary posting to Aberdeen. In the 5 working days from Friday 13 February I operated on 25 sectors with almost 21 flying hours and truly enjoyed the change.

On 12 March the first fully modified Viscount 701 (V701X) with a high-density seating layout plus an integral forward door air-stair was brought out from the hanger. BEA Chief Executive Anthony Millward with 29 other VIPs boarded G-ALWF for a 30 minute flight. Captain Watts flew to be overhead Brighton and return whilst the guests looked over the 60 seater aircraft. As the trip had no catering I was the Flight Clerk.

An Air France DC6 (F-BHVA) took 3 Flight Clerks and myself to Nice on 10 May for a 5 day Riviera jaunt. We visited the usual places then onto Monte Carlo for an expensive night (I still avoid casinos) before crossing the Italian border to get badly sun-burned in San Remo. Living is an education - we learnt painfully.

Below is a list of Flight Clerks for mid-summer 1959:

Base	Staff Numbers	Control Flight Clerk
Glasgow	21)	Don Campbell
Aberdeen	3)	
Jersey	25)	John le Fondre
Guernsey	4)	
Gatwick	18	Paddy O'Connor
Heathrow	28	Alec Jenkinson
Manchester	27	Norman Stott

With an increase in the number of flights at Heathrow there was a shortage of staff to cover the schedules. From 23 May Viscount aircraft had to be rostered with one Flight Clerk instead of two. This despite the fact that most of these aircraft had more than 50 passenger seats fitted. A re-design of the cabin layout on many versions brought this number up to 71 seats by the following year. Surprisingly, the crews seemed to accept this but I thought it was unwise for safety reasons, and against CAA regulations.

In June I heard there was to be a Station Superintendent based in Moscow for the new BEA Air Service which had started in May. For some reason the job appealed to me. Shopping for Russian phrase books was not easy and finding a tutor, even in London, was impossible on my salary. But I was keen and spent countless hours with some help from a friend learning parts of the basic language. When advertised I applied for the post and with 5 other candidates had an interview on 17 July. On reflection I was lucky not to be chosen. The LHR Control Flight Clerk job with its variety and often long hours kept me fully satisfied.

With another Flight Clerk I thought a visit to Moscow would be interesting. We bought our subload tickets and applied to Intourist (the official Russian agency) for accommodation and got a visa stamped in our passports for the trip. Because of a weight restriction on the Viscount aircraft from Moscow, which routed via Copenhagen, during August BEA imposed a staff travel ban on the route. Our plans were thwarted.

Athens, Beirut and Cyprus were the places chosen for 10 days annual leave from 13 September. With a work colleague we used our 90% rebate airline tickets and selected hotels which gave staff half price rates. Athens was more interesting than I imagined and on our final evening a visit to the annual wine festival was a must. About 20 attractive girls each dressed in regional costumes were giving free samples of their local wine. There was a happy atmosphere. I was happy and getting happier by the glass full. By 0200 whilst waiting for the coach to the airport my happiness turned to illness. I can just about remember daybreak and boarding the Viscount for Beirut.

Beirut was beautiful with cedar trees, wide avenues and a happy cosmopolitan mix of local and French cultures. This was reflected in the variety of the shops. The 4 day visit from 15 September passed quickly with daytime swimming on fine beaches and evenings reserved for eating and enjoying a beer at vari-

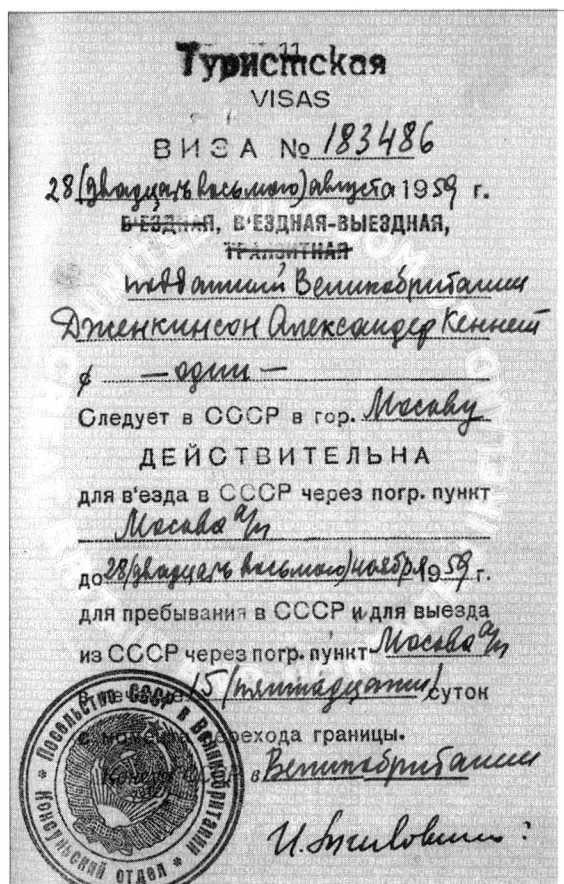

Tourist
VISA
VISA No 183486
28th (twenty-eighth) August 1959
ENTRY AND EXIT
British subject
Jenkinson, Alexander Kenneth
Unaccompanied
Travelling to the USSR, to the city of Moscow
VALID
for entry to the USSR via the border point of
Moscow airport
by 28th (twenty eighth) November 1959,
for presence within the USSR and for exit
from the USSR via the border point
of *Moscow airport.*
within 15 (*fifteen*) days
of crossing the border
from *Great Britain*
[signature]

ous pavement cafes. Visits to 2 night clubs can best be described as illuminating.. The biggest shock - a visit to a local meat market with its adjoining abattoir. The sights, smells and sounds will be remembered all my life.

Nicosia Airport, Cyprus, was our next stopping point on 18 September. On arrival the British Military Police, who controlled the immigration facilities, noticed the Russian visa in my passport. I was questioned at some length. Had they caught a Russian spy on a recognisance trip ? Eventually my airline documents were proof enough to clear me for the holiday. We stayed at the luxurious Dome Hotel in Kyrenia enjoying its facilities and the surrounding area. Some years later after partition of the island Kyrenia became part of the Turkish sector.

Whilst in transit at Athens airport on 22 September an Immigration Officer saw that I was travelling on a Jersey passport. After checking with his superiors they decided that this British-style document was not acceptable in Greece. Despite my explanation that I was in transit to London and that 9 days earlier I had been in Athens on holiday they put me 'behind bars'. I protested and asked for the BEA Duty Officer. After 15 minutes I was escorted to the London aircraft without apology or explanation. By phone I complained to the Foreign Office in London who said the Greek Immigration Officers were wrong but my solution was to get a new British passport issued in London.

Fog (it really was smog) would often blanket huge areas of Britain in the autumn and winter periods during the 1950s and 1960s. Most transport was affected but more so the planes. At times records show LHR was closed totally for up to 48 hours. On 01 December after a scheduled Birmingham night-stop most of Southern England was smog-bound. The Pionair crew and I waited at foggy Birmingham's Elmdon airport until after lunch before returning to our Coventry hotel for another night. The next morning the weather had improved but a Manchester Flight Clerk was missing so I had to operate a Viscount service to Manchester and then onward to LHR. Flight Clerks were prepared for flexible working days and this was one of the joys of the job for me, well usually anyway.

On 19 December my duty was the evening return flight to Manchester. The aircraft (G-AOYP) was one of the first to wear the new BEA colour scheme.

To end the year I flew to Jersey. It was on the Leopard aircraft 'Lima Tango Tango' operating two hours late. My scheduled return flight had departed and there was no alternative but to nightstop on Jersey. But with just a sweater to replace my uniform jacket it was a dispirited New Years Eve.

1960

By 0800 on New Years Day I was at Jersey airport preparing a Pionair for LHR. The 32 passengers were quiet and I was not elated at having missed a dance-party in London.

My first jet aircraft flight was on G-APMB a Comet 4B to Zurich on 30 January. Captain Owens commanded this 'training flight'. It was a thrill to feel the powerful acceleration along the runway and the steep climb. Such a contrast to the lumbering efforts of a Dakota.

Five weeks later I experienced the first and only engine failure on a DC-3 during more than 1130 such flights. It happened on G-AGHJ operating BE L07 on 05 March. Almost 15 minutes after take-off the oil pressure fell and the port engine was feathered. It happened near Alderney and the 50 degree North reporting point. We returned to Jersey. After a change of aircraft we left for LHR with 30 passengers and almost 100 kilos of Post Office mail.

During the period 10 May 1956 to 15 March 1960 my log book shows operating figures of:

1,508 flights. 1,724.22 flying hours carrying 38,601 passengers. Landed at 26 UK airports plus 4 in Europe. Sectors by aircraft type were:
Pionairs - 1077. Leopards - 60. Elizabethans - 45.
Viscount 701 - 111. V802 - 112. V806 - 103 (figures exclude positioning and passenger flights).

BEA leased several Viscount aircraft from Fred Olsen and this required a one day training course held on 30 March. G-APZP (A V779D) had differences - which in my view were relatively minor for cabin crew. This aircraft on 13 April was allocated to 6 sectors. I flew on all 6 during a 14 hour day for in-flight training on many Flight Clerks. In the next 5 weeks I was also kept very busy with check flights on the new temporary staff.

Jersey Flight Clerk John Hervieu with a monetary grant was building his flying hours at every opportunity with the aim of getting a commercial licence. Twice in the summer of 1960 I flew as a passenger with him from Elstree Airfield on cross country flights to Kidlington, Oxford. These were my first light aircraft flights and first attempts at ground and air map reading. John became a BEA pilot and retired as a Captain from the BAC 1-11 fleet.

Another lesson I learned from John was not

to bet on horses. Together we went to Windsor Race Course on a fine sunny day. Later I wished it had snowed. I bet 10 shillings here and 10 bob there, here a bet, there a bet but only one winner. John had more luck but I had squandered more than three quarters of my week's pay. For the next 7 days I can remember feeling very poor and had to borrow from a friend. Since that day I have never bet on a horse (except in an office sweepstake) and have never again been to a race course.

On an empty positioning Pionair flight to Jersey on 23 September the Captain asked if I would like to experience weightlessness. Keen to try anything new I stood in the cabin aisle with a hand on each luggage rack. The crew pulled the aircraft nose up and then steeply down. My legs lifted off the floor and on the third attempt my body was almost horizontal –briefly free of gravity.

Charter flights, whether at home or away, added a little more zest to life. On 09 November I flew as an extra crew member to Ostend on a V802 to prepare the 'ships papers' for the return flight. (A few years later inherited nautical terms such as 'ships papers' were changed to 'flight documents').

Seating layouts varied on and between the different BEA Viscount fleets. The V701 series aircraft had either 52, 54 or 61 seats. The V802 usually had 66 or 71 seats whereas the V806 had a standard 58 seats to allow it to operate the two-class flights. Whatever version there was just one Flight Clerk who occupied a rear door crew seat for emergency evacuation reasons. There was no intercom with the flight crew. Each passenger seat pocket stored an emergency procedures card. A brief mention of this was made during our public address announcements. Safety was taken for granted and as cabin crew none of us were worried. Such a laid-back approach would not be allowed today.

BEA arranged press and television coverage for the last scheduled flight of a Pionair. It was to be a return flight from London to Birmingham. Assistant Flight Manager Captain Griffin flew G-AGZB with Flight Clerk Kay Hart on 31 October. At Birmingham the television crews waited in the murky conditions whilst the aircraft circled. Eventually the aircraft landed too far along the runway and overran into the soft ground ahead. Nobody was seriously injured but the press and television had a good story. That plane was repaired but did not fly again with BEA. Some time later after another mishap it ended its days on the Isle of Wight.

31 October 1961 was a sad day as it was the day the Flight Clerk Unit was disbanded. This picture was taken on the roof garden of LHR Terminal 1, overlooking the tarmac.

9
THE YEAR OF EXPANSION THEN CESSATION

There was a local newspaper advertisement for temporary Flight Clerks at LHR in January 1961. The wage mentioned was £9.19.6 per week plus £2.0.0. flying pay. The basic amount was equal to that offered for ground check-in staff. There was a similar advert in the paper for Cabin Staff but the starting pay was not mentioned although it was almost 30% greater.

Vickers Vanguard aircraft were in production and flying on a few scheduled BEA services. On 27 January I took my first training flight on a Vanguard 951 (G-APEE) to Le Bourget, Paris. Flight Number BE 327 was flown by Captain Mitchell. Many of us attended a 3 day Vanguard conversion course held from 30 January to 01 February. This was followed by two familiarisation flights. Both of mine were to Paris, flying on G-APEF on 08 February and G-APEE on the 18th.

Some BEA flight numbers changed to 4 numerics commencing with an '8' from 1 April. This was linked with an air traffic control need to avoid VHF radio confusion with similar aircraft registration call signs.

For some unknown reason Pionair G-AMKE was in Jersey. To return it to London it was planned to operate a passenger service on 16 April as BE 0849A. It left the island at 1648 flown by Captains Law and Coleman. There were 27 passengers including one with a medical problem lying on a stretcher. I had specially rostered myself for the flight thinking it might be my last operating service on a Dakota. It was. (However I flew as a passenger in several overseas countries years later).

On 31 May I made a two day visit to the Paris Air Show. An Air France Super G Constellation (F-BGNH) took me from LHR to Orly. The return flight from Le Bourget was on a BOAC DC7C aircraft (G-AOIA) which had been hired by BEA to meet the demand for seats.

Meanwhile back in the office morale was high as we waited for the date of the first Flight Clerk operated Vanguard service. It happened on 7 July, with little prior notice, as G-APED was allocated to BE 8804. With Captain Liver in command we left for Manchester at 0609 carrying 94 passengers. Maurice Hill and I were the Flight Clerks. There were 63 passengers on the return flight BE 8807. Although exciting it did not have the true thrill of first flights.

A Vanguard of the 953 series (G-APEI) flew the next service from LHR to Manchester on 22 August. It was a substitute for the normal Viscount service and used as a crew training flight with Captain Gray in command. Northbound I did a check flight on Cecilia Boyce and during the return flight (BE 8831) I cleared Gwen Chaston.

We had great expectations but it turned out to be much ado about nothing as that was the fourth and last Vanguard sector operated by Flight Clerks. With 132 seats on the aircraft there had to be at least 3 cabin crew, although it was rumoured that some flight crew wanted 4 as a minimum. Productivity and utilisation were looming problems.

'Prepare to meet thy end' was the sombre message given to the 5 Control Flight Clerks at a Head Office meeting at Bealine House, Ruislip, on 4 September. Flight Clerk bases–except in Scotland–were to be disbanded on 31 October. The staff options were: become a Steward/Stewardess or transfer to a Ground Services job or leave the Corporation. My diary does not list the decisions made by most people but I chose a training programme in various traffic (ground services) departments at LHR.

Comet 4B G-ARJL flew my mother and I to Gibraltar on 21 September for a weeks holiday on the Costa del Sol. It was an interesting visit to the then unspoilt Torremolinos with authentic, and sometimes spontaneous, flamenco dancing in small non-tourist tavernas. The trip included seeing my first bull-fight at nearby Malaga.

There was a Flight Clerks' farewell party on 27 October held at the Hounslow home of Jane Priest. The 60 or more who attended judged it a great success. It was an easy-going party which captured the true feelings of happiness, loyalty and joy of being a member of a prestigious unit called 'Flight Clerks'. We were, and still are, proud of the job we did during those developing years and making a niche in the history of BEA.

My last Flight Clerk duty was the regular Birmingham night-stop flying on G-AOYK with Captain Thom on BE 8882. The next morning Tuesday 31 October was my last operating flight, BE 8857, with the same aircraft and crew. We left Birmingham at 0803 and arrived at LHR at 0834. When I got off the aircraft this ended my five and a half years as a Flight Clerk.

Statistics from my log books covering the period May 1956 to October 1961 as an Operating Flight Clerk show:

Number of Flying Hours	2,107.10
Number of Flights	1,906
Number of different aircraft	133
Number of Passengers carried	54,876
Calculated miles flown	343,000

1,138 sectors were flown on Pionairs or Leopards; 45 were on Elizabethans, 4 were on Vanguards. 719 were on various types of Viscount aircraft.

In addition to the 'Operating Flying Hours' of 2,107.10 must be added 134.15 hours as extra crew, positioning or on training-familiarisation flights. The total then becomes 2,241.25 duty flying hours.

(If my personal passenger flying figure of 342.15 hours is included the grand total is 2,583.40 flying hours).

Above: When BEA retired its Pionair aircraft, Viscounts and later Herald aircraft were used on the Scottish Highlands and Islands services. This photo taken in May 1966 shows two Viscount 800s at Abbots-inch Airport, Glasgow. (BA)

A 953 Series Vanguard showing the slightly modified forward passenger airstair. The onboard airstairs carried a slight weight penalty but were a great blessing to passengers for speedy disembarkation. (BA)

10
THE BEA GROUND DUTY YEARS

Ministry of Civil Aviation (MCA) staff provided most of the service functions at LHR. The porters and baggage handling staff went on unofficial strike from 06-12 November. BEA managerial and some supervisory people (which included me) were drafted in to do their work. I was allocated to loading and driving a baggage truck to and from the aircraft.

From 20 November 1961 until the end of March 1962 I was attached, on a supernumerary basis, to 8 traffic (ground services) units and attended several courses to supplement the on-site training.

Canary Islands–the name had a magic and romantic ring to it. Very few holiday brochures listed the area and there was just one flight a day from the mainland. Iberia Airlines gave the prestigious flight number 1B 001 to its Madrid to Las Palmas service flown by a Super G Constellation aircraft. On 25 January my friend Brenda and I spent a most interesting 2 days in Madrid before flying on the Connie EC-AQM to Las Palmas. The luxury hotel, Isobelle, (at a discounted rate to us) had prize winning gardens and was not too far from the beach. Most of the tourists we met were from Scandinavia–barely a Brit in sight.

With rebate tickets we flew on 1 February across to Tenerife (surprise, surprise it was on a Dakota EC-AEU) to do some sightseeing. The next day we flew from Los Rodeos Airport to Madrid on another Connie EC-AMQ. At the end of such a wonderful holiday with happy memories, a good suntan plus some silly souvenirs we were ready to go home. But the only seats available from Madrid were on an Iberia Convair Metropolitan aircraft which boringly bumped and battled against a head wind for five and a quarter hours to LHR.

At work I was posted to the 'Station Control' unit on 08 April. This involved talking on UHF radio to mobile 'observers' who patrolled sections of the airport apron and reported on the readiness of aircraft for departure. We could hold the boarding process if a delay seemed likely. The observer system evolved into the 'Redcap' in use today for liaison and control of departure formalities.

My diary shows I bought a new Mini-van on 12 April for £404.10.0. The van model was cheaper as it was exempt from Government purchase tax.

Promotion to Station Controller (shift supervisor of the unit) came on 13 June when 5 of us were upgraded to scale M2 after an internal selection board from the 22 staff eligible. Our office was the co-ordinating nerve centre for all BEA movements–in and out–plus more than 12 foreign airlines handled by BEA. Arrival information such as zone / finals / landing times with the allocated stand and gate number were passed by ticker tape from the MCA. This was broadcast via a tannoy-type system to relevant BEA units from station control.

We had incredible power and authority making almost instant decisions to ensure aircraft departed on time. Examples were: 8 passengers for Paris not on board the aircraft (i.e. missing) at 5 minutes before departure would be refused for that flight. The Captain was advised, flight documents were changed, the aircraft door shut by S.T.D. minus 3 minutes and the aircraft would taxi off its stand on schedule. Cargo late at the aircraft side was another occasion when the slang term 'chop and go' might be used.

There were 5 station Duty Officers, also on a rota basis, to whom we were directly responsible. Our roster system was basically: 6 days on with 4 days off, or to cover leave 6 on and 2 off. The shift time changes were at 0730, 1430 and 2130. Often we worked under extreme pressure of time with the added irritation of apportioning blame and getting a late-departure report from the guilty section supervisor. After two years I began to dislike the job but stayed for another 12 months until the summer of 1975.

To see again places with childhood memories is often a mistake. But my Gran and I spent 09 October visiting the Fareham, Hampshire area. Little had changed in Fayre Road and the Junior School appeared almost the same. Alas, the cow fields where we played or collected bomb shrapnel in the war were modern housing estates. That day quashed my yearnings to re-live old memories.

Continuous freezing fog paralysed Heathrow for 3 days. Not one aircraft landed or took off on 5, 6 or 7 December.

On Boxing Day evening it started to snow at LHR and there were intermittent heavy falls during the next 3 weeks.

1963

Sub-zero temperatures affected the airport (and of course very many other parts of Britain) until 26 January.

Vans had a 40 mph vehicle speed limit. One evening going to work on an unrestricted dual carriageway my van overtook a line of traffic. A police Daimler Dart sports car in the convoy did not like being overtaken. Blue lights appeared from behind. On 21 March my mistake cost me a £4 fine. In almost 40 years of driving this was the only time I was caught.

College friend Peter Harte then living in Denver, USA was about to marry a girl who did not like travel. He wanted to see parts of Europe before settling down to life in America. His planned itinerary was to visit 12 cities in 7 countries in 11 days. In mid-April I went with him and we made 11 flights on 5 airlines. It was really silly to try and appreciate the sights or even get a realistic feeling and flavour of the different cultures. The countries visited were France, West Germany, East Berlin (crossing at 'Check Point Charlie'), Holland, Denmark, Norway and Sweden.

A few other memories from those days: Finnair had a daily flight by a Convair 440 aircraft routing Helsinki-Hamburg-Amsterdam-Heathrow. In 1963 the flight number was AY831. Now (in 1999) after 36 years Finnair uses the same flight number, which must surely be a record for consistency. In the mid-1960s I used this flight several times from Helsinki, which was then flown by a Caravelle aircraft.

Night shift on 20 May was quiet apart from trying to get the three Argosy freighter aircraft to depart on schedule loaded with their 8 pallets. With a colleague I wanted to see the Air Traffic Control Units in the tower.

To say I was fascinated understates the situation. At every opportunity, which meant at least fortnightly, I would sit in the 'Approach Control' area to watch planes being radar vectored from the Watford or Epsom beacons onto the I L S (Instrument Landing System). On foggy nights some aircraft would be 'talked-down' using (PAR) Precision Approach Radar up to the half-mile-from-touch-down point for a visual landing.

Soon afterward I bought an aircraft band VHF radio which when at home was switched onto frequency 119.2 (or 120.4) for approach control or 118.2 for the tower. This habit became addictive. In the mornings I had to switch on the VHF radio to London Volmet (met bulletins) before hearing the BBC News. (I was cured of the obsession when I joined BOAC and was posted to Nigeria).

On 8 August a weekly magazine, *The Aeroplane and Commercial Aviation News*, carried a letter to the Editor written by me titled 'Wanted for the SST: a new airport'. In it I suggested a new airport be built on Salisbury Plain, just south of Airway Green One, solely for the use of the expected influx of Concorde aircraft. My primary thoughts were to separate fast and slow moving craft for Air Traffic reasons and to overcome the expected objections from high noise levels. The proposal included a fast monorail link to Heathrow before speeding to Central London on the then under-discussion elevated system to be built over the existing A4 road. Further I suggested that Check-in, together with Customs and Immigration staff could ride on the train to Salisbury Plain and thus expedite the formalities for Concorde passengers.

(Although not directly relevant to the above paragraph, it is interesting to note that by the Spring of 1999 Air Traffic Control were able to maintain a sustained landing rate of up to 38 aircraft an hour at LHR. This could only apply in perfect weather conditions to remain within the legal vortex separation distances, and with aircrew co-operation. The same rate could also apply to departing aircraft. Modern radar technology and not least skilful air traffic controllers have made huge forward strides since I wrote that article.)

Picking wild mushrooms in season was an awakening adventure at dawn. Towards the end of a nightshift up to 6 of us would get clearance from air traffic to search the grass between the two main runways. Some of the best mushrooms were picked near the aircraft compass-swing area to the east of Terminal One. The idea fell from favour when a nursing sister warned us to beware of the thin film of engine kerosene deposit covering the mushrooms.

They say that nearly everyone remembers what they were doing when President Kennedy was shot. I was on a late shift when an aircraft tarmac observer called on his UHF radio to give us the news quoting a BBC radio news flash. The date of course was 22 November.

An elderly lady sitting beside the emergency exit window on a Viscount being readied for departure to Paris noticed the window was rain smeared. She had told the cabin crew that she wanted to have a good view. Above the window was a sign: TO OPEN–PULL. She did. The heavy frame fell into her lap. An engineer tried to re-fit and re-seal the window. He couldn't. The aircraft was changed and the flight departed almost an hour late. The now wiser and contrite dear old soul was sitting by a clean non-emergency window.

Trident aircraft were being hailed as the new super-jet for BEA. Staff training was needed before it entered commercial service. I was an eager volunteer for a 'Proving flight' on 14 December when the newly delivered G-ARPE was allocated to fly an all-staff special to Nice.

To provide realism we had to check-in with a suitcase weighing 15 kilos and follow usual departure procedures. However, at that time UK Customs would not allow duty free purchases on a day trip. Time-and-motion experts logged every activity including the breakfast service outbound and refreshments served on the return journey.

Test pilot 'Cats Eyes' Cunningham was the Commander with BEA Training Captains Angus, Brown and Carter also in the cockpit. The flight was fast. About 65 minutes after wheels-up from LHR we were overhead a clear and sunny Nice airport at well above 20 thousand feet. The crew told us the engines would be put into 'reverse thrust' to quickly reduce speed followed by a very steep descent. The engines were a bit noisy, then near silence when the aircraft nose was pitched downward. I can now only assume it was a descent rate well in excess of 7 thousand feet a minute. To me it was a thrill. To some others it was sheer fear with a few muted screams to heighten the excitement.

1964

New Years day morning at work was quiet as almost a third of BEA flights were cancelled. None went to Scotland. Many foreign airlines flew their services. In general passenger numbers were mostly low. Some people were refused travel when they were foolish enough to 'top up' their spirit level in the departure lounge. I was called to help restrain 3 boisterous Scandinavians before the police arrived. The shift log book showed 13 passengers did not fly that morning due excess alcohol. The reasoning: if someone was incapable at Heathrow's elevation of 80 feet above sea level, how might they react in an aircraft cabin pressurised at about 5 or 6 thousand feet?

Since my first flight in August 1955 until 01 January 1964 I had made 426 flights on 26 different aircraft types to accumulate 602 hrs 15 mins flying time. These totals exclude the flight Clerk operational figures.

United Airlines had a stewardess training school in Denver, Colorado and after graduating some came to London for a few days. An American friend gave my phone number to about a dozen during the summer. I met most of them. It was a double fascinating period for me. Firstly the girls were refreshingly different. A few were brash and worldly but the others mostly from small-town America showed charm and delight with almost all they saw. An extra interest for me was their knowledge of London and I learned much through their tourist eyes.

Shift working with irregular eating caused me to put on weight. A strict diet brought this down to 12 stone by year's end.

1965

This was a year of change and happiness. BEA management decided to change working conditions for supervisory staff with scant notice. None of us cared much for trade unions but a local panel which represented our grades (M1-M4) suggested we join 'ASSET' as a short term solution to get talks started. Reluctantly most of us did so. The trade union officer recommended we form a traffic-branch 'Steering Committee' to advise the union official. Almost 30 staff met in the control tower canteen on 18 February to elect a committee. Partly in ignorance I agreed to be Secretary. Later I was voted onto the staff panel as one of the three reps. It was exciting in the early months. Staff meetings, then management panel meetings plus union branch meetings at the engineering base steadily eroded my enthusiasm but I stayed for the elected year. In the autumn I attended, as an observer, the official Conference of the union at Eastborne. Clive Jenkins was the General Secretary. The name 'ASSET' became 'ASTMS'. Within two years my membership lapsed. I learned much on human behaviour and how a few fragile words could inflame or settle a small simple problem. Later in life these experiences helped me in dealing with staff relations–a smile was better than three scowls.

My mother and I wanted to re-visit our wartime home on the Isle of Arran. With a hired car we had a good week touring places with childhood memories. We stayed at the Lagg Hotel in Kilmorie near the old school. On 01 June the sun warmed the sand ahead of an incoming tide. On a deserted beach I could not resist a swim in the warm shallow water, but in my underpants. Impulsive actions are fun and long remembered.

Ten days later with friend Brenda I flew to Helsinki to meet some of her university friends. We all had a great time and were invited to return for their mid-summer festivities. Brenda and I arrived by BEA Comet on 17 June and stayed until the 28th. We smuggled many extra bottles of spirits through customs which ensured we had an even warmer welcome. (From memory hard spirits were rationed in Finland and sold only to licensed users on a quota basis at exorbitant prices from just 5 shops in Helsinki).

With a group of students we toured many camp sites and upcountry lakes sleeping in log cabins or under canvas. Saunas with birch twigs were exhilarating but the big party was mid-summer night. All 200 people from a village gathered near a bonfire from 2100 until 0300 or whenever to eat, drink, dance, be merry and sing, especially when the church bells rang at midnight. Yes, I could read a newspaper during the night at a latitude of 60 degrees North..

During the party I met Eeva. She was fun and liked to talk in English. One of her friends, a chap named Hannu, seemed to keep a watchful eye on us. I liked the Finnish people I met and in the following six months I made 5 more visits. Was it love or infatuation ? The language fascinated me and I mostly flew Finnair to try my limited vocabulary on the stewardesses. On

An interesting photo showing part of LHR Terminal 1 (now Terminal 2) with a Viscount parked on Stand Number 7. Taken in June 1960 before the ATC Control Tower was extended skyward. In the background is an aircraft just airborne from Runway 28 right. (BA)

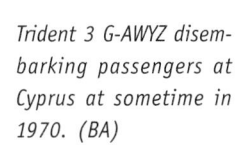

Trident 3 G-AWYZ disembarking passengers at Cyprus at sometime in 1970. (BA)

Above: Passengers boarding a Trident 1C, G-ARPL, at LHR from a coach in July 1970. It looks a 'messy' scene but most people accepted these sort of conditions. (BA)

Left: Passengers about to board a Pionair during a rare charter flight. This one was to the Lake District for United Steel executives in October 1958. I was the Flight Clerk to do the flight documents.

11 December when staying overnight at Loppi with Hannu and his parents the evening temperature was -28° Celsius–which remains my all-time coldest experience. Loppi was a village just 60 kms north of Helsinki where the next day Eeva took me Christmas shopping. Stockmann's department store had the most magnificent and breathtaking displays I have ever seen anywhere. Over a four year period I visited Finland 15 times. After Britain it is my favourite country.

There were other happenings in 1965. BEA shuffled some staff and I happily moved from station control on 26 July to become a supervisor at International check-in. It needed 3 of us on the morning shift to control the surge of up to 400 passengers an hour in a congested area. Every day some passengers were unable to reach check-in before the deadline and missed their flights.

Nightshifts were not a favourite with me as some foreign airlines departed during the 'dozzy-hours' period between 0330 and 0530. Before midnight there was a 132 seat Vanguard to Palma, Majorca with flight no. BE 010. The excursion fare was cheap and the flight was popular. To meet demand a string of extras followed the prime flight at between 15 and 30 minute intervals subject to the ability of ground handling to cope. Alertness was needed at check-in and boarding as the 'extras' were numbered with an Alpha suffix, BE 010A/B/C/D and I can remember a 5th as BE 010E. We were grateful that a high percentage of these night flight passengers checked in at the West London Air Terminal and used the coach service to LHR.

One unforgettable short break holiday was in a small family hotel on the Costa Capirica south of Lisbon from 5 September. Breakfast was sardines or other fish straight from boats on the beach to the kitchen grill, then served with chunky home made bread. Other meals were also so good they attracted the local people. An unspoilt beach area made it easy to relax and enjoy life slowly.

That was the year that was–lots of fun, variety and joy.

1966

New Year for me started in Scotland. After playing the 'first-footing' ritual on a few of my mother's neighbours I did a quality control job. Scottish water was tasted from one or more bottles. I slept well.

After lunch the next day our family and friends met at St. Margaret's Church in Dunfermline for the baptism of my niece. She was named Nicola Alexandra and I was honoured to be her godfather.

Robert Burns was depicted on a set of post office stamps issued on 25 January. I flew to Scotland and then travelled by train from coast to coast posting first day covers at special locations such as Alloway in Ayrshire, Burn's birthplace. These covers were given different commemorative handstamps.

Aerophilately seemed the next logical interest. Four UK country stamps were issued on 02 May. Just after midnight I was in a queue at London's all-night post office in Trafalgar Square. I bought sheets of the more rare phosphor lined stamps, but most were of the Scottish and Northern Ireland values. Using pre-overprinted post office covers I spent the rest of the night affixing stamps to them. 100 were prepared and flown to Belfast for its first day of issue postmark.

Cairngorms was the scene on the Scottish stamp. 100 covers with this stamp and the one shilling BEA airways letter service label were carried by me to Glasgow. But there were differences. I flew on the first BEA Comet jet flight Heathrow to Glasgow which was the first aircraft to land at the new Abbotsinch airport. The Comet 4B aircraft was G-ARJN flown by Captain David Jack who kindly signed some of my covers during the flight. After a cursory look around the bedecked Abbotsinch my priority was to get the 100 flown covers into Glasgow central post office for the first day handstamp.

America was the big event of the year. In the summer Reggie (for Regina) Le Geyt, a former Jersey flight Clerk with whom I had kept in contact, asked if she could use some of my rebate cargo concessions. In 100 kilo consignments we packed and shipped via BOAC all her belongings to New York. Reggie was to marry Captain J P Tristani USMC, a test pilot based at the US Naval Air Test Center, Patuxent River, Maryland.

With an invite to the wedding I planned my first USA visit to include an extension to Denver and return home via Bermuda. On Saturday 26 November my first long haul flight was on BA 501 a Super VC-10 G-ASGD from LHR to JFK. It departed 3 hours late awaiting the incoming aircraft. On arrival it was a taxi ride to New York's La Guardia Airport for the $14 pay-in-flight Eastern Airlines B727 Shuttle Service to Washington National airport. (Many years later BEA copied both the idea of a 'Shuttle' and its pay-on-board system to its prime UK domestic flights.) The plane was almost empty - it was Thanksgiving holiday weekend.

Reggie and JP met and drove me around parts of the city before a 2 hour journey to their home in Lexington Park, Maryland. It was at about 0300 when we arrived. Reggie was a very good cook and I can clearly remember some superb meals she prepared in the next few days. First visits to countries are rarely forgotten, and for me, this one never will be.

Patuxent Air Base was huge with all kinds of aircraft types in various stages of development and evaluation. J P showed me over a few planes but I suspect there were many others hidden away and still on the 'secret' list.

On 30 November I flew from Dulles Airport Washington to Denver–the Mile High City at the foot of the Rockies. Peter Harte met me from the TWA B707 at 1855 Mountain Standard Time. Early next morning we got security clearance to visit the 'Denver Center' of air traffic control. At one time I was surprised to see on a radar screen 8 or 9 aircraft out over the desert in a straight line for the landing runway.

The ATC jargon differed from that used in London but I had not expected the clock times to be that of good old British GMT.

Rocky Mountains were next. Peter drove me there where a sign said:

> Loveland Pass
> Continental Divide
> Elevation: 11,988 feet
> Arapaho

It was truly breath-taking and the beautiful snowy scenery made me vow to return. I did a few years later.

Denver had cold crisp air on 2 December and it was a quick morning tour of the city. By 1410 I was airborne on a TWA B707 back to Washington. Continuous moderate to severe turbulence, which the Captain attributed to a jetstream, encouraged the crew to climb to 41,000 feet. This remains my highest ever subsonic cruising height. The schedule was 3 hours 20 minutes but the plane landed 45 minutes early.

At Washington City air terminal former flight Clerk Joan Wood and her husband Graham Hughes (of BOAC) met me for the drive to Lexington Park for J.P's stag party.

Wedding bells rang at 1500 on Saturday 3 December when Reggie and J P were married. At least 10 Britons were among the 50 guests at the lavish reception.

Bleary eyed at sunrise a stewardess Gail and I were driven to Washington airport for a flight on a National Airlines Electra aircraft via Philadelphia to New York. As it was a Sunday our tour of some of the sights was almost hassle-free.

Next morning Gail showed me more of the city including Christmas displays in Macys department store before a snack lunch at Madison Square. My first visit to New York lasted just more than 24 hours. I left on a BOAC VC-10 aircraft for the 2 hour flight South to Bermuda on 5 December.

Isobel and Howard Rouse, friends from my school days in Bermuda some 16 years earlier, met and drove me to their home in Somerset parish. The purpose of the visit was to see again by bicycle the places I knew so well as a young teenager. In general not a lot seemed to have changed. Although not sunny I felt compelled to have a swim. I did and enjoyed it. The two day visit passed quickly.

At 2110 Atlantic Standard time on 7 December B707 G-APFL left Bermuda for the 7 hour night flight to Heathrow. About 3200 miles later we landed on a damp, dreary day. But that first trip to America will remain the most memorable.

1967

January was routine but from then onwards the year gathered momentum and my life changed direction, and by December I was working for BOAC (British Overseas Airways Corporation).

Aer Lingus offered some supervisors an 'interline tour' via Shannon to New York for just a few pounds. Naturally I leapt at the opportunity. On 13 May the B707 developed a technical fault during a routine stop at Boston which delayed us by 3 hours.

Reggie and J P Tristani met me at Kennedy airport and then kindly filled the next four days with an amazing variety of adventures. Boat trips, Broadway shows, lavish meals, less flash snacks in Greenwich Village, plus most of the regular tourist sights and seeing a working session of the United Nations. Next it was upstate to visit West Point Military Academy. Then home via Dublin after a week of intense enjoyment.

'BEACON', the BEA reservations computer was on trial installation at LHR from May onward. There were teething problems, mostly with the dedicated line to West London Air Terminal. At first glance I thought it was just a novelty and paid little heed to its operation. One of the 5 supervisors on the ticket desk moved and I asked to be the replacement although I had very little detailed knowledge of fares. In early June I attended a 2 day course on how to operate 'BEACON' and an engineer showed a few of us how to boot (reset) the computer when it went down.

Flying lessons had long interested me but the cost was too great. The Airways Aero Club at Booker offered attractive rates and in July I started a course flying on Beagle Terrier aircraft. The registrations were G-ASAD, G-ASDL, G-ARZT, G-ARZU. After 9 flights around High Wycombe and Henley-on-Thames I stopped for financial reasons.

Although content with life I had a yearning to move somewhere–almost anywhere. Using the staff vacancy notice system I applied for four jobs during September and October. One was at LHR Station Control (promotion in grade), one was for Station Manager at Aberdeen, another was at Manchester and the fourth was with BOAC (British Overseas Airways Corporation). The interviews were spread over many weeks and the results were: LHR offered and a week later BOAC also said yes. Manchester rejected my application and Aberdeen was late with an interview date.

Another visit to America had been planned and I left LHR on 11 November for Denver to see Peter Harte and his wife. Once again I went sightseeing in the Rockies before going to Salt Lake City (the Mormon capital of the world). Next it was further west to see Los Angeles and San Francisco. All of which fascinated me. However during this trip the British Government devalued the pound sterling, and this curtailed some sightseeing.

On my return to London there was a letter with an interview date for the Aberdeen job and another from BOAC saying I had to have a full medical for overseas duties. As a result of the letters I rushed to Aberdeen for the interview and later that day had my medical at LHR. I was passed as fit. BEA refused to release me to BOAC for two weeks as a result of the upheaval in fares following the Government devaluation. Finally on 11 December I joined BOAC at the Victoria Air Terminal in central London with the title 'Reservations Officer Overseas (Pool)'.

This is the notice that excited me to transfer jobs from BEA to BOAC for world-wide travel. After interviews and medical clearance I joined BOAC on 11 December 1967.

BOAC STAFF VACANCY NOTICE

694 CENTRAL LONDON

POST: RESERVATIONS ASSISTANT (POOL)

SCALE: 'M.2' £1316 per annum rising to £1516 per annum

A vacancy exists for a Reservations Assistant on the Reservations Manager's Pool based at Airways Terminal.

DUTIES:

1. Relief duties at overseas stations

2. Assist at overseas stations during peak traffic periods

3. Perform "on the job" training at overseas stations

4. Ensuring that the proper standard of reservations service is maintained during temporary posting

5. Investigating reservation discrepancies and complaints on behalf of Regional Reservations Superintendents during periods at Airways Terminal

6. Undertaking any reservations duties world-wide as directed by Reservations Manager

11
JOINING BOAC AND OVERSEAS POSTINGS

New Years Day in 1968 was on a Monday and I was one of 12 students attending an Advanced Fares study course. Held at the BOAC training centre located opposite the Victoria Air Terminal in Buckingham Palace Road, London, it was an unhappy week for me. This level three course was well beyond my basic (BEA) knowledge of global fares and tariff constructions. On a later course I achieved a better result.

Lagos was my first overseas posting. There was a well established pre-departure check list: medical jabs and tabs (pills), work permit, tropical clothing, travellers cheques (UK law required the amount be entered in our passports), plus up to 20 kilos of 'goodies' such as non-obtainable items of food or medicines for the expatriate staff.

VC-10 G-ARVE operating BA 275 on 21 February carried me via Frankfurt and Kano on the 11 hour flight to Ikeja Airport, Lagos.

Anthony Farnfield met and skilfully escorted me through the many chaotic arrival formalities including the brazen 'dash' points. ('Dash' equates to an almost compulsory tip or fee given under duress). For the next 7 weeks my home was at the Farnfield's house in the city suburb of Apapa. His wife Judith had arranged a light lunch before Anthony and I drove to the town office to meet the management team and local reservations staff.

BBC World Service News was a feature after supper when the 3 young Farnfields, aged from 3 to 8 years, were put to bed. The adults supped cool beer on the patio which was surrounded with anti-mosquito repellents. Patrolling the grounds was a 'night-watchman' armed with a club. Most expatriate houses had a 'guard' as a status symbol.

Week One for me was giving an induction course to 6 staff. Two were from the Northern Nigerian offices in Kano and Kaduna and both were from the Haussa tribe. The main purpose of my posting however was to be leave relief for Anthony as Chief Reservations Officer (CRO). I had to learn a lot quickly such as: checking daily the sales shop ticket issues, collecting ticket stock from the main vault at Barclays Bank, controlling the seat allocation on all Northbound flights and watching for local irregularities in many of the reservations functions. Airport Manager Rod Hoare gave me support and guidance before the passenger list was released to the airport.

Senior expatriates of major British companies wanted and got priority personal attention. Their annual First Class - often round the world - holiday was valuable revenue for BA.

Sales Manager Western Africa was Marcus Buck and after one of his territorial trips to nearby Cotonou in Dahomey (now Benin) and Lome in Togo I was fascinated by the depth and content of his sales report. It kindled in me a yearning to see and learn more about different countries.

Temperatures averaged near 30 degrees C with high humidity. The increasingly heavy showers were a prelude to the rainy season which could give up to 12 inches in a month.

BOAC owned a generous sized cabin (5 rooms could sleep 8) situated on Tarqua Beach. The families of other multi-national companies shared the area. At weekends we boarded a 10 seater motorboat for a short trip across a bay to the sandy beach before a 50 yards walk through the spruce-like trees to the cabin. The BOAC families shared the picnic foods with chilled liquids and a happy relaxing time was had by all.

Weekday life had so many frustrations that the carefree picnic was a necessity. Electricity outages daily lasted from minutes to many hours. The half-speed SITA Communications link with London and the telephones behaved no better. Driving, which was then on the left-hand side of the road, was not fun. Indiscipline with congestion plus good sized pot holes were a challenge almost like bumper-car driving. Military security road blocks which varied from nuisance delays to frightening gun point searches were also a part of life.

Europeans were usually not much troubled by the Biafran War although tribal matters did not feature in our conversations. One afternoon we watched a noisy frenzied group fracas from the BOAC office. After some cheering the crowd dispersed. Lying in a bloody mess was a mutilated person. It was thought he was an enemy - an Ibo tribesman from the Port Harcourt area of Nigeria.

Africa, whether North, South, East or West, had many surprises and not all were agreeable. Over a 12 year period I had more than 20 visits ranging from 5 days to 8 months. This first memorable posting ended on 09 April when

G-ARVE flew me on the daylight flight to Heathrow via Accra and Tripoli.

(As a postscipt to my experiences in Lagos, the Federal Capital of Nigeria moved to Abuja at the end of May 1999 to coincide with a change to civilian Government.)

Just 5 days later I was on the move again. I had one day at Head Office, a two day trip to Scotland visiting my mother and family loaded with tropical fruits from Lagos, and just two days at my Windsor flat before I was at LHR with a BOAC boarding pass for Lusaka, in Zambia.

Easter Sunday evening, 14 April, was spent on another VC-10 with a stop at Frankfurt before crossing the Equator minutes ahead of landing at Nairobi. At that time most airlines made a fuss over the symbolic crossing into the Southern hemisphere and gave passengers a certificate during flight. BOAC stopped this practice soon afterwards. Next the plane called at Ndola in Northern Zambia before its final destination of Lusaka. The elapsed journey time from London had been just less than 16 hours.

Chief Reservations Officer Peter Hodd, for whom I was his leave relief, met me and despite my fatigue explained his role and duties at the airport.

Cairo Road in Lusaka, the main high street, was a fine wide avenue intended by some colonial gents many years ago to be part of a continental-long highway stretching from Cape Town to Cairo. The BA Sales shop was an annexe in the only down town hotel on this road. This meant my bedroom and the office were only about 50 yards apart.

Friday night was music night. Andy Ogilvie, the BA Airport Manager, knew some English nurses at the local hospital. My accommodation was the BA house in select Nairn Close with spacious grounds and large swimming pool. The word 'party' was heard by some ex-pats of the local airline Zambia Airways (QZ) who offered to bring themselves, bar-b-que equipment and good music. Crates of beer plus beefy T-bone steaks and sausages set the scene for merriment. Many of the 10 to 20 guests had a midnight splash in the pool to end the evening. A current hit record was Tom Jones singing 'Delilah'. Even today this song revives happy romantic memories of those parties.

Rhodesia under Prime Minister Ian Smith had declared UDI (Unilateral Declaration of Independence) and was under economic sanctions. On the Zambian border at Victoria Falls the rail bridge line was blocked. There were at least 3 road crossings where formalities were minimal every time I used them. Quirks existed in the sanctions. One example I saw. A Lusaka supermarket sold cans of baked beans marked 'Product of Kenya' When that consignment finished the next supply of tins were labelled 'Product of Rhodesia'.

Dave Harrison, the Zambia Airways Reservations Officer, was one of the Brits I would meet for an after-work beer. On the May Day holiday Dave and I drove across the Rhodesian border at the Kariba Dam. It was a majestic and almost unbelievable structure. Under an earlier Central African Federation treaty some of the Kariba generated electricity was for Zambia. As a tourist I knew no more.

Work permits were necessary for most postings. To renew them we had to leave the country. On 12 June I left Lusaka for Nairobi and took the opportunity to visit Mombassa on the Kenyan coast flying down on an F27, 5Y-AAB, returning two days later. Most of the internal flights in Zambia were flown by a BAC1-11 aircraft RJ-RCI.

Mike McGuire, the expat Zambia Airways Manager at Livingstone, and his wife Jeannette accommodated me for two weekend visits. The wonder of the Victoria Falls almost challenges description - and I visited it four more times. Other adventures included one escorted and two free range safari trips to a nearby game reserve. Tourists were few. The more rare wild animals were car-shy, took patience to find but the sightings were worth the effort.

Saturday night at the Victoria Falls Hotel across the bridge in Rhodesia, was the formal dinner dance of the week. On 22 June the three of us went for dinner and then to the hotel casino. Many of the gamblers were Rhodesian tobacco farmers. We left at 0200 for the 10 minute drive to Zambia - happy but minus much money.

Sunday afternoon I boarded an Air Rhodesia Viscount, VP-WAT, for the 75 minute flight from Victoria Falls airport to Salisbury. For the next three nights my home was the well known Meikles Hotel, with its glorious refinements and colonial furnishings.

Regional headquarters of BOAC and a Sales shop were maintained in Salisbury during the entire period of UDI.

BOAC pilots were on strike. In order to get home I was booked on South African Airways flight SA 218 on 26 June. The B707 ZS-EUX, routed Johannesburg-Salisbury-Luanda (Angola)-Las Palmas-Frankfurt-London. The stop at Luanda was for fuel (although local mosquitoes were waiting in the open air transit area for their night meal). At the Las Palmas stop there was a crew change whilst passengers could gulp fresh cool dawn air on the tarmac, well away from the stuffy and crowded fuselage where we had endured the night. My seat was the middle one of three in the rear row - where the toilet queue began. 15 hours 45 minutes was the flying time and the total elapsed time was 18 hours 40 minutes.

Despite rain at LHR when we finally landed at 1355 I was so pleased to be home. On the following day, 28 June, I reported back to the Victoria Air Terminal in London.

Zambia posting number 2 started on 14 July when I left LHR via Nairobi for Lusaka. The purpose of this visit was to be Acting Airport Manager at Ndola when Alan Hillman went on leave. I enjoyed being close to the majestic VC10 aircraft. There was a small Sales and Reservations unit in the town run efficiently by two women whose husbands were on contract from South Africa. I enjoyed the variety of tasks and meeting many people at the Expatriate Club. However on 15 August my time at Ndola was up and I flew to Lusaka.

French airline, UTA, on a once weekly service, was the only direct link between Zambia and South Africa. On 16 August I flew on F-BIUZ to be met at Johannesburg Airport by Dave Williams. He was the BA Area Reservations Liaison Officer and I was to be his leave relief.

Working in the SAA (South African Airways) central reservations office my job was decision making. At 48 hours before departure BA London space (seat) control released the flight to the boarding point. Although SAA was the official handling agent I had the authority to over-ride any decision and further over-book/or undersell London bound flights.

Regional Manager Peter Baker thought it would be useful for me to see the BA coastal sales shops to better understand their problems with late bookings. On 29 September I visited Durban, met Gerry MacGilvray, the District Sales manager and the five reservations girls. Two days later I flew on another B727 to Port Elizabeth where the office was small. Areas on the outskirts of the town had large craters caused by recent flash floods. On 02 October it was on to Cape Town for the weekend. Parents of Johannesburg Sales Representative Tertius Van Zyl kindly showed me the area including the vineyards at Stellenbosch, the Simonstown dockyard plus the incredibly beautiful coastline and of course Table Mountain.

Apartheid rules were different in Cape Province. I was surprised to find, for example, that the upper deck on a bus was not segregated. During one short journey as the bus started to fill a black man sat beside me and I felt a revulsion. In just 6 weeks in South Africa I had grown used to segregation. On 06 October I returned to Jo'burg and then on 23 October I took the daylight BA 108 via Entebbe to London.

Looking back now on that 10 week posting I learned much about life in South Africa and was intrigued at the various strands and divisions within everyday life. My work was interesting, my social life was varied with good food, parties and fun. Overall it was an enlightening educational experience.

During some UK leave on 02 November I met my grandmother at Formby and we visited her family grave at St. James Church, Orrell near Wigan, Lancashire. After seeing the state of the cemetery she decided against being buried there and opted for cremation.

India was my next posting and I left LHR on 11 November for New Delhi. Also sitting in the rear row of the VC10 G-ARVK was Peter Spencer on his first overseas training assignment. (By 1999 Peter was Director Americas for BA). As the aircraft roared along runway 10 Right at LHR some catering equipment fell on the galley floor and he appeared nervous. During conversation he said there was another trainee on the same flight.

After five and a half hours we landed at Baghdad and I met Phil Dunnington. He was outside in the transit area looking to record aircraft registrations - as plane spotters do. Our flight continued via Bahrain and Doha landing at Delhi at 0545 local time. The 3 of us stayed at the Ashoka Hotel which was on the outskirts of Delhi.

Saftarjong Airport was a small private airfield just across the road from our hotel. Seeing little planes pass over made me seek flying lessons. I was told no, but 'sightseeing' flights were possible. This meant therefore that I got four unofficial flying lessons on the home-built Pushpak aircraft which I greatly enjoyed. Registrations were VT-DMY and VT-DTR. Political relations with Pakistan were unstable. Non-Indian nationals were limited in their activities and this included flying. Several times during my stay the air-raid sirens were tested.

Sightseeing is a must in this area and like all good tourists I took the Taj Express train to the Taj Mahal and Agra on 08 December. To list the numerous sights and experiences I had would be like reciting from a holiday brochure. The Ashoka Hotel was packed with oddities or maybe time honoured traditions. The sitar band at dinner every night at 19.36 would faithfully play "Down Mexico Way". The temperature in Delhi was beginning to resemble England in Autumn and we found the hotel swimming pool almost too chilly. But overall the happenings, events and cultural experiences in Delhi will long be remembered.

Collecting souvenirs and other memorabilia and starting to pack for my return to London was abruptly halted on 14 December. I got a shock memo from Jack Cowley, our Admin. Assistant at Head office saying "We have in mind to translate you to Calcutta for Christmas. The CRO there has asked for leave and we thought you might be good enough, since you are nearby, to take over his duties for a month. I am sorry this is short notice but Christmas in Calcutta might make a contrasting change for you". I could have said no but my sense of adventure said yes.

Early morning on 18 December I was aboard an Indian Airlines Caravelle from Delhi to Calcutta. The local CRO Malcolm D'Netto met and drove me through some streets crowded with people, cars, bicycles and cows. The density of the city was almost unreal and I was surprised by the shabbiness of most people and buildings. It had to be a fast learning curve for me in a busy reservations office.

Midnight Mass at Christ the King Cathedral was almost unbearable due to the congestion inside. After the two hour service my hosts for the evening, an Anglo-Indian family who had befriended me, celebrated with a late dinner party.

Christmas Dinner was spent with John Blows, Regional Manager, and his family. By late afternoon I was weary and returned to the Grand Hotel. From the roof I saw some local riots where tram cars were burnt and riot police in action. This behaviour was not too infrequent in Calcutta but it took me unawares. Yes, Jack Cowley was right. It was a contrasting Christmas.

Boxing Day until New Years Eve was a period of work punctuated by parties, which became almost boring. But on 31 December there was a mammoth party with 600 guests at the home of a rather wealthy gentleman. Eating, drinking and making small talk gets tedious after five hours and by 0400 I was glad to get back to the hotel.

1969

Bed rolls in the gutter did not arouse my curiosity as I walked the half mile from hotel to the office. The staff asked if the dead bodies wrapped in the bed rolls upset me. After that I took a taxi to work. Night time temperatures in Calcutta got near to freezing and this killed the weakest beggars who were left for the authorities to collect each morning.

Seeing three waifs holding down a bitch dog to suckle milk from it was one of the saddest sights I saw in India. In an alleyway near the BOAC Office the children held the dog and with little resistance from it managed to get a few mouthfuls of nourishment.

Cockroaches in the tea pot at breakfast did not appeal to me. After two consecutive mornings, I moved from the old-type imperious Grand Hotel to the modern Park Hotel. On the pavement outside was a young beggar with a large open sore above his knee. To avoid being pestered, I never gave money to street beggars. One morning, I noticed he was missing. I asked a nearby news vendor who just pointed to a bed roll in the gutter. To this day I regret I did not donate even five rupees (5 shillings or 25 pence) to allow the chap at least one decent meal before he died.

Thai Airways Caravelle Aircraft HS-TGL flew me from Calcutta to Kathmandu on 22 January. The runway had recently been extended to allow Caravelle operations provided the jet was fitted with a parachute breaking system. This was a novel experience for me. I stayed at the de-luxe Hotel De L'Annapurna. In contrast I visited a seedy pension where an assortment of hippies of the times lived or visited to indulge in their drug habits. The squalor so nauseated me that I was never tempted to try drugs.

Royal Nepal Airlines flew a once weekly sightseeing trip around Mount Everest. On 23 January I took this tour on an F27 aircraft, registered 9N-AAR. It was a perfect cloudless morning and some passengers, including me, visited the cockpit to get a panoramic view. The high-wing design of the plane did give a good overall aspect but many of us were a little disappointed as the mountain range looked so similar with little idea of perspective. Mount Everest was not immediately apparent even though it was the highest peak at 29,098 feet.

Indian Airlines F27 VT-DVG took me back from Kathmandu to Calcutta on 24 January. A few hours later I boarded BA 799, G-ARVJ, for London. A snow storm at Teheran caused the plane to divert to Karachi. With luck, BA 921 was in transit just 90 minutes later and we got seats on the B707, G-APFO, via Rome to arrive at LHR 20 hours 45 minutes after leaving Calcutta. The date was 25 January.

Next excitement was a double lightening

strike on Vanguard G-APEB whilst in the holding pattern at Watford (or was it Garston at that time?). It was on 06 February and I was returning from a few days holiday in Scotland. The Captain was not happy and we got immediate air traffic clearance well below cloud base for a 'quickie' landing at LHR. (I think we landed on runway 23 Left.)

BOADICEA–the BOAC reservations computer system - was spreading across the airline network. Six of us were given the full formal 2 week training course from 10 February. This was followed by a few days of practice in the telephone sales unit.

Tripoli in Libya was my next posting when I left LHR on 04 March on BA 143. The local reservations official had been splitting sales commission with a travel agent. My brief was to restore confidence in BA as a non-corrupt organisation in an environment where bribery was not unknown. For me to be politically squeaky clean, I had to remove all the St Michael labels from my clothing before leaving London. (The St Michael brand was considered to be a Jewish company.) King Idris was on the throne. The Colonel Gadaffi days were still to come. I visited several nearby tourist places including the ruins at Sabrata.

Kingdom of Libya Airlines (KLA) Caravelle 5A-DAE took me on 22 March via Benghazi to Cairo. The next 3 days were crowded with the usual touristy adventures such as visiting the pyramids, riding a camel, tour of the city museum, trip to Suez Canal plus the near obligatory visit to a naughty night-club.

Ethiopian Airlines on a delayed B720 flew me via Asmara to Addis Ababa on 25 March. Haile Sellasie was still the ruler in Ethiopia. To justify my stay in the country I did spend at least 2 hours visiting the BA Manager in his one-room sales office. After 3 days of tours and sightseeing I flew to Nairobi.

30 March was my next move - again to Zambia, but based at Ndola. My main task was to assist in the reservations unit but the new District Manager, Chris Preece was keen for me to visit the travel agents in 4 towns on the copper belt. They were Kitwe, Chingola, Luanshya and Mufulira on the border of Zaire near Lubumbashi. Not too far from Kitwe was the simple monument of stones erected near the spot where UN Secretary General Dag Hammershold had died in a plane crash. That 4 week posting was one of the happiest due mainly to the kindness of Chris and Ann Preece.

East African Airways Comet 5Y-AAA flew me from Ndola to Nairobi on 26 April to renew my work permit. The original document was valid for a month but by leaving the country for a minimum of 24 hours a further 28 day extension was granted. The next afternoon a VC10 returned me to Ndola.

Sadness was in the air on 30 April. The last BOAC flight to leave Ndola was G-ARVL. The runway was of sufficient length but it was of sub-standard width. Zambia Airways operated DC8 aircraft to London and their engines overlapped the runway. Being uncompetitive, the Zambian Government withdrew the BOAC licence. Chris Preece with Jenny Pickering, from the small reservations unit, and myself raised a toast as Victor Lima taxied out. Moments later the full throttle vibrations from the Conway engines shook our beer glasses as the VC10 roared down the runway. I hate to use a cliché –but–it really was the end of an era.

East African Airways Comet, 5H-AAF operating EC 892 was the very last big jet to leave Ndola. It was Saturday 03 May and I was on board for Nairobi with a few farewell drinks inside me.

Panafric Hotel in Nairobi was the usual crew rest stopover place. After one night there, I continued to London on G-ARVC the Sunday daylight flight via Cairo.

Staff travel regulations required family members to be accompanied on rebate journeys. On 08 May, I flew with my mother to New York on her first visit to the USA. Reggie and JP showed my mother, her friend Lily and me around the city and parts of New Jersey. My mother continued her holiday for another 3 weeks. I returned to London on 12 May. Both Atlantic flights were by VC10 aircraft.

Posting number 4 to Zambia was on 17 May to relieve the acting chief Reservations Officer. Then for work permit purposes, I flew on 5X-UVJ, a super VC10 of EAAC from Lusaka to Dar Es Salaam for a 3 day visit. Ernie Alsina who was the acting CRO there drove me to the local market where I bought 30 kilos of fresh prawns on 18 June. They were loaded in the aircraft hold. The plane developed a fault and left 5 hours late. The prawns were baked in the hold and were 'off' on arrival at Lusaka. Harry Cabel Manager Zambia and his wife Marcelle were just 2 of the disappointed friends that evening. After a spell at Ndola, I returned to Lusaka on a grand old DC3 of Zambia Airways. The plane was 9J-RDR and the date was 25 June. Then on 02 July, I flew to LHR via Nairobi and Tripoli for some UK leave.

With my grandmother on 15 July I made my first hovercraft flight from the Isle of Wight to Portsmouth. We were on a day trip from

Sutton. My grandmother usually spent part of each year with friends, Mr and Mrs Mumme, at Carshalton Beeches, Sutton in Surrey and at other times stayed with her niece Clare Smith. Tom, Clare and their 5 children lived at Freshfield, Formby in Lancashire.

Bombay was my next posting when I left LHR on 20 July. BA 764, G-ARVF, routed via Frankfurt, Beirut, Kuwait and Abu Dhabi. Neil Armstrong landed on the moon just minutes after we landed at Kuwait. Captain Sledge relayed the BBC World Service over the Aircraft Intercom System from 2015 GMT. Despite atmospherics, the excitement of the occasion echoed round the aircraft cabin.

To register as an alcoholic was almost a ritual for tourists upon arrival at Bombay Airport. Who was I to break with tradition? To buy beer or liquor, a permit was needed even for visitors. A ration card was marked for every unit purchased and there was a monthly allocation.

Twenty two staff were engaged in the reservations and sales shop functions. The units were usually frantically busy helping to facilitate would-be migrants to obtain entry permits for the UK. Most of them were uneducated near relatives of a resident British sponsor. All related paperwork, including getting a passport, was done for them by BA staff. At the airport the migrants were shown a 'mock' aircraft toilet to avoid 'accidents' during flight. The training programme in this and other accepted Western ways took about 4 hours.

Monsoon rains fall in July. The average of 24 inches seemed to fall on me that month. But it did not stop my attempts to try and play golf and even have a swim in the sea. Willie McKie, the Area Manager, and his wife Dolde had a flat in the same block as the Airport Manager and I. This was very convenient for sharing the staff car to and from the office.

Colombo in Ceylon (later Sri Lanka) was my next destination. Early on 08 August, I flew to Colombo for a short visit and meeting with the BA sales agents Air Ceylon. The next day a Qantas B707 carried me to Singapore via Kuala Lumpur. After a Sunday meeting in Singapore, I flew on BA 725 to Calcutta for an overnight stop. Finally the next day an Indian Airlines Caravelle returned me to Bombay.

Amhedabad in Gujerat State (via Baroda) was my next two day duty visit from 26 August to check on the local non-regular ticketing agents. I arrived with 5 bottles of alcohol and received the warmest of welcomes! The area scenery was beautiful and there was just time for me to visit a shrine to Mahatma Ghandi.

Bye, bye, Bombay (or Mumbai to use its current name) was on 4 September when I boarded Swissair HB-IDE for Bangkok. The Vietnam War was raging and American troops were on R and R chasing beer and birds–living while they could. But for me sightseeing: the floating market, Buddhist temples, cruel cock fighting, elegant Thai dancing and more were crammed into 3 days.

Three hours on BA 922, G-APFH, took me to Hong Kong on 07 September. The local manager showed me some of the sights during the two day visit. I was impressed but not overawed. A later visit gave me a better feeling of atmosphere in the Colony.

Tokyo was next. Logically, I was going the wrong way from Bombay to get home to London via Japan. During my time on the overseas pool, the BA managers I met were kind and considerate and allowed reasonable flexibility with my travel plans. Weariness had caught up with me and despite a tour of the usual places-to-see, Tokyo left me little to remember. It rained and was cold. I probably missed a lot but of all the capital cities I ever visited it left the least impression.

Thursday evening 11 September BA 851, G-ATZD, left Tokyo on the Polar route, crossed the International Date Line, to arrive at Anchorage 6 hours 15 minutes later on the same day. There were a few interesting hours of daylight to see the vast ice shelves below before more hours of darkness. The plane landed at LHR at 0800 BST on 12 September to give a flying time of 15 hours 10 minutes. I remember thinking how lovely it was to be home.

Three training courses and some UK leave took up the time until 29 November when I was sent to Johannesburg to give new staff some training. The VC10 left LHR with snow on the ground and had to divert to Khartoum en route to Entebbe due to low cloud but we were only 2 hours late arriving in Jo'burg. My accommodation was the Moulin Rouge Hotel in Hillbrow, near where it all 'happened' in the city.

Unscheduled movements were either the fun or the curse of being 'available' on the overseas pools. It was suggested that I stop off at Nairobi on 14 December whilst on the way home as the CRO had fallen ill with a leg injury. That break in my journey was to last for 5 months.

Christmas, New Year and Easter were all spent in Nairobi. The office work was often demanding, but the rewards of excursions and the expatriate social life were the big plus benefits.

Diary entry for 25 December reads: Noon, drinks and Christmas lunch at John and Beth Webb's house with six other BA staff. Excellent. 1800 returned Intercontinental Hotel, siesta. 2000 until midnight drinks and a second Christmas dinner at Lloyd and Christa Paxton's house. What an orgy of food, drink and good company!

New Year's Eve ended with a morning full of work followed by the final 1969 round of festivities. I had lunch at the Thorn Tree Hotel with Mike and Lynda Wickings, others joined us later for drinks. The last few hours of the year were spent enjoying a briflace (an African word for barbecue) at a Country Club outside of Nairobi where we all celebrated in traditional fashion.

1970

Ten hours into the New Year I was driving with the Wickings to Negure and then to the Flamingo Lake to see the majestic birds. Later we continued to Thompsons Falls to view the beauty of that area. This meant we had to cross the magical Equator line and celebrated with a good old fashioned British cup of tea at a wayside restaurant on the 'line'.

Social life was hectic. Many Head Office personnel arranged visits to East Africa to escape the cold London weather. As the acting CRO I had to entertain (or at least be polite to!) people like auditors and escort them to nearby game reserves and other attractions. Bob Geddes was Regional Sales Manager and Roy Rogers was the District Sales Manager Out of hours I would meet Airport Manager Alan Hillman and his wife Kit as well as Mike and Lyn Wickings plus Martin and Margaret Rhoades. Mike and Martin were on secondment from BA to EAAC as training officers in the reservations department.

Manager Kenya, Geoff Bridges, was very understanding that my duties often involved irregular working hours. The BA reservations unit was open 24 hours daily, every day and I was responsible for the seat control of up to 26 flights a week. My job in Nairobi embraced more than just the reservations function. The Sales Shop was the least trouble with the most problems arising from over-bookings. Some over-sales were the result of the standard VC10 operating in lieu of the larger Super version. Occasional technical or weather problems had their own impact when delays put pressure on the town office to contact passengers. At weekends or in the evenings it was not unusual for the duty town staff to phone me for advice. The airport too, would call for help when the staff were under extreme commercial or operational pressure. Daily there was a London bound flight at 0030. My sleep was rationed on bad nights!

Staff numbers in reservations fluctuated around the 25 to 30 figure to allow for shift workings. One of the main-stays was Tony D'Souza, who although born in Kenya had a short term problem with his work permit in 1970, but is still in 1999 employed as the BA East African Reservations Officer. He had a stabalising effect during some of the turbulent reservations re-organisations and was a great help to me. During my posting in Nairobi, and also at other places, I sat on several selection panels for reservations staff and a few of those chosen are still with BA in 1999.

Mauritius sounded like an exciting place to visit and renew my Kenyan work permit. On 15 February I flew on 5X-UVA, an EAAC Super VC10, via Dar es Salaam for a 36 hour visit. I was most impressed with the island and crammed as much as I could into the time available. The 4 hour return flight on G-ARVF gave me the chance to catch up on sleep. Renewing a work permit was a good way to snatch a break in another country.

Zanzibar also sounded fascinating. On 27 March I flew on 5H-MMT, a VC10, to Dar es Salaam and stayed at the Kilimanjaro Hotel. Chris Waters was the District Manager and Mike Ramshaw was the CRO at Dar. On the Saturday afternoon they entertained me at the Gymkhana Club. On Sunday the 29th with a special visa I took a day trip to Zanzibar on a Twin Otter aircraft 5H-MVK. The 10 hour tour of the island was organised and discretely monitored by the authorities. Some years earlier the British Government had issued a 'D Notice' on the territory. I was pleased I went but being escorted throughout there were probably many more interesting places and sights on the island that I was unable to see. The Comet 4 flight on 5Y-ALF from Dar via Mombassa to Nairobi on the following afternoon was an exciting end to the long weekend.

Cyprus was a new stopping point from Nairobi to London for the VC10 from 02 April. Alan Hillman and I prepared some First Flight Covers.

Blantyre in Malawi attracted my attention. A visit to the GSA (Air Malawi) was arranged for 17 April. The BA aircraft and crew operated the round trip with a 6 hour stop-over. Captain Paddy Ward, on G-ARVE, allowed me to ride on the jump seat there and back. Regrettably there was nothing over impressive for me to see in Blantyre during the short time available. However, on the return flight to Nairobi, there was excitement galore. Two lines of thunderstorms with active centres lit the evening sky and highlighted the superb towering cunimb clouds. I was fascinated as the Captain hand-flew the plane to avoid the turbulence and the vicious looking dark thunder clouds. Because of the bumpiness some passengers didn't eat their meal but I didn't care. I ate mine. That evening in the hotel I bought the crew a thank you drink.

May Day holiday was spent in Kampala when I flew to Entebbe Airport on 5H-MOG. Neil Attwood the CRO met and showed me some of the nearby places of interest. I stayed at the de luxe Apollo Hotel which was the pride and joy of President Milton Oboto. (The Idi Amin era was to follow.) Three days later Comet 5Y-AAA flew me back to Nairobi.

Tropical fruit and vegetables of most varieties seemed to be available all year round in the large Nairobi produce market. Kenya straddled the Equator and the different terrain plus climatic conditions with contrasting rainy seasons meant most fruits were always available. Avocados, mangoes, paw paw and strawberries were common items in the house. Most air crews had a permanent order to carry 15 kilos of fruit wrapped in rush mat containers as 'part' of their personal baggage allowance.

Two farewell parties later, on 05 May, I left Nairobi via Zurich for London. That long unplanned posting ranks as either number One or number Two on my favourite list (mainly for enjoyment mixed with a good variety of hard work and excursions both local and to neighbouring countries).

Staff training was needed in South Africa as BA expanded its operations. On 19 May I left London via Frankfurt and Nairobi for Johannesburg. Teaching new staff was rather tedious for me. I was pleased to meet for an evening beer some ex-BEA colleagues such as Dave McKewan. However, I had to restrain myself from becoming a 'social' creature like many in the Sales Department!

Johannesburg had a private flying club at the Rand City Airport. I joined and started flying lessons on a Piper Cherokee 140 aircraft, usually ZS-PMC. After one impulsive, unescorted and unauthorised solo taxi session around the airstrip my membership was withdrawn.

Once a month the local Chamber of Commerce took guests on a tour to an underground gold mine at Welkom in the Orange Free State. There was a long waiting list but a cancellation on 18 June gave me the chance. A DC3 aircraft, ZS-DRJ, of private airline COMAIR flew about 20 of us on the 70 minute journey from Germinston Rand Airport. On arrival we were given a full briefing, kitted up and taken 4,300 feet below ground level to experience the conditions of drilling for gold. The area ground elevation meant we were not below sea level. The working tunnels were impressively huge and the air temperature was uncomfortably high. But at the mining face it was almost claustrophobic as thousands of cubic metres of black soil rumbled along the belts. It was a carefully escorted and orchestrated tour to show how well the native workers were treated and included visits to their hostel accomodation. After lunch the tour continued as we saw gold being poured from a smoulter. Then a quick peep into a guarded strong room - but there was no freebie!

Six days later I boarded BA 006 from Jo'burg via Nairobi and Zurich for London. During the transit at Zurich I met the Airport Manager Graham Hughes, an old friend, who persuaded me to disembark and spend the night with him and his family. It was a pleasant reunion. His wife Joan had been a Fight Clerk and there was therefore some reminiscing. The next day, 25 June, I took a BEA Trident to London.

My last posting, although I didn't know it at the time, started on 02 July when I left for Port of Spain in Trinidad. BA 691 operated by G-ASGG flew via Bermuda, Antigua and Barbados on a 13 and a half hour journey. The island was under partial military curfew from a foiled coup. I was accommodated at a delightful small hotel, the Chaconia Inn, a few miles out of town. The purpose of my visit was to relieve the local CRO, Mrs Myrna Hadeed, who was pregnant. The ten reservations staff were all friendly and helpful and there was a happy atmosphere in the office. That 15 week posting to Trinidad vies with Nairobi as my most enjoyable. A week after my arrival the local DSM, Leslie Joseph, had arranged a get-together buffet lunch for the Port of Spain travel agents at the Holiday Inn. A well known steel band attracted much attention and it was estimated that gate-crashers put the attendance figure at over 200. Music from steel bands became infectious and I still love the sound today.

Trinidad was more a commercial centre than a holiday point in the Caribbean. Business for BOAC remained steady with 18 flight departures a week. Peter Anderson was Manager Trinidad and Tobago and always helpful to me and receptive to my suggestions to visit other islands and places. During the posting I visited 'on duty' Caracas, Lima plus the islands of Barbados, Grenada, St Vincent, St Lucia, Dominica and many times to Tobago. I flew on PanAm to Caracas then with Alitalia onto Lima with the return journey on Aero Peru DC8 registered OB-R-931 via Bogota. The inter-Caribbean island flights were mostly on Leeward Island Air Transport (LIAT) using HS 748 aircraft. Arawak Airlines used Beechcraft 99 aeroplanes between Piarco, Trinidad and Crown Point Airport, Tobago.

Interviews and tests for promotion meant I had a 4 day visit to London from 06 September. There was a re-organisation at Head Office. Two months later I got one of the new jobs and my days on the overseas pool were over. Meanwhile, I was enjoying the work, the many parties and island hopping. Somehow there were 3 farewell parties for me in Port of Spain but on 18 October it was the final farewell to a fine bunch of staff. There was just one task left, across the water in South America.

G-ASGE carried me on the 55 minute flight to Georgetown, Guyana (formally British Guiana). My job was to open a new BOAC office which had been delayed for numerous reasons. The new District Manager was John Bustard who had skilfully co-ordinated the arrangements with Guyana Airways. I helped train some staff for the new sales shop and office in the Tower Hotel.

Three times weekly the seven-sector BA 537 arrived at Timehri Airport, Georgetown having started at Manchester, via Prestwick, New York, Antigua, Barbados and Port of Spain. The crews, and all BA visiting staff, stayed at the BA Associate Hotel the Pegasus which was built (probably unwisely) slightly below sea level at the junction of the Demerara River and Atlantic Ocean. The hotel was leaning at a few degrees toward the sea which was a murky shade of muddy brown.

At noon on 31 October the Guyanese Minister of Tourism officially opened the new BOAC office in the Tower Hotel and the usual party followed.

Kaieteur Waterfall at 721 feet is one of the longest single sheer drop waterfalls in the world. On 01 November I took a tour to see this sight using a Guyana Airways Twin Otter Aircraft, 8R-GDC for the one hour journey mostly over dense forest. It was an unspoilt beauty area, interesting to see and worthy of a postcard home.

Adios South America. On 12 November G-ASGM took 5 minutes short of 13 hours to carry me home from my last posting. London was not unexpectedly cold and wet. I went from LHR to Victoria Air Terminal to see my boss, Dave Gould. As from 16 November I was appointed Reservations Officer Western Routes.

Christmas was spent with my mother, brother and family at Dunfermline, Scotland but I celebrated the New Year at a party in Windsor, Berkshire. Here endeth 1970.

On a duty visit to Tobago while based in Port of Spain, Trinidad, July 1970.

12
ON THE GROUND BUT IN THE AIR

Freezing fog conditions in January 1971 were a reminder of life in London years ago. Working normal office hours was a shock to the system. As the junior member of a three man team it was difficult for me to accept the tedious and often repetitive duties of investigating problems encountered by passengers such as missing their special flight meal or being left behind on overbooked flights. I was not happy but thought the experience would be useful in the future.

Jumbo Jets were about to enter service with BOAC in the Spring. I was lucky enough to get a ticket for a staff proving flight on BA 4001 on 04 April from Heathrow to Kennedy with a one hour stop at Toronto. G-ANWE was a B747-136 with Captain Barrow in command. It also gave me the chance to visit the complex reservations centre in New York for two days. I tagged on some leave to this visit and flew aboard another B747 of Eastern Airlines to Miami. It was 09 April and the plane operated flight number EA9 for the 2 hour 45 minute journey. I stayed at the splendid Fontanbleu Hotel on Miami Beach and was shown around the area by Rae-Ann Gilder, a friend from my Bermuda days. A B707 returned me to London 2 days later.

Iceland was a country off the normal tourist circuit. An offer of an Interline trip became available for just a few pounds. On 29 May with 15 other airline staff I travelled on FI 201 from LHR to Keflavik. It was a B727 registered TF-TIA. We stayed at the Saga Hotel in Reykjavik and the 4 day tour was organised by Icelandair. Now this place really did impress me. Cold glacial-type rivers flowed only a few miles from hot geyser springs and the landscape although mostly barren had lush areas of greenery. From memory, even bananas were growing under glass sustained by the hot moist air. We were treated to a sightseeing flight on an F27 from Reykjavik to Sekki to view the tundra. There are only a few hours of darkness at the end of May and even after our excursions we were still able to wine, dine and dance until who knows when. I felt satisfied yet sad when the time came to return to London on 01 June.

To celebrate the 90th birthday of my grandmother I drove her from Newbury to Bath for lunch and then on to visit the SS Great Britain docked in Bristol. Gran was an incredibly active person for her age and enjoyed adventures and day trips. The date was 25 July.

Tarbay Farm, Windsor had been my address for some years but the daily drive to work in central London was tedious in the extreme. In early August I moved to another flat at Kew Gardens near Richmond.

Office work was generally dull and I therefore welcomed a two week advanced course of training concerning the BOAC computer system called BOADICEA. This started on 27 September.

A strange phone call in early November invited me to join a group of mainly airline people who for £100 would buy a share in a hot air balloon. I had only ever seen such a thing floating across my TV screen to advertise Nimble bread. The phone call came from Phil Dunnington, the BOAC trainee I had met in Delhi. I dithered for a minute or two, he persisted and I then said yes. That decision, made so casually, led to my life being drastically changed.

At the Swan Pub beside the river Thames at Staines on 11 November I attended a meeting of the balloon group members. Decisions on the size of the balloon, its colour scheme, its name were just a few topics discussed every Friday evening over a pint or two. Eleven of us paid our £100, BOAC sponsored the balloon for £500 to carry its Speedbird logo. The name DANTE was chosen (an abbreviation of Dante's Inferno), the size was middle of the available range at 65,000 cubic feet (AX7), and the colour scheme was a blue and white chequered design. Cameron Balloons of Bristol were to build it.

Sunday 05 December was a damp, dreary, dull and calm day. The Nut Tree Inn at Murcott, Oxfordshire was the pub assembly point and by 1300 Don Cameron arrived with DANTE. A crowd of about 300 gathered to watch the balloon being prepared for flight. There were only 14 other active hot air balloons in Britain at that time. Roger Burnell and I were drawn as third priority for a flight. Don Cameron did 2 tethered (captive) displays with the balloon and then as third in line Roger and I got aboard. To our surprise and delight Don decided to fly free. With no wind we lingered over the launch site before drifting about 200 yards in 12 minutes. We landed in the next field at 1448. It was a real joy to be on the

Maiden flight and photographs of the occasion show I was clutching a bottle of champagne. What else? The balloon, registered G-AZIP, took off again with two other group members. It was a day I will never forget.

Christmas was spent with my mother and family in Scotland. That year I used my rebate tickets on British Caledonian Airways from Gatwick to Edinburgh flying on BAC1-11 aircraft G-AXJM returning on G-ASJC.

Above: This Super VC10 seen landing at LHR wears yet another BA livery. The registration was G-ASGP shown in early 1976. (BA)

Pilot Roger Barrett (foreground) took this picture of himself and Bob White flying in their balloon 'London Pride I' practising for the Observer Balloon Meet, Easter 1971.

13
GETTING A LICENCE TO FLY HOT AIR BALLOONS

Reservations Inspectors were introduced by BOAC on 05 January 1972. The thinking behind this was to have available a few experienced staff who were able to undertake quality control visits at short notice or relief duties as required. Still eager for travel and adventure I joined the unit.

Ballooning took over my life. With some of the group we tethered Dante for rides at almost any suitable location and this despite the fact that we did not have a licensed pilot. The first group Annual Dinner Dance was held on 08 January at the Monkey Island Hotel, Bray, Berkshire. Dinner jackets were, and still are, mandatory for this function. Monika Schade, who was visiting London from BA Hamburg, accompanied me to the dinner. The following afternoon the balloon was again tethered in Windsor Park and I was 'airborne' for 12 minutes.

Needed was a permanent base to store the balloon within easy reach of London and outside controlled air space. My grandmother was staying with friends, Olive and Arthur Hayes, at Newbury. I asked my Gran - to ask her friend - to ask their son - to ask at school - to ask a farmer if anyone knew of a field for us to fly a balloon. Richard Liddiard asked his father, David, who was the tenant farmer of many fields at Bradfords Farm, Marsh Benham just south of the A4 to the west of Newbury and better still miles from any controlled air space. Shortly before 0900 on Sunday 30 January I got a phone call from David inviting me to fly the balloon from his farm that day.

Thrusting myself into top gear I had to find a pilot and crew members quickly. Peter Langford agreed to fly the balloon and Pete Bish with Celia Redhead said yes to be the crew. The balloon was in my garage at Kew Gardens, refuelled and ready to go. My Mini car towed the trailer with balloon down the M4 at speeds maybe above the legal limit. We reached the farm at 1110 to be met by David, his family and some friends plus to our surprise newspaper reporters and photographers from the Newbury Weekly News.

There was a cold northerly wind and the temperature was minus 2 degrees Centigrade. Peter Langford allowed me to do the balloon inflation believing I was experienced. In fact it was the first time I had handled the controls. At 1255 Dante got airborne with Peter as pilot. When in level flight he let me fly but the erratic nature of my control soon alerted him to ask the question "How many flying hours have you got?". When he heard the answer "12 minutes" he said "Perhaps you had better watch me this time". We flew relatively low but a faster moving snow laden cloud overtook us. It sprinkled snow flakes in passing and this flurry seemed attracted to and drifted around the balloon.

Binley in Hampshire was our landing place at 1425. As we approached a suitable field Peter released the trail rope over some trees and this noticeably reduced our speed for a gentle landing. That was Dante's 4th free flight: my 2nd but most important of all the First flight from Marsh Benham. From that day forth Dante was based there and David's farm became the centre of British ballooning for the next five years and more.

It is difficult to exaggerate but I am sure that more than 1500 different pilots flew from the site. Best estimates are that probably more than 8000 balloon flights were made from Bradfords Farm in the 20 years to January 1992.

Competition was intense amongst five of us in the group to get our balloon licence quickly. The legal minimum flying time required was 12 hours before a check flight by an examiner which was then followed by a 30 minute solo flight. Balloonists were required to pass the same exams as those for a powered pilot's licence, with an additional paper on Aerostation (lighter than air flight).

Freezing fog conditions existed on my drive to Newbury on 10 February for a proposed flight. Kevin Meehan with his girlfriend Jennifer and I laid out Dante over the hoar-frosted grass with less than 50 yards visibility in the field. A fast approaching warm front with southerly winds was forecast. There was no wind when just the 3 of us inflated the balloon and as soon as a glimmer of weak sunshine peeked through the low clouds we took off. It was 0950. Some time later the sun gave the balloon a silhouette effect over a foggy field. Pilot Kevin was amused as he flapped his arms which on the clouds below gave the image of a bird. I was flying the balloon but unaware the propane fuel tank was almost empty. The balloon started to descend rapidly. I did not know how to change cylinders. We penetrated the fog and luckily there was a ploughed field beneath us. As an ex-Navy man Kevin said some earthy words as we thumped into the ground. I thought the flight was over and released the trail rope - such was my inexperience. Kevin reconnected the fuel system and we climbed away dragging the trail rope behind us. A barbed wire fence snagged the end of the rope and smartly pulled us back to earth. With brute force we unsnagged the rope but the balloon was too cold to climb. A lengthy drag across the field scooped much soil on board. The final irony was another blessed barbed wire fence which speared the balloon in dozens of places. My third flight of 35 minutes was over.

From a farm near Hungerford and with Pilot Laurie Ryan I had my next flights on 22 March. The wind was light and variable and after takeoff at 0945 we crossed the A4 road northwards. At 500 feet the wind took us south to again cross the A4. What fun! We tried this again and repeated the novelty. Motorists were equally intrigued and caused an obstruction in both directions. Then patrolmen in a police car who were not so amused used their loud hailer and told us to move on. Laurie taught me a lot and we had several intermediate landings. The idea was to give member Dave Munson, who was doing the retrieve, a spell of flying but with the quirky winds we could not linger too long on the ground. Next we had a marvellous 4 or 5 mile trip of low level contour flying at heights below 100 feet, which really tested my skill and concentration. Such was the openness of the country that roads were few. Pilot Laurie let me bounce the balloon across 2 fields until the fuel gauges were reading below the contingency level. The 2 hour flight was the most instructive I ever had and as a trainee pilot the most enjoyable.

Traditionally the Heineken International Balloon Meeting was held over the Easter weekend. That year it was held at Stanford Hall near Rugby from 31 March to 03 April. British Bank Holidays are often wet and windy - this was no exception. All the Dante group members attended and it was a good education seeing what to do and what not to do in bad weather. With our white BOAC overalls we attracted some attention from the seasoned balloonists who were intrigued by the offer of free access to fly from Marsh Benham. Most of us witnessed our first accident. A balloon tried but failed to get airborne. For 400 yards it sailed along at about 50 feet above ground level straight into the branches of a waiting tree. No one was badly hurt but pride was dented. The balloon fabric (ripstop nylon) was vigorously shredded in the strong wind.

BBAC (British Balloon and Airship Club) was the controlling body of the sport. The CAA (Civil Aviation Authority) vested the licensing of pilots, their balloons and all associated matters to the BBAC. This is similar to the authority given to the British Gliding Association. I joined the BBAC on 22 March. Later I took an active part in many aspects in the administration of the Club.

Munster in Westphalia, Germany was the first overseas trip for the Dante Group. Eight of us boarded the ferry–dare I mention its' name–the 'Herald of Free Enterprise'–at Dover at 2315 on 18 May for a crossing to Zeebrugge, Belgium. Then it was a 6 hour drive through Belgium and Holland to Munster. We all had at least one flight in a mildly competitive event. Most of us remember the happy social aspect, good food, wine, beer and meeting balloonists from five other countries. After thanking organiser Arno Seiger we wearily returned to Dover on 23 May.

For work Mexico City was next. BA 675 on 29 May flown by G-ASGC took slightly more than 13 flying hours for the journey via Bermuda and Nassau. There had been accounting discrepancies with the reservations sales reports. With a London auditor my job was to tighten the local procedures. Mexico, at 7300 feet above sea level, is set in a basin of the Sierra Madre Mountain Range. There was very poor air quality in the city. A weekend in Acapulco was planned from 03 June. My reason was to get some fresh air - or if that sounds implausible, have a swim in the Pacific Ocean. An AeroMexico DC9, XA-SOD flew me there and a Mexicana B727, XA-SEN brought me back. The Hilton Hotel on the sea front was a relaxing break from the stuffiness of the Fiesta Palace Hotel in Mexico City. There was not much time for sightseeing, but I did get to the Pyramids, before leaving on 10 June for London via Freeport and Bermuda. Other trips to Mexico were to follow.

Ballooning took up most of my free time. It was either trying to get a training flight or acting as a ground crew member for others. On 24 June many group members inflated Dante at the BOAC Family Day event at Heston near Heathrow.

Bermuda was due for an inspection visit. I left LHR on 25 June aboard G-ASZF and was met by Nat Chambers the CRO. Nat was a Scotsman who had become a naturalised Bermudian. The 3 day visit went very quickly and revived again some of the memories of my youth. I returned home via JFK using the daily

Taken on 18 May 1972 outside the BOAC Head Office, central London, as we left for Munster, Germany, on the first overseas trip of the Dante Balloon Group.

		Certificate Number
		G-BDSE/R1

UNITED KINGDOM
CIVIL AVIATION AUTHORITY

CERTIFICATE OF REGISTRATION OF AIRCRAFT

1. Nationality or Common Mark and Registration Mark	2. Manufacturer and Manufacturer's Designation of Aircraft	3. Aircraft Serial Number
G-BDSE	Cameron Balloons Limited Cameron O-77 (Hot Air) Free Balloon	210

4. Name of Owner

British Airways Board

5. Address of Owner

British Airways Victoria Terminal
Buckingham Palace Road,
London SW1W 9SR

It is hereby certified that the above described aircraft has been duly entered on the United Kingdom Register in accordance with the Convention on International Civil Aviation dated 7 December 1944, and with the Air Navigation Order 1974.

K. F. Allan
For the Civil Aviation Authority
Aircraft Registration
Shell Mex House
Strand
London WC2R 0DP

Date of issue 27 February 1976

NOTES. (a) The person in whose name an aircraft is registered may or may not be its legal owner. Prospective purchasers are warned, therefore, that this Certificate of Registration is not proof of legal ownership.
(b) No entries or endorsements may be made in this certificate except by the Civil Aviation Authority.

CA Form 71

SEE FURTHER NOTES OVERLEAF

British Airways owned balloon G-BDSE as part of its fleet!

B747, BA 491, before transferring to a VC10 for LHR.

Lima, in Peru was my next overseas destination when I left LHR 13 days later on 11 July. The B707 operated via Antigua and Caracas. CRO Eduardo Ramos and Sales Rep Ian Gillespie met and drove me to the Hotel Crillon. My task was a routine inspection of the reservations functions done on behalf of BOAC by the General Sales Agent PSNC (Pacific Steam Navigation Company). The Sales Shop was in a prominent position beside the main square and the interior was palatial. Five well educated girls in the office gave it an aura of superiority.

On the morning before I left, 15 July, Ian Gillespie drove me high into the Andes - to a point just over 16000 feet - where there were magnificent views. On the way down we stopped at the bustling town of Chisica, very alive with a Saturday market. There were 2 or 3 steam train engines ready to return villagers to their dwelling areas before nightfall. I was totally fascinated by almost everything I saw. The variety of the peoples, their different styles of clothing and even the contrasting manners between the groups intrigued me. My only dislike was a bad-tempered llama which tried hard to take a bite out of my arm.

An Aerolineas Argentinas B707 flew me on the two and three quarter hour sector to Bogota, Colombia. Eldorado Airport was, and still is, at 8355 feet the highest airport on the BA network. It was 16 July and the CRO Carlos Navarro met and drove me to the Hotel Tequendama. Another inspection visit of the reservations unit followed. The most memorable sight from this visit was a large graveyard for old and antique aircraft where more than twenty planes were in varying degrees of decay. At that time BOAC had just one flight a week to London and on 21 July I boarded G-AXGW, complete with my complimentary 2 kilo packet of coffee, via Caracas and Antigua.

Security was lax at many smaller airports. At that time Antigua was, in my opinion, the slackest of all International Airports served by BA. In transit I could walk to the open air 'transit lounge', continue through the coffee shop, past the check-in area and out onto the street and the taxi rank. During my transit on this flight I met the District Manager, Antigua, Roland Cobbold who was attending to a problem at the check-in area.

Heavy rain and strong winds almost ruined the Official Opening of the Dante Balloon Centre at Marsh Benham, Newbury on 06 August. The celebrations were subdued, not all guests arrived, but the ceremony took place and none of the food or champagne was wasted.

17 days after my Grandmother's 91st Birthday she enjoyed a tethered flight in Dante at Marsh Benham. 11 August had promised to be a calm day but it was just outside flying limits, particularly with the press around. Her photo with a brief story appeared in the local newspaper.

Caribbean time again as I left LHR on 15 August for a combined duty visit and holiday. Antigua was first, staying at the Blue Waters Hotel, with its excellent sandy beach but mediocre facilities. (Could it be that I was spoilt by staying at too many superior hotels?) On 18 August I made a day trip to the nearby island of Guadeloupe using a LIAT HS 748. One of the attractions of this island was the semi-dormant volcano where one could walk through the sulphur fumes to the bubbling mud pools. As this is French territory I took the opportunity to enjoy an excellent lunch generously laced with garlic which helped replace the sulphur odour on my clothes. The capital, Point a Pitre, had an interesting combination of old colonial buildings adapted for and mixed with Caribbean styles. The sight of armed French gendarmes on the streets was a surprise.

On 21 August the LIAT aircraft to Vigie Airport on St Lucia routed from Antigua via Guadeloupe, Dominica and Martinique. The inspection visit of the BA Reservations office and Sales Shop was satisfactory. The sightseeing and relaxation days were also good. On 29 August I used a Piper Cherokee aircraft to fly between the downtown airport and the International one at Hewanorra. With only the local pilot and myself on board it was a bumpy old night with thunderstorm activity nearby. I won't say that the pilot lost his way but it took a while to find the airport in the dark. The London plane was overbooked and I ended my tour by being up-graded to the First Class cabin for the return journey.

September was a month of lost ballooning opportunities but I did have two good training flights with Nigel Tasker in his larger 84000 cubic foot balloon named *Oberon*. I also took my written exam papers on air law, navigation, meteorology and aerostation. The navigation paper confused me and I had to retake it.

The Dream Machine was the name given to a new balloon by Joe Phelp. To inaugurate its first flight he invited many seasoned balloonists to a lunch party before the ceremony. I was privileged to attend and took Dante along and

How not to end a balloon flight! Roger Barrett was practising for the First World Hot Air Championships in Albuquerque, USA, and over-estimated his rate of descent. This mishap occurred during the 1st Icicle Meet on 7 January 1973. He escaped by sliding down the trail rope but only his pride was injured!

had a 65 minute flight ending at Holdenby in Northants. It was Sunday 01 October.

Kampala in Uganda was the next adventure. When I got to the office on 02 October I was asked if I would fly to Uganda that night to deliver 3000 airline tickets. The urgency of the trip was because General Idi Amin was expelling the Asians from Uganda. At 2000 that evening an East African Airways Super VC10 left LHR almost empty for Entebbe and landed at 0540 local time. The local Customs officials welcomed me and the boxes of airline tickets, which they knew were needed for the departure of the Asians.

Manager Eastern Africa, Willie McKie, hosted a small dinner party on 4 October for the 11 BOAC staff, 7 of whom were on detachment from London, to say well done for the task we did in ticketing and expediting the Asian families for travel. Peter Welek was the CRO and had the job of co-ordinating our workload during the 10 to 12 hour shifts. It was hard tedious work with the documentation required. Although extra flights operated it was not easy to match demand with capacity. Working along side us were 5 British Caledonian Airways staff from London and there was a great spirit of co-operation. BA staff were on a meal allowance system, the BCAL staff ate at the hotel on a re-charge basis. It was not unknown for BA staff to be guests of BCAL for dinner. It was also not unknown for a hungry BCAL staff member to have the finest steak in the hotel with a lobster thermidor as a side salad!

During my stay I had twinges of pain in my back which suggested that my posture was not right and this was affecting my spine. It was sore enough to prevent me swimming in the hotel pool and it gave discomfort at night. I was also aware that on a few occasions I appeared to stagger on the walk from the office to hotel in the evening particularly when tired. Symptoms such as an unstable and irregular gait and occasional apparent 'slipped disc' problems became more frequent during 1973 and 1974. In May 1975 after exhaustive checks Multiple Sclerosis was diagnosed.

Exhausted after 9 full working days I was happy to board BR 212, a BCAL Super VC10, for London on 12 October. The flight routed Entebbe-Nairobi-Tunis to arrive at Gatwick at 0145 on Friday the 13th. I caught the 0306 train from Gatwick station to Victoria and then a taxi to my flat at Putney arriving at 0410. Maybe I was overtired but after just three hours sleep I went to the office for de-briefing. Writing this now it seems I was foolish to put myself under pressure and lead a life of such stress.

More interesting balloon training flights followed in October and November. Our group bought a new larger sized balloon of 84,000 cubic feet capacity. We named it Beatrice (who was Dante's lover) and it was registered G-BAGY.

Saturday 25 November was a good day. In the morning I flew on the maiden flight of Beatrice for a good landing at Stratfield Saye (Hants) after 1 hour 25 mins. At 1410 on the same balloon I undertook my check-flight with Don Cameron. It was a dual check with Alan Root (of Kenya). We both passed the flying test and landed at Upper Bucklebury. Normally I would have continued in the balloon to fly solo for 30 minutes to qualify for my pilot's licence. The wind was strengthening and Don was concerned that the London TMA (Control Zone) was too close based on my projected track. I was happy but not elated that my solo had to be postponed.

David Liddiard had on the next morning got examiner Mark Westwood to undertake his check flight and solo. I hurried to Newbury and by early afternoon had found Beatrice lingering in the sky near Linkenholt. The balloon landed. David and Mark got out and I got aboard, alone. There was almost no wind. The balloon was very light–just half a tank of fuel. I gave the burner a ten second blast and very quickly shot up to at least 500 feet! After that I learned to be more judicious with the burner despite the fact that there were high tension power wires beneath me. After 45 minutes I saw a perfect landing field ahead. To reduce height I pulled the vent rope which broke and I was left holding half a burnt line. The main Andover road lay ahead and after crossing that I firmly opened the velcro rip panel and made a positive landing (which is parlance for a thumping touchdown). I had passed my solo and was now a balloon pilot. 26 November was also a good day.

My purple covered Pilots Licence, number 100107, arrived from the CAA ten days later. Then on 17 December I made my first balloon pilot-in-command flight in Beatrice. The flight to Ramsbury lasted just 45 minutes. That was the year that was.

Some American authorities in 1973 would not allow the Concorde aircraft to operate from London to New York. As a mini protest Don Cameron flew this banner beneath his balloon at the First World Hot Air Balloon Championships at Albuquerque in February 1973.

At the first British Balloon Meet I ever attended I saw Don Cameron carry this cover on the first balloon built for Norway.

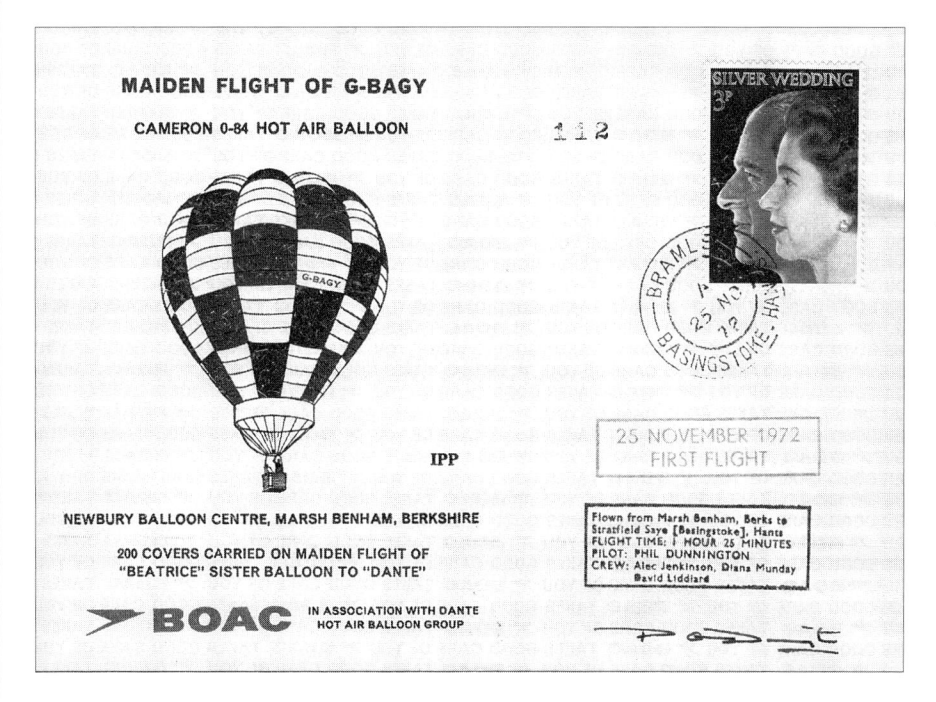

I was crewman aboard the maiden flight of 'Beatrice' on 25 November 1972. Later that day I had my check flight on this same balloon.

Gwen Bellew was one of the first women pilots in Britain and was soon nicknamed 'The Flying Grandmother'. She carried this cover at the World's First Women Pilot's Balloon Meet. The date was 12 July 1975. I helped organise the event.

14
A LOT OF 'FIRSTS' CROWDED INTO 1973

There was an annual open-to-all balloonists event called The Icicle Meet held on the first week-end of the New Year at Marsh Benham. This attracted pilots from 17 countries including Australia, Hong Kong, USA and Eastern Europe most of whom came with their own balloons. 'Registration spotters' had a field day - in more ways than one. In 1978 on January 7 and 8 in good weather 85 balloons made 179 flights at that Icicle Meet which was, at that time, a record. During the 1987 Icicle event 117 balloons flew making 186 flights. At the Icicle Meets, organised as usual by the Dante Group, I did various jobs including giving pilots the meteorological briefing and acting as social secretary.

Icicle Meet Number One was held on 06-07 January 1973 but the weather was below flying limits. I gave the pilot met briefing at 1015 in murky conditions, a ragged low cloud base and cold Easterly wind. Balloonists are a determined lot, particularly when gathered in a flock. The first few got airborne at 1130 and inevitably others started to follow. Tim Stafford with his balloon G-AZRN was very keen and I had agreed to fly him. He inflated the balloon and reluctantly I took off at 1155. We crossed a railway line, then the Kennet and Avon Canal, headed south west and floated gently over some ploughed fields. Below we saw 2 balloons had landed and the pilots shouted warnings to us of power lines ahead which we could not see in the fog. I decided to abort the flight there and then much to the annoyance of Tim and his wife Tot. We had been airborne just 15 minutes but it took us more than 90 minutes to carry all parts of the balloon to a side road.

History was made next morning Sunday 7th January. Don Cameron and Dr Teddy Hall surprised us all when they appeared overhead the balloon launch site flying in the world's first hot air airship. The wind, still from the east, was stronger than on Saturday and this strange looking craft was having difficulty, with it's low powered modified VW engine, manoeuvring in the sky. After two irregular circuits the pilots guided the airship into wind for a near perfect landing on the balloon field. The project had been a well guarded secret and everybody stood in awe, amazement and almost disbelief. On Monday morning the Times newspaper printed a photograph of the airship on its front page.

Not so much a secret, just a hot air milestone. Thunder Balloons had built up publicity for the unveiling of its first balloon. Tom Donnelly, Dick Wirth with Kenneth Simmonds wanted to be a competitive manufacturer to Cameron Balloons. An earlier company, Western Balloons controlled by Gerry Turnbull, no longer made these craft. The first Thunder was of 77000 cubic foot capacity, in the colours of the Union Jack, given the name Jumpin' Jack (Flash) and registered G-BAIR. At lunch time the balloon made its maiden flight. There were many happy photographers that day, including me.

Amongst the 27 balloons I flew Beatrice for 55 minutes to cross into Wiltshire landing at Shalbourne. Commemorative Flight Covers with illustrations of the balloons Dante and Beatrice were carried on both days.

Two Sundays later on 21 January I flew for almost 11 hours on a B707, G-AWHU, from LHR to Georgetown, Guyana via Antigua, Barbados and Port of Spain. The purpose was an inspection visit. On the 25th I flew to Barbados to report my findings and attend the regional managers meeting. Was I just lucky or what? At the Southern Palms Hotel there was a steel band playing on the beach - just as I finished my swim and - just before my first rum cocktail and - just as the barbecue started. Oh to be in Barbados.... especially at that time of the year....

Caracas in Venezuela was my next inspection visit. To get there I had to spend the night of 27 January in Port of Spain. The next day I had breakfast with Kathy Lawrence the Reservations Supervisor who had been so kind and helpful to me during my posting there. I then flew on a Viasa DC9 aircraft, YV-C-AVR to Caracas. Yet another Sunday flight before meeting Manager Keith MacGaul at the Hilton Hotel poolside. It was a hectic 3 days used partly as a public relations visit to the travel agents. On 01 February the same DC9 flew me back to Barbados to connect with BA 688 via Bermuda for LHR.

Albuquerque, New Mexico, USA had the greatest number and highest concentration of hot air balloons in the world. Local pilot Sid Cutter together with Ed Yost and others applied to the FAI (Federation Aeronautique Internationale) in Paris to host the First World

Hot Air Balloon Championships. The attraction for me was irresistible. Using my 90% rebate airline tickets I left LHR on 13 February aboard G-AWND for JFK. I made a quick taxi transfer to La Guardia airport to catch a TWA B727 via Oklahoma City for Albuquerque. With a 7 hour time difference it was 0315 when I arrived.

Strong winds on Monday 12 February had caused cancellation of the first day's competition. On Tuesday, as I was not yet in Albuquerque, I also missed the 'Spot Landing Contest'. Valentine's Day morning, just 6 hours after my arrival, I went to the downtown Fairground where the event was being staged. The weather was good and the pilot's second task was a 'Level Flight Barograph Test'. A barograph is a revolving drum on which a needle linked to an altimeter records the altitude path followed by an aircraft in flight. In addition to the competitors there were other balloons on fun-flights which got the name 'Fiesta Flying' and produced a carnival atmosphere in the huge stadium. Although free of charge it was a shame so few people attended. I considered myself to be privileged to be at this first World Event. The organisation was amateurish by today's standards but it was a great joy, even as a spectator, to feel part of the occasion.

Task number 3 was a Step-profile Barograph Test on Thursday the 15th. By next morning it was snowing. The wind was calm, the visibility was about 50 yards and the sky obscured. The organisers coerced the pilots to fly in what was virtually a white-out condition. The task was a series of Tunnel-climb and Level Flight Control manoeuvres. There had to be a minimum of 4 tasks to constitute a World Championship and this was the last opportunity available to the organisers.

Countries were allowed to enter a maximum of 4 pilots. The Britons were: Terry Adams, Roger Barrett, Don Cameron and Peter Langford. The declared winner was Dennis Floden of USA with Sid Cutter, USA, in second position and Janne Balkedal of Sweden third.

Good weather allowed a mass ascent on Saturday morning 17 February and this encouraged more Albuquerque folk to come and see the balloons. The press and television loved the spectacle and it got nation-wide coverage. Shortly after lunch I had to catch a TWA aircraft for Chicago to connect with BA 570, G-ARVL, for London.

During February and early March I twice visited my grandmother in hospital near Wigan, Lancashire, after she underwent a major skin graft covering almost two thirds of her back. The surgeons were pleased with her recovery and their skilful efforts on a 91 year old. The case history was written up in their medical journals. Her accident was caused when a hot ember from a coal fire is thought to have burnt into a shawl and smouldered on the bed when she went to rest. She recovered completely and lived for another three and a half years.

Reggie and J P Tristani, from New Jersey, visited London and we had three flights together in Dante. Nine days later on 18 March I took Austrian airline pilot Joe Starkbaum for a training flight in his new balloon, G-BAMA, called 'Poferl'. The weather around this period was good and on 21 March we had another training session which allowed 17 intermediate landings during a 75 minute flight. In mid April David Watkins was under training in 'Holker Hall', G-BAAX, and we had 4 good flights and one not so good. On 15 April sudden gusty winds caused the balloon to hit 4 fences and the landing could be described as 'uncomfortable'. David needed a hospital X-ray for severe bruising. Later I flew a number of other trainee pilots including David Dokk-Olsen in 'Pied Piper', Allan Snook in 'Jack O' Newbury', Jenny Greaves in 'Jules Verne' and John Green in 'Gemini'.

Whitsun weekend, 05-07 May, was spent at Alton Towers with a balloon ready to fly. The weather was foul. Complimentary rides on the funfair attractions were fun. In the next four years there were at least a dozen public events I attended with a balloon where flying was thwarted by bad weather.

Belgium was next. On 01 June six members of the Dante Group sailed from Dover to Zeebrugge with both Dante and Beatrice for a balloon meet at Kasterlee. Rain and wind threatened to disrupt the event. However I did manage to get a 20 minute flight in Dante on 02 June and another 20 minutes in Beatrice the next day. We were well wined and dined and enjoyed the reception given by the Mayor of Kasterlee.

It was a 7 hour drive, in my beloved little green Mini towing Beatrice, via Cologne to Iserlohn in Germany. Here the weather was hot and sunny but with a strong wind on 04 and 05 June. Meet organiser Eugene Wothe was under pressure from the sponsor for us to fly. On Wednesday the 6th a more sheltered site was found on a British Army Camp base.

Some German Army cadets were drafted in to 'assist'. By mid afternoon they were inflating our balloons whilst we were resting in the

'Dante', the BOAC sponsored balloon, visited Montreal, Canada on a promotional tour in June 1973. The newly amalgamated BOAC and BEA airline was to be called British Airways and we carried a banner with the new name.

The World's First Hot Air Airship, seen preparing to land after its first public flight. This venture was such a well-kept secret that even the Civil Aviation Authority did not know. It amazed spectators at the Icicle Meet, Newbury as it made a difficult approach in windy conditions. The date was 7 January 1973. Don Cameron and Dr Teddy Hall were at the controls.

An anxious ground crew wondering if the balloon 'Promethius' would clear the trees. It did.

The main British Balloon and Airship Club Committee plus some co-opted members taken at a meeting in 1974. I was elected as a full member for a 2 year term in the Spring of 1973.

hotel. Pilot John Collier and myself sped to the launch field and were pressured into flying Beatrice. Much against my will, I finally agreed to take off but only if John came with me. I flatly refused to carry the allocated passengers. With such unstable thermic conditions, it really was unsafe - as the landing tally confirmed. One French pilot incurred a broken leg, another got a fractured wrist and almost every flyer had cuts or bruises. As for balloons, one draped over a lamppost, two landed in trees, one bumped into a house and another demolished a garden greenhouse. For us in Beatrice, our problem was a fast approach which ended in a dog-house landing across a small paddock. A dog-house landing is when the basket is dragged upside down along the ground with the occupants trapped inside. Luckily, a German family in a nearby house saw the accident and rescued John and I from the basket. We were both injured, but I more so than John. X-rays at the British garrison Hospital showed my ribs were just bruised and the fluid on my swollen knee was not too serious. The doctors then cleared me to fly home the next day on a BEA Trident 3 aircraft from Dusseldorf.

Lord Bathurst gave permission for Cirencester Park, Gloucestershire, to be the site for Air-Britain (Historians) to stage an International Balloon Meet to commemorate its 25th Anniversary. This company was the world's leading exponent on aircraft registrations and modern aviation news. The Daily Express newspaper and Society for the Prevention of Cot Deaths helped to sponsor the event and British Airways donated a trophy. The Dante Balloon Group assisted Air-Britain to arrange the balloon entries.

First balloon flights were at 0810 on Saturday 16 June with another wave departing in the late afternoon. The next morning was wet and windy. Some of the 7 hydrogen gas balloons again took off at 1700 on the Sunday. That weekend was the first time I had ever seen these craft which took up to two hours to become inflated and ready for take off.

Coloured commemorative illustrated balloon-post covers were carried aloft by all the pilots and most were signed by them. At least 2500 covers were flown. Blocks of 50 went in the different gas balloons and some were posted on landing as far away as Coventry. The Post Office, for a modest fee, hand-stamped the other covers with a special one-day illustrated Cirencester post mark which I had organised.

Montreal, Canada, was next. BA 601, G-ASGJ, on 18 June took Phil Dunnington, Dave and Merilyn Munson and I on a BOAC Fly-the-Flag Promotion in association with Export A (beer). On the following afternoon local pilot Larry Horrack led us to Markham (Ontario) where both Phil and I had short P1 flights in Dante. Niagra Falls was only a short plane ride away. Dave, with his commercial pilot's licence, tried to hire a small aircraft for us to see the Falls. Sadly none was available on 21 June. That evening on Canadian TV Phil appeared with an American pilot who down-graded us British as a 'bunch of amateur cowboys'. To counteract this at 0710 the next morning, with my hackles up, I was interviewed live on the nation-wide 'Canada AM' programme. However my fellow interviewee was a gentle Canadian who mollified the situation.

Strawberries and champagne were served at the 0600 press reception in a downtown Montreal park on 23 June. The organisers then gave the pilots a weather forecast. As the wind would take the balloons out over Lake Ontario for miles, life jackets were being sought for all crew members. The local radio stations were asked to broadcast appeals for all boat owners to stand by to rescue balloonists from the water. Without hesitation Phil, Dave and I said 'No thanks'. Ten American and Canadian balloons took off and eight of them had accidents on landing, such as hitting dockside warehouses, knocking over part of a pier, smashing into lampposts on the quayside or even in two cases landing on water. We tethered Dante in the park for about an hour and got more TV and press coverage for not flying.

Midsummer morning started with heavy rain and thunder. Having risen at 0400 we went to the morning briefing. The planned display (with the reduced number of serviceable balloons) was cancelled. At 2010 that evening, 24 June, together with the balloon we all returned to London on G-AWND. That was the first time Dante had travelled in the hold of a Jumbo Jet. (This B747 ended its life when blown up on the tarmac at Kuwait Airport during the Gulf War in 1990.)

Friday 13 July was a day of appointments for me. I became the first Advertising Manager (an overrated name for a relatively menial task) of the British Balloon and Airship Club journal Aerostat. I was also appointed the first Safety Officer of the BBAC. This job stemmed from a division of the Flying and Technical Committees. There was a perceived need to keep track of the increasing number of incidents with the growing number of new balloons in Britain. Roger Barrett, Chairman of the BBAC, who had his office not far from the BOAC Victoria Air Terminal persuaded me to accept both jobs during a lunch time meeting.

With help from Peter Langford, of the BBAC Flying Committee, I instituted an Incident Report Form. This was to be used by all pilots involved in any irregular flying experience either of a technical or human nature. Other ballooning countries around the world liked this feedback system and fairly soon produced a similar form to meet their local requirements. It took a lot of my time to get it accepted by pilots. Most were suspicious and I had to guarantee their anonymity when reporting flying foibles.

The Red Arrows Display Team and a hot air balloon flying in close proximity are not a recommended mix. On 11 August I was training a pilot on The Mary Gloster (G-BBCK) from Duntisbourne Abbotts and drifting gently towards Kemble Airfield, Gloucestershire, which I mistakenly thought was closed on Saturdays. Suddenly out of the blue streaked nine nice red jets on a downwind circuit before landing at Kemble. After a quick prayer I rapidly descended and landed on the first available patch of grass. We hurriedly packed away the balloon and left the area.

Duty visits to 9 Caribbean Islands started on 21 August. I flew 19 sectors in 17 days. Without detailing all that happened I flew from LHR to JFK then to Puerto Rico, before visiting Tortola in the British Virgin Islands - what a delightful place. Next it was the turn of the US Virgin Islands, the less attractive St Thomas and St Croix. The real excitement here was my first ride in a sea plane. It was an Antilles Airboat Grumman Goose, N74588, on a scheduled 25 minute inter-island trip from St Thomas. I also stayed overnight on the islands of St Kitts, Dominica and St Vincent.

All the towns in the West Indies are different. From my hotel bedroom near Roseau, the capital of Dominica, on the morning of 30 August I was surprised to see two lines of 'ant-like' figures. They were carrying peduncles of bananas on their shoulders along a wooden jetty for loading onto a tender to carry to the mother-ship in the bay. Bananas were the principal source of revenue for the Colony. I liked all three islands, in varying degrees, but Dominica was one of the most interesting since the road from town to the airport crossed a mountain rain forest, at least 1500 feet high.

On 01 September a very happy me travelled in the co-pilot's seat on a LIAT Islander aircraft, VP-LAG, from St Vincent to Grenada with an intermediate stop at a tiny airstrip on Cariacou. The runway had been hacked from the local grasses into a semi-flat condition but tall palm trees surrounded two sides. There was no VHF radio contact so landing clearance was given to the pilot by the one ground employee by means of three blinks from a hand held torch. I admired this primitive type of air operation. The name LIAT stands for Leeward Island Air Transport but many of the islanders preferred 'Leave Island Any Time'.

Two days later after inspecting the Grenada office I flew out of Pearls Airport. This was a tarmac strip built on some flat ground jutting out over part of the sea with a very steep high hill at the other end of the runway. LIAT 748 aircraft were allowed only to land and take-off from the sea-ward end of the runway. This made for some interesting flights!

After a night at the Barbados Hilton on 03 September I called on the BA Manager Mike McDonald the next day before catching a northbound B707.

The LIAT Reservations Manager was based in Antigua and I reported my findings to him. BOAC Head Office was concerned that LIAT as it's General Sales Agent was functioning below par. My problem was to define the word 'par'. The swimming was lovely, the people were friendly, the islands had their own charm and despite the concentrated nature of my tour I enjoyed the experiences.

Antigua had been planned as a 24 hour visit. On 05 September BA 686 was oversold and as a staff passenger I was 'bumped', i.e. offloaded, and had another night on the island. The following morning I tried to reach New York on BWIA (British West Indian Airways) but there was no space. Next along was a Pan Am B707 going to San Juan, Puerto Rico. It had seats available so I travelled. Then it was a change to another Pan Am flight to JFK where by luck, at least for me, BA 508 was delayed so I made a connection for LHR to arrive at 1215 on 07 September. Not only were my visits overseas full of surprise, adventure and novelty but the flying parts were also unpredictable. I rarely got exasperated at the irregularities in life. I could get frustrated and angry but generally preferred to accept what came along.

Named 'British Airways' G-BBAC was the third balloon bought by the Dante Group with financial help from BA. Its maiden flight was on 16 September and I was at Marsh Benham to see the event. I enjoyed flying this balloon because with it's 77000 cubic foot capacity it was more responsive. Regrettably the balloon was written off on 31 July 1976 when it landed in a field of cut hay and both the hay and balloon were consumed by flames.

Inspectors from the Civil Aviation Accident Investigation Branch asked me, as BBAC Safety Officer, on 01 October, to examine a balloon named 'Carousel'. This craft had been involved in an accident at RAF Yeovilton when an old design 'banana rip' panel opened in flight and it landed very heavily injuring two passengers, one seriously. The balloon registered G-AZOO did fly again after modifications and safeguards had been made.

Full medical examination was carried out on me by BA Medical Branch on 08 November. It had a dual purpose to give me full medical clearance for BA overseas duties and to continue the validity of my balloon pilot's licence. The pressure and stress of my work and private life did not show in any of the rigorous tests.

Christmas was spent as in most years with my mother and family at Dunfermline, Scotland. I escaped south before the New Year to avoid too much drink and maybe getting involved in stromach problems. My final ballooning task of the year was to test inflate and check 4 balloons in order to renew their certificates of airworthiness. This was done at Newbury on 29 December.

'Jambo' a helium-filled gas balloon seen on a 2 hour 40 minute flight on 29 August, 1966. The owner (and pilot) Anthony Smith carried Malcolm Brighton, Roger Barrett and a BBC reporter. The balloon was first flown from Zanzibar, (Africa) in January 1962 but sadly was destroyed by fire after landing in Sussex in July 1968.

15

MORE HOME AND AWAY-FOR WORK OR BALLOONING

Four European pilots were amongst those who attended the 2nd annual Icicle Meet held on 05 and 06 January 1974. Despite my optimism when giving the pilots the met briefing at 0930 there were strong winds, with rain showers, on both days. However 16 balloons made free flights and 2 of these were involved in landing mishaps. In opportunistic lulls in the wind these balloons made a total of 25 flights. The emphasis switched to the social aspect held at the nearby Elcot Park Hotel which remained the focal point for all non-flying activities for many years. As the Icicle event became more popular with balloonists the resources of the hotel became over-stretched, with up to 200 for the Saturday evening buffet. The Elcot was irreverently nicknamed 'Fawlty Towers'.

At work my manager permitted me to combine some overseas duty visits with leave - which in my case meant attending balloon events. On 03 February I left LHR for Panama City via Bermuda and Kingston aboard G-ASGK for the 14 hour journey. The tour was to check the reservations and sales standards being offered to BA passengers by the general sales agents in Panama, San Jose (Costa Rica) and Guatemala City. The itinerary I had planned was much more sensible than my over-zealous island hopping on the previous tour. Built into the time-table was enough freedom to allow for sightseeing.

Panama was memorable because of two evening visits to different locations along the Canal. Early morning on 07 February I boarded a plane of the local airline TACA, registration YS-17C, for the 1 hour flight to San Jose, the tranquil capital of Costa Rica. I went on an excursion tour to the interesting extinct volcano named Iraza at 10,420 feet, near the ancient capital city of Cartago. The waters in the basin of the volcano were the deepest blue I had ever seen. On Saturday the 9th a Pan Am B707 flew me to Guatemala City. I took a whole day coach tour to the mountainous interior region to a native market settlement called Chichicastanango. Every Sunday villagers from neighbouring localities walked miles with items, home made or grown, they wanted to barter (or perhaps sell) at the market. It was not a tourist haunt - there were just 3 other coaches from the city. We wandered around for 75 minutes admiring the simplicity of it all before leaving for Lake Atillan. An hour or more later we had lunch, time for a swim, or even a siesta. For me the adventures and sights of the day far outweighed the rather boring conversation by some of the passengers, who were mainly 'blue-rinse' American widows.

Guatemala City to Mexico City was a 1 hour 50 minute flight on the same TACA aircraft. It was 13 February. After 2 days of careful investigation of local procedures in the office another weekend came along for local sightseeing. I was invited to the Sunday afternoon bull fight on the outskirts of the city on 17 February. The stadium appeared to have seats for tens of thousands and were all occupied by a noisy, but well behaved, crowd in a carnival atmosphere. At 1600 the lesser known bull fighters entered the arena and in the next 2 hours the atmosphere became highly charged as the decibel level soared. As I recall only 2 matadors were injured. I was surprised at the stamina of a few bulls and this seemed to incite the crowd to even greater fervour.

Western Airlines first class breakfast service from Mexico City to Los Angeles on 19 February was memorable but not for its on-board amenities. The local manager had given me a first class seat into an almost empty cabin. Copious quantities of champagne were offered but very little food on the 3 hours 50 minute flight. That afternoon I had another tour of the Los Angeles area with a friend who was a local airline Sales Manager.

Trans Texas International Airlines flew me the next morning to Albuquerque and the DC9 landed in the unfavourable conditions of a snow storm. My first job was to clear the balloon G-BBAC from the local customs shed where it had been shipped from London via Chicago to await my arrival. British Airways Cargo was very good in arranging to have the balloon flown to where it was wanted. After checking in to the hotel I went to the official pilot briefing that evening.

British Airways had sponsored my appearance at this the 3rd International Albuquerque Balloon Fiesta from 21 to 24 February. The BA Regional Sales Manager, Dick Muir, and two sales representatives attended to watch part of the event. On the first morning, after a delay in refuelling, I had a 45 minute flight across the city. There were many receptions, side shows and other interesting balloon related happenings. Local radio station, KDEF, wanted me for live interviews on its breakfast programme before I hurried back to the Fair Ground site. At 1240 on 22 February I took off with a local newspaper reporter cum photographer, again across the city with a view of the Rio Grande River, to land 50 minutes later in Benatillo County. Don Cameron, who was there with the 'Lady Budget' balloon, and I had exchanged balloon burners for some now forgotten reason and this was a mistake as I had a minor rego valve propane fire in flight. Luckily I kept the fear to myself and the reporter was not aware that the landing was sooner than intended to extinguish the flames. That evening at a buffet reception I returned Don's faulty burner without thanks.

Strong winds on the 23rd prevented all flying which disappointed the Saturday spectators. That evening there was a Grand Banquet Dinner with traditional New Mexico fare, drink, speeches and prizes. The next morning, without admitting that I did not feel like flying I nevertheless inflated the balloon but before take off I aborted when the wind strengthened on the unsheltered launch site. After a lunch time barbecue I helped a well known American pilot, Bill Murtoff, make many attempts to fly his old Piccard balloon from the West Mesa. The wind defeated us all.

Monday morning was anti-climatic when I boarded a Continental Airlines B727 for the two and a half hour flight from Albuquerque to Chicago O'Hare. In the evening I boarded the BA Jumbo G-AWNB for LHR to arrive at 0840 on 26 February.

BEA and BOAC were officially dissolved at the end of March to become British Airways.

Cardington (Bedfordshire) Airship Hanger was used on 06 April for tests on the balloon Carousel, G-AZOO, after repairs following its accident. Peter Langford was there as chairman of the BBAC Technical Committee and I as the BBAC Safety Officer. That evening I attended 2 further meetings. First was on the forthcoming Cirencester Balloon Meet and then the BBAC Main Committee meeting which lasted until 2300. This was a Saturday and looking through my diary there are very few Saturdays and Sundays when I was not involved with ballooning.

Weekends in May were as follows: 1) Drove with balloon to Newark Agricultural Show (Nottinghamshire). No flights - too windy. 2) Took balloon G-BBAC to Penshurst Place Show (Kent). Did 2 inflations - too windy for free flights. 3) Flew in my first Thunder Balloon, 'Rocinante' G-BBOX, with Norman Pritchard and David Calkin under training. Flying at about 800 feet we saw a smaller Thunder Balloon beneath us hit some power wires. We were pleased to see the two occupants scramble away apparently unhurt. 4) Spent 11 hours 10 minutes sitting in B707, G-AXGX, en route to Kingston via Nassau and Montego Bay. 5) This is cheating a bit but it was Saturday 01 June when I returned from Jamaica after a 9 hours 40 minute flight.

Butlins Holiday Camp at Bognor Regis was where I went the next day. The reason was to visit my mother, brother, his wife and daughter, Nicola, who were there on a Whitsun weekend break.

British Rail from Waterloo to Southampton on 06 June to catch 'Viking II', an overnight ferry to Le Havre, was the next adventure. Thence by car via Paris and Rouen for the French Balloon Meet at Montbard organised by Robbie Noirclerc where we arrived in time for the evening reception. Some balloons flew on Saturday 08 June before a barbecue dinner (four whole sheep had been roasting all day over a spit). There was also the most unforgettable vat of punch. The word 'unforgettable' has many meanings. Some of us took a few sips of the delightful and seemingly innocuous cocktail but soon found ourselves legless and with a pronounced slur of the English language. Seemingly there was rain later in the evening. I vaguely remember lying on the bonnet of a car for a quick nap. I was sound asleep when it rained heavily. It did not wake me. Some kind souls rescued and saw me safely to bed in the hotel.

Without a hangover on the following morning I went to the balloon site, a well protected valley location, intending to fly with Dick Wirth of Thunder Balloons. My stomach was unsettled and I opted out - which meant I did not get a flight that weekend. However with other Group members we won an inflation race with Dante in the late afternoon. I 'hitched' a lift with Pete Bish and Phil Dunnington to central Paris where we arrived at 0030. Then followed a tour by road and foot around a few of the nightclub areas before a late-night snack. Robbie Noirclerc had kindly let us spend the night in his flat. Less than 12 hours later I was on a BEA Trident 3 from Orly to LHR. The date was 10 June.

'Balloons around the World' a 28 page booklet written by me, to sell at 20p, was the first attempt to record all known balloons and registrations. It was published on 14 June and went on sale at the Cirencester Meet..

85 Balloons made 188 free flights on 15 and 16 June from Cirencester Park. This was a record number of flights on any occasion outside of the USA. There were pilots from eleven countries. The event was the Daily Express International Balloon Meet, largely organised by the Dante Group. There was a record of 9 hydrogen gas balloons present. During the weekend many firsts occurred including the then largest balloon of 375,000 cubic feet capacity (Daffodil II) appeared with the smallest radio controlled model of 2,000 cubic feet (Mercury). I flew the British Airways balloon, G-BBAC, from the park on both days.

Indianola in Iowa, was the annual venue for the American National Balloon Championships. On 03 August I flew from LHR to Chicago on G-AWNO to connect with a United Airlines B727 to Des Moines which was the nearest airport to Indianola. Accomodation for balloonists was available at Simpson University, which was just yards away from the launch site. Don Cameron and I shared a room. The local aviation inspectors insisted that an American Licence was necessary for us to fly a US registered balloon. After some haggling Don and I finally qualified for the US licence on the afternoon of 04 August. As 'fun flyers' we took off after the competitors. I flew N90903 'Weathering Heights' a new Cameron O-65 balloon with its owner Larry Allen under training.

It is easy to run out of superlatives when describing a gathering of balloons. The more outstanding and memorable happenings from this meeting were:

1) Not too far ahead of us in the air was manufacturer Tracy Barnes in his all black solar tetrahedron balloon. This works on the principle of heat from the sun warming the air inside the envelope which then produces lift. During this flight, some cirrus cloud partly obscured the sun forcing the balloon to descend and land involuntarily. The 4th solar flight had lasted just 15 minutes.

2) Captain Eddie Allen, a gutsy 78 year old, flew his smoke balloon on Sunday evening the 4th. This was the first such flight in the US for six years, and I was lucky to be there. His rate of climb was put at 800 feet a minute. At about 3000 feet the balloon cooled, then distorted before inverting itself to release the smoke. The astounded crowd, estimated at 25000, then watched the pilot parachute away from the smoking canopy to land safely.

3) 120 of the most competitive pilots had 4 tasks in which to prove their superiority. The winner was 19 year old Chuck Ehrler. This was surprising because he had got his licence just 3 weeks before the event and had been ballooning for only 3 months.

There was a myriad of sideline attractions. These included parties, food, drink, bric-a-brac stalls and almost anything to keep happy the estimated 45000 visitors that week.

A 600 mile car drive from Indianola to Ann Arbor, Michigan sounded like a good idea at the time. With a mandatory 50 mph road speed limit it turned out to be boring. We arrived with Tucker Comstock at 0200 on 10 August. Later that day we played at balloon inflations to measure output performances.

Delta Airlines flew me the next day from Detroit to Miami for an overnight stop. Then it was British Airways business that took me to the Cayman Islands using a LACSA jet, TI-LRJ, on 12 August. My assignment was to check on the local sales agency and visit the 2 travel agents. There was an amazing turtle farm where at least 5000 turtles were reared and their eggs exported to many nearby countries in a conservation programme. The Holiday Inn served turtle steak as a delicacy at dinner. I thought the flesh was tough and almost tasteless. It was a relaxing few days before a 1 hour 50 minute flight to Kingston, Jamaica on 16 August to report my findings to Area Manager David Creedy. That evening I boarded a B707 for LHR via Nassau.

Hang-gliding was becoming a more popular fringe activity. There was a championship competition near Stroud in Glostershire on 25 August and I visited the event in the rain. I was not over-impressed with what I saw.

Another weekend was spent at a UK balloon meeting. From 06 to 08 September I was at the Gliffaes Hotel in Wales ready to fly G-BBAC along with another 20 invited pilots. Severe storms kept us isolated but the social gathering, food and drink were great.

Reims in France was the next weekend experience. On Friday the 13th I drove with Dick Wirth, Mo Fisher and Tina Shand from London to Dover for the ferry to Calais. We arrived at our hotel in Reims after a leisurely 12 hour journey. The next afternoon in almost flat calm conditions I took off in G-BBAC with Tina Shand. We were still almost overhead the launch site at 7500 feet. I decided to climb a little higher as two balloons ahead had done. When Tina complained of feeling cold I again checked the altimeter and was surprised to find it read 9500 feet. I will not confess to being in the base of a French airway but a Caravelle jet some miles away seemed low! Making a semi-controlled rapid descent I found we were drifting back towards the city. Traditionally, Dante members were non-competitive, flying purely for fun. By mistake, I won a silver cup for landing nearest to the declared goal. This was in spite of my efforts to satisfy the judges by entering my take-off co-ordinates on the landing form, handed in before take-off.

Walking along cool, dark corridors in a deep underground cellar before breakfast on a Sunday morning may seem rather odd. Veuve Cliquot had invited a dozen of us to visit their well managed and secure champagne cellars on 15 September. The loving care shown to the quarter-million bottles lying peacefully in their racks was impressive. Next we were treated to a champagne breakfast. I cannot forget the generous hospitality but then can remember little else! Rather than free fly the balloon in the afternoon I gave tethered displays. I still retain happy memories of this second French balloon event. We left early the next morning for the drive to Calais then the Dover ferry. I was at home in London by 1830.

Meanwhile back at the office on 30 September there was a double farewell party. Jack Cowley who had been an assistant to Martin Hyland, BOAC Reservations Manager, was retiring. Jack had been the Head Office 'guardian' on our overseas duties. Bill George, who had been my boss, moved from Southern Division to another post.

"Balloon accident at Birmingham - 2 dead." That was the garbled phone call I got at work on Tuesday afternoon 08 October. Minutes later Geoff Holton, an Air Accident Investigator of the CAA, phoned to ask if I could accompany him to the accident site. An official car arrived at the BOAC Victoria Terminal to take Peter Langford, BBAC Technical Committee, Dick Wirth, a partner in Thunder Balloons and myself as Safety Officer to Birmingham. The balloon, G-BOCG named 'Free N Easy' had crashed beside a canal just minutes after take-off when the rip panel opened in flight. The police were guarding the area and in heavy rain we examined the basket and balloon envelope. The following morning we had to visit the local police station and make a brief report at the Coroners Court before further examination of the balloon. I found it a distressing experience. This was the first known fatal balloon accident in the UK. The pilot was Mike Adams and his passenger was Mike Sparks. They had taken off in unfavourable weather as part of a public relations exercise for a fork lift company.

Nineteen flying hours were added to my total when I made a 4 day visit to Caracas from 19 November. It was an audit to assess the workload versus staff numbers ratio. Outbound the daylight flight called at Antigua but

A midday flight with me piloting the British Airways Balloon, G-BBAC, on 22 February 1974. Below is the city of Albuquerque, New Mexico, with the Rio Grande River in the background.

the return journey, also by B707 aircraft, was a night flight. There was no audio or visual entertainment on these planes and I had a strong dislike of the boredom when flying at night.

When news got out that a gas airship club was looking for members to finalise plans to launch a project I became interested. On 01 December I drove to a meeting in a pub before visiting the airship, partially inflated with air, in a hanger at Wroughton Airfield, near Swindon, Wiltshire. As secretary Andrew Lloyd had the task of trying to mollify the strongly differing opinions of some members. Harold Wingham had been an early instigator to produce an airship. It was at the pub meetings that I met Max Woosnam who was to become a friend and help when I moved to Malmesbury 11 years later.

BEA and BOAC were officially dissolved by April 1974. The amalgamated companies took the name British Airways. I attended a one week residential course at the BOAC Staff Training College at Burnham Beeches in Buckinghamshire from 02-06 December. This was one of many staff-progression courses I attended over many years.

This BA photo shows the 3rd balloon sponsored by the airline and used on promotional tours by the Dante Group.

The unusual shape of a 'smoke' balloon being filled by means of a kerosene burner for flight on 4 August 1974. The place was Indianola, Iowa, and the event was the US National Championships.

The balloon assumed a more conventional shape. When very hot the balloon was released from its restraining rope and rose at about 800 feet per minute.

The only American practising this unusual spectacle was a 78 year old named Captain Eddie Allen. He dangled below on a parachute line. When the balloon cooled at about 3000 feet he released himself and floated back to earth.

US manufacturer Tracey Barnes built this tetrahedron-shaped balloon. The direct rays from the sun penetrate the black material and heats the air inside to produce lift. Also photographed at Indianola in August 1974.

16
STILL MANY ACTIVITIES DESPITE HEALTH PROBLEMS

Savernake Forest in Wiltshire was used as the launch site for the 3rd annual Icicle Meet due to the strong winds around Marsh Benham and to avoid overflying the Greenham Common Air Base. I again gave pilots the met briefing at 0845 on Saturday 04 January 1975. My records show 35 balloons flew that day.

Incident report forms had been summarised by me and were presented at the main BBAC Committee Meeting held in London on 28 January. Roger Barrett, Chairman of the BBAC, was very adept at running a strict meeting and this I appreciated. Throughout life I have been intolerant of people who waffle at meetings. For me the only good assembly of communicators is when subject matters are dealt with succinctly.

Not really for economy reasons, but I bought a new Renault 5TL on 01 February which despite a few weaknesses served me well until the dial read 99,964 miles.

St Valentine's Day gave me a touch of luxury as I was upgraded to First Class for the 14 hour flight to Mexico City via Bermuda and Freeport. It was a VC10, G-ASGI which gave a quieter, smoother ride than the B707. The purpose of my visit was to 'assist' in the move to another sales shop and reservations office. In London we had forgotten to add time for the 'manana' factor. Five days later the move was still not fully complete but I had another engagement. It was to attend a ballooning event in Albuquerque.

Complimentary tickets on other airlines were easy for me to obtain as a 'Reservations Officer'. On 21 February I flew on a Braniff B727 from Mexico City to Dallas Fort Worth to connect with a Continental Airlines flight to Albuquerque. Bob and Marge Ruppenthal met me at the airport and I stayed with them for the next 3 days of the annual Balloon Fiesta. Although there was snow that evening we attended the pilot briefing and reception.

There was almost 2 feet of lying snow when we woke on Saturday morning the 22nd. Their house, named 'Eagles Nest' was situated in the hills above the city. It took the family with British pilot Terry Adams and myself nearly two hours to clear the snow from the garage entrance and exit road. We finally arrived at the State Fair Ground at 0930 to learn that a few 'balloonatics' had flown. We did not offer to retrieve them! However that evening we did venture out to the banquet at a city motel.

Raven Balloons via Sid Cutter the next morning kindly lent me a Raven Rally RX6 Balloon to fly and evaluate. This was a new model with an aluminum gondola (basket). Despite the thick layer of snow I flew N7306L from the State Fair Ground with Terry Adams as P2. Using my USA pilots licence I was able to sign him out as an American balloon pilot. We landed just inside the forbidden territory of an Indian Reservation and quickly 'floated' the balloon back over the fence onto a snow covered side road. Then we left the area promptly.

By late afternoon some of the snow had melted. The West Mesa was a large tract of scrub land outside Albuquerque and Marge Ruppenthal asked me to fly her in 'Cactus Jack'. This was the second balloon built by Thunder, the first to be exported, and briefly registered G-BARK before becoming N711CJ. We had a pleasant 45 minute flight to re-establish the confidence Marge had lost in a nasty balloon incident a year earlier. To complete a very full day I had dinner at the home of Tom and Linda Rutherford. Tom was a keen balloonist and a Deputy Governor of the State of New Mexico. I greatly appreciated the gesture when he gave me an honorary State Award.

Continental Airlines flew me to Denver via Colorado Springs on the morning of 24 February. A TWA B707 then carried me to JFK where after a 4 hour transit a BA B747 took me to LHR. The elapsed journey time was almost 17 hours. After an afternoon siesta I attended the monthly BBAC main Committee Meeting. I was really doing my health no favours with such a hectic life style.

The BBAC AGM was held while I was in Albuquerque. There had been a postal ballot for a place on the main Committee and I was elected. At that time I did not realise I was getting involved in so much balloon work. When I did realise, I handed over the job of the Safety Committee Chairman on 10 March to Bernard Hockley. However I retained the less demanding role of Social Secretary. This allowed me more time to gather information for the ambitious project I had set myself. It was to prepare a comprehensive book to be called 'Balloons Around the World' - a Register of all known hot air and gas balloons with modern and historical notes. It turned out to be 90 pages long.

A neurologist at Charing Cross Hospital, Fulham Palace Road, London, saw me on 08 April. This led to a two week stay as an in-patient from 13 May for a very thorough series of investigations.

Stockholm sounded like a pleasant place to spend a weekend. The Dante balloon G-BBAC was delayed returning from a promotional visit to Kingston, Jamaica. Nevertheless I kept my plans and flew to Stockholm on 02 May to stay with prominent journalist and balloonist Seve Ungermark and family outside the city. After sightseeing on Saturday morning, 03 May, I was honoured to be a guest at a meeting of the 75th anniversary of the Swedish Balloon Federation. At tea time there was a mini-meet of balloons in a city park plus the launch of many hundred paper balloons by school children. Gusty winds kept the big balloons tethered. When the adults had become exhausted we replaced our food and liquid levels by attending two sumptuous parties.

Sunday morning 04 May was still too windy to launch the 4 balloons from the city park. The Swedish newspapers proudly carried the story of the 75th anniversary. By late afternoon I was on my way to the new Arlanda International Airport, some 45 kms from the city, for a First Class seat in a Trident 3 to LHR.

Hospitals are not usually considered to be a place of relaxation. On 13 May I was admitted to Charing Cross Hospital initially for one week and a series of tests. The neurologist was somewhat mystified by the symptoms of unstable walking and little else. The hospital was a teaching establishment and I was considered a prime subject for any number of medical problems with a background of so much overseas travel. Ailments such as bilharzia, brain tumour or other nasties were suggested to the students to exclude from the list of afflictions. I had my own en suite bedroom and treated with some reverence. When told I would have to return for a second week I remember feeling elated. Those two weeks in that ward, strange as it may sound, were one of the happiest and most relaxing periods I could remember. Although some of the tests were irksome I was free from external pressure and anxiety. A deficiency of Vitamin B12 was an interim diagnosis and I was given daily injections. On 23 May I was discharged after all major tests proved negative. No mention was ever made of 'disseminated sclerosis' (now re-named 'multiple sclerosis').

'Balloons Around the World' was printed in Belfast. A friend collected the first batch whilst I was on weekend leave from the hospital. About 100 copies were posted at London's Trafalgar Square Post Office on Sunday 18 May. Distribution of the bulk supply followed slowly over the next 3 months but retail sales were well below my estimated target. The disappointing lack of sales did not justify the amount of effort, time and stress I had so lavishly placed on the project.

Temperatures that summer were well above average. In the London area in May, June and August my diary lists figures in the mid-eighties Fahrenheit (low thirties in Celsius) and this was almost unbearable for me. The hospital had given me 12 weeks sick leave. Some of this time I spent in a cooler Scotland. At the end of May I helped my mother move to a new house but still in Rosyth near Dunfermline, Fife.

Cirencester Park was again the site for a summer balloon meeting. Many pilots stayed at the Kings Head Hotel for the two day event on 14 and 15 June. On Friday 13th I had flown to Belfast, Trident out - Tristar back, to collect more copies of my book. On Saturday the long awaited display by the Gloster Airship, G-AWVR, nearly took place. Whilst the envelope was being inflated with cold air the glue joints on the panels had reached their use-by dates and gradually split. As a member of the Gloster Airship Society I was saddened to see our project collapse in such a way.

Instability with my walking was not improving. My GP gave me a walking stick and prescribed a course of ACTH (steroid) injections on 17 June. When complete I saw him again and finally he used the word 'sclerosis' on 25 June. A much fuller explanation was needed but Dr Crowley gave me a rather woolly prognosis. I left his surgery feeling annoyed, confused and upset. The secrecy at not being told sooner still irks me today but even with this knowledge it made no difference to the way I lived my life. Is it not better to plough ahead into the unknown than sit back and fear it?

The World's First Women Pilots Balloon Meet took place on 12 and 13 July. Veuve Cliquot sponsored the event at Castle Ashby, Northamptonshire. I attended and helped Anne Lewis-Smith with part of the organisation and enjoyed seeing the pilots and their crews, dressed in their best balloon finery. The weather was not kind - windy from late Saturday morning with rain on the Sunday. My collection of flown balloon-post covers shows that 12 balloons made free flights. Other reports (and my memory of the event) think that some of the balloons had made only captive ascents.

Cardington Airship hanger was an ideal building to test-inflate experimental craft. On 18 July Don Cameron was testing alterations to G-BAMK (the world's first hot air airship) and I wanted to be there. In a corner of the hanger was The Santos-Dumont, G-BAWL, the recently designed and homebuilt gas airship of Anthony Smith. I liked to keep an interest in new developments and the Cardington hangers usually had creative air vehicles around the site. My diary shows that I undertook Certificate of Airworthiness checks on 9 balloons, mostly brand new for export and mostly Thunder made, during the first 7 months of the year.

The Daily Express was part sponsor of the BBAC Summer Balloon Meet held at Weston Park on 13 and 14 September. For a change I had opted out of the organisation to run the event and attended just as a spectator. Printed accounts show different figures for the number of balloons both attending and or flying. My estimate is that more than 75 hot air balloons flew plus probably 7 gas balloons. There is no record of any flying on Sunday 14th due to wind and rain, which may be just as well as the Saturday night Survivors Dinner was a staggering success.

World Hot Air Balloon Championships Number Two was next. On 02 October I travelled on a BA Jumbo from LHR to Chicago then onward by Continental Airlines to Albuquerque. It was planned to be a big gathering. 34 International pilots from 15 countries had entered. To run concurrently there was the annual Fiesta Rally which attracted about 130 'fun flyers'. The Albuquerqueans who organised the events did a superb job based mostly on their experience of two years earlier. A member of the Panel of Judges reported that there were 1,289 launchings (including the Fiesta balloons) in 9 days with 48 tasks set and scored.

Dick Brown, Editor of the Balloon Federation of America journal 'Ballooning' took me for a 40 minute flight in his balloon N616DB on 04 October and we landed near the Rio Grande river. There was an amazing and immense variety of commercial activity at the Convention Centre. Added to this was an almost infinite number of minor and major banquets throughout the city. The problem for most of us was finding time to sleep. It really was a fun-packed eleven days where I made new friends, saw interesting flying, visited nearby natural attractions and never found time to be bored. On 12 October I flew on Continental Airlines to Chicago and then caught the BA flight to London that evening.

On the eve of Guy Fawkes Day I prepared the first ever colour edition of the BBAC journal 'Aerostat'. Editor Anne Lewis-Smith entrusted me to assemble the information and colour artwork. Most issues thereafter were in colour - though not quite so elaborate for cost reasons.

British Airways wanted me to have meetings in the Bahamas on communication problems. On 09 November I flew to Nassau via Bermuda. Then it was a day trip across to Freeport for more talks, which were only partly productive (and for me boring). 12 November was a day of rest and relaxation, plus report writing, at the Nassau Beach Hotel before flying to LHR that evening.

To maintain the variety in my life I organised the BBAC Christmas party - dinner and dance - at the Charing Cross Hotel in Central London on 06 December.

Christmas was spent with my mother and family in Scotland. To avoid the usual congestion at Heathrow I travelled on the 1210 'Aberdonian' express train from Kings Cross on 24 December and for a change returned on an overnight sleeper on the 28th.

1976

Strong almost gale force winds affected Southern England on Friday evening 02 January as I drove to the Elcott Park Hotel, Newbury to night stop for the 4th Icicle Meet. The hotel was without electricity until after midday on the Saturday. The hardy balloonists attended a pilot briefing at 0800 but the storm force winds continued and all flying was abandoned for the day. The hotel had attached a large marquee to the building, well anchored, with enough space to accommodate 200 people for a social evening. I had organised a Pilots Forum, several film shows and a buffet dinner. On the Sunday morning the launch site was moved to a sheltered place in Savernake Forest and I saw more than 25 balloons fly. By lunch time most pilots and crews had left to go home.

Anne Lewis-Smith held a dinner party at her house at Potsgrove near Henley-on-Thames on 09 January as a prelude to passing over the editor's position on Aerostat to Alan Noble. It was a pleasant evening and we talked until the wee small hours.

From 20 January until 23 February I was away from work on sick leave, caused mainly by tension and weakness. The doctor prescribed a course of Parentovite injections from 22 January. When completed Anne Lewis-Smith kindly invited me to spend a week with her at her cottage at Cwarre, Newcastle Emlyn, Cenarth to help me unwind. On 31 January the drive to Wales took less than 6 hours.

Outdoor frozen pipes were just one of the problems confronting us and a partly blocked chimney gave unwanted amounts of smoke indoors. Almost everything that happened in the next five days was so much better than I could ever had imagined. Occasional snow showers did not stop interesting visits to places such as Cardigan Bay and Camarthan Market, plus of course a few distinctive public houses where generous portions of local foods were served. I enjoyed seeing life on two neighbouring farms and the company of the hard working owners. For me that visit to Wales was relaxation with good food, good company and happiness.

A 15 day duty visit to the Caribbean started on 25 April when I left LHR for Antigua. It was a 25 minute connection onto a LIAT Avro 748 to Montserrat where I stayed at the Vue Point Hotel. (Regrettably this beautiful island has now been almost decimated by volcanic activity in the mid 1990's.) The next day Eric Camacho, the CRO from Antigua, joined me on a visit to the local BA agent before we flew out that evening to St Kitts. After breakfast on the 27th we visited the capital, Basseterre, to meet the local representative and enjoy a sightseeing tour of another delightful island, unspoilt and unsullied by commercialism.

Mid-morning on the 28th I continued my island hopping alone, flying northwards to St Maarten. I was met by the local manager and stayed at the delightful Hotel Caravenserai. My bedroom was only yards from a white sandy beach and gentle blue water on the leeward side of the island. This duty trip was more like a luxury tour. Then it was onward to the British Virgin Islands. The Puerto Rican airline, Prinair, carried me in a Heron aircraft for the 40 minutes to the airport on Beef Island. The local agency manager, Russell McGregor, drove me across the bridge to Tortola (the main island) where I visited his office in the capital, Road Town. I met a number of people influential in the travel trade, linked to some rich yacht owners who had homes in Britain. It was Thursday 29 April and the weekend was approaching. The Prospect Reef Hotel and its facilities were too good for me to vacate.

St Thomas, one of the US Virgin Islands, was my next port of call on 02 May. I was there for less than 24 hours before catching a LIAT flight on the 3rd to Antigua. The plane landed at St Croix, St Maarten and St Kitts. Yet the flying time for the 4 sectors was just 1 hour 50 minutes. Early the next morning with Eric Camacho we flew on a 7 seater Islander for a 9 hour day trip to Nevis. This was another small yet beautiful island and we had time to explore some sugar mills and meet a few eccentric expats who had moved there. Although I had work to do there were occasions such as this when the hassle of life in London could be forgotten.

The London to Port of Spain aircraft on 05 May carried me from Antigua to Barbados. I reported my findings to Regional Manager, Tim Kelly. I then carried out an inspection visit of the Barbados reservations functions. Andrew Lang, who was Manager Barbados, had organised a public relations gathering which included bringing 'Miss Speedbird', Ross Hanby, from London. There was a poolside barbecue at his house which lasted until 0200.

Good fortune had been with me throughout this tour and even continued with the flight home. I disliked night flights but on 08 May the evening flight to London was operated by a half-empty B747 which allowed me room to stretch out on three seats.

With a slowly worsening ability to walk unaided my doctor would not renew the medical certificate for my balloon pilots licence. Therefore my last solo tethered balloon ascent and very short free flight was on 05 June. The balloon was home built by Angela Smith based on the Cameron O-31 size, named 'Cheeky Devil', and registered G-BDYM. It was at a charity event at Navestock in Essex.

From 18 to 20 June I attended another balloon meet at Cirencester Park and saw 56 flights over 2 days. The weather was a mixture of hot thermic conditions and heavy rain showers. My diary shows that the temperature in London on 26 June was a record 95 degrees Fahrenheit.

British Airways decided to integrate the reservations officers at Victoria with a number of traffic officers at LHR to form a joint 'Customer Service Unit'. This involved us attending five courses and studying from 'trainaid' manuals to qualify in ground service functions. The training started in late June and culminated in a series of written exams in the week ending 26 November. I and most of my colleagues found it very hard work, which was not helped by the hot summer weather. We received certificates in: Ground Operations I and II, Cargo, Customer Service and Fares,

Load Sheets plus Balance Charts for VC10, B707 freighter, B747 and even the Concorde aircraft. We had a celabratory party in the belief that we were the most qualified and up-to-date multi-functional customer service staff in the airline. Our elation was short lived as a change of management at Head Office decided to abandon the previously much heralded multi-functional staff scheme. Disenchantment was just one of the emotions we all felt.

My grandmother who had been staying with her niece Clare Smith and family at Formby, Lancashire celebrated her 95th birthday on 25 July. Gran had developed an infection and spent the occasion in Southport Hospital where I visited her. Although weak physically she was mentally very alert but died on 29 July. At her request only Clare and I attended a simple Catholic cremation service on 31 July. I had been very close to my grandmother from childhood and was saddened by her death.

The Route Superintendent had doubts that the BA staff in the Nairobi office would find it easy to complete the conversion course to the BABS computer system. The Nairobi staff were brought to London for the two week training and most achieved good results. Our Nairobi office was the first in Africa to be mechanised. On 14 October five of us from London took the overnight B747 to Nairobi to prepare for the 'cutover' to BABS. On Saturday afternoon the 16th, together with a number of Kenyan staff, we started to 'mesh' the manual Sales Record Cards into the computer. By 1300 the next day the job was done and we all had a festive Sunday lunch at the nearby Hilton Hotel. Shortly after midnight most of us were flying back to London to arrive just after breakfast-time on 18 October.

Eight days over Christmas was spent with my mother and family for the usual family get-together.

A certificate of which I am very proud. BA posted this memento to every passenger some weeks after their flight.

British airways Concorde

presented to

Alec Jenkinson

who flew supersonically on Concorde

between *Washington–London* on *14 August 1977*

17

A HIGHLY CHARGED YEAR AND WITH SPEED-CONCORDE

Good weather, calm winds and a clear sky, on Saturday 08 January made my job easy as the met man at the Icicle Meet. There were 84 flights that day. Strong winds on Sunday the 9th kept all balloonists grounded. The official BBAC statistics for 31 December 1976 showed there were 123 hot air balloons in the UK and 54 of these flew at the 1977 Icicle–an indication of the popularity of this event. For the record there were 138 known active pilots resident in the UK on the same date.

Ahead was another year of exciting events, much mileage on duty trips, my first flight on a Concorde aircraft and upheaval in my personal life. The first overseas journey was another Atlantic crossing, this time by B Cal (British Caledonian Airways) from Gatwick to Caracas. The nine and a half hour flight was aboard a B707 on 11 January. The UK to South America routes were operated by B Cal but BA retained sales shops in Caracas, Bogota and Lima. My mission was to check the standards in the offices. After 3 days in Caracas I flew on a VIASA DC8 plane to Bogota, which at an altitude of almost 8500 feet, was never one of my favourite capital cities. It seemed squalid and disorderly although the Tequendama Hotel where I stayed was first class.

On 18 January the planned flight onward to Lima was delayed. Luck was on my side and I transferred to a passing B Cal aircraft which routed via Quito (in Ecuador). Ian Gillespie in Lima met me and as on my previous visits tried to arrange a visit to Cuzco and Machupicchu for me to see the Inca ruins. Fortune was not with me as the daily flight was booked for days ahead. On 21 January another B Cal B707 returned me to Gatwick via Bogota and Caracas with a flying time of 13 hours 45 minutes.

BA wanted an active sales agency in Santo Domingo in the Domincan Republic and I was sent to sound out the reaction of Eastern Airlines on the island. To get there I travelled BA from LHR to JFK thence an Eastern Tristar to San Juan (Puerto Rico) on 07 February. The following morning I had talks with the EA Regional Manager and his staff where my reception was cool. Using Eastern B727's for the 45 minute inter-island flights I made a day trip to Santo Domingo on 10 February and was fascinated to see two Constellation aircraft of the local airline on the tarmac being prepared for departure. After another night stop in San Juan I flew to Miami on 11 February again on an EA Tristar to connect with a BA Jumbo for LHR. The final outcome of my visit to the Dominican Republic was not a success, Eastern Airlines locally was not interested in taking on any work for BA.

Balloon meetings still attracted me and on 11 March I stayed at the Albany Inn Hotel at Crick for the Stanford Hall Meet. On Saturday the 12th the pilot briefing was at 0600 and 18 balloons flew in the morning with more in the afternoon. With strong winds on Sunday the event was abandoned at midday.

During the next six weeks I made several visits to Charing Cross Hospital, mostly to see Dr G D Perkin who arranged a number of tests including eye sight, bladder pressure and stability in walking following a course of ACTH (steroid) injections. Life was a little on the cheerless and dreary side. Therefore I was surprised and uplifted to see my photograph with David Liddiard on the front cover of the April issue of our balloon magazine Aerostat. It was to commemorate my first flight from Bradfords Farm 5 years earlier.

Moving house is a stressful time for most people and this time I found it even more irksome. On 16 May I left Lytton Grove, Putney and moved to a flat at Kew Gardens. This was intended as a short term solution but for numerous reasons I did not take possession of a new house at Thatcham near Newbury until 29 December 1978.

Multi-millionaire Malcolm Forbes owned the Chateau de Balleroy in Normandy, France and in June held an extravaganza balloon assembly there. Through his Meet organiser, Anne Lewis-Smith, I was honoured to be one of the four British balloonists invited to the 3rd International event held from 10 to 12 June. David Liddiard, nurse Sandra Lusby and I sailed on the Townsend ferry, Viking Valiant, from Southampton to Le Harve on 09 June with the balloon 'Concorde', G-BDSE. (Officially this balloon was part of the BA aircraft fleet and therefore had comprehensive airline insurance of £150 million !) On Friday the 10th there was a de luxe buffet supper followed by a totally spectacular computer programmed sequence of fireworks accompanied by music.

Just after daybreak on Saturday, say around 0515, we saw from our bedroom window rain falling from an overcast sky and the trees swaying. At the pilot briefing it was confirmed that flying was off. We took the chance to visit the famous tapestry in Bayeux. It was only a short drive to the beaches at Omaha and Arromanches of World War II fame plus their associated museums. We also saw the wartime graves so well maintained. That evening two sheep had been barbecued along with other meats and these were served to about 80 invited guests in the cellar of the Chateau. It was an excellent feast. Then there was a slide and film show by American pilot Ed Yost. This related to his recent World Distance and Endurance gas balloon record flight of 2475 miles in 107 hours 37 minutes. He, like some others before, had tried to be the first person to cross the Atlantic by balloon, but had to abandon the attempt near the Azores.

On Sunday 12 June in almost flat calm conditions I inflated 'Concorde' and gently lifted off with David Liddiard at 0735. We drifted just above tree top height with a wind speed of maybe 3 knots. It required my concentration to keep the balloon in equilibrium but the challenge was worth it. 27 minutes later a clearing in the forest appeared and I landed to allow Sandra to have a flight. By mid morning it started to rain but we continued by road to the nearby town of St Lo for a good lunch. Later after saying our 'thank you's and goodbye's' at the Chateau we drove to Le Harve for the overnight ferry crossing to Southampton.

As part of the London celebrations for the Queen's Silver Jubilee, the BBAC, in conjunction with the Sports Council, got special permission from the Civil Aviation Authority for hot air balloons to take off from and fly over Central London. Saturday 23 July was the allocated date with Sunday as the reserve day. 54 balloons had clearance to fly from Hyde Park Corner, subject to several strict conditions. The CAA stipulated: the wind must be around 8 knots, the direction must have an element of westerly in it, the balloons must not impede the jets landing at Heathrow and there must be at least 2 hours fuel on board.

Scores of pilots and crews had afternoon tea in the garden of the Hyde Park Hotel on the Saturday. However the surface wind remained above the permitted speed and reluctantly flying was postponed until the next day. One commentator wrote "Next time balloonists have a tea party before flying they should avoid eating cucumber sandwiches as I suspect this generates wind!". As a minor official for the launch procedures I again turned up on the Sunday. The wind remained outside limits and with regret the well planned balloon extravaganza was cancelled.

August 1977 was an important and special month for me. All 4 Sundays were significant.

On the 7th: After many years absence from the Church I saw Father Michael Hollings and had a long spiritual talk culminating in my making a long overdue confession.

On the 14th: I flew on a scheduled BA Concorde flight from Washington (Dulles) Airport to LHR in 3 hours 35 minutes at a speed of Mach 2.02.

On the 21st: Attended Mass and received Holy Communion at my local parish church at Kew Gardens.

On the 28th: With 3 other Dante members I was in my favourite country, Finland, at an airshow near Helsinki. We drove up country to find a launch site but bad weather prevented the balloon from getting airborne.

The morning after seeing Father Hollings I flew on a duty tour to St Lucia via Antigua for an inspection visit. On 10 August I flew to Dominica via Martinique for another quick inspection of the reservations unit. With barely enough time to write my report I left the next day for Barbados via Martinique and St Lucia. The LIAT planes seemed to spend all day just island-hopping and it was rare to be able to get a direct flight to the main hub points. I had great admiration for the LIAT pilots who frequently flew more than 10 sectors a day and some respect for the HS 748 aircraft which rarely seemed to break down when flying almost double that number of flights a day.

On 12 August I reported my findings to the BA Regional Manager and after a snack lunch sped to the airport with a ticket for an American Airlines flight to JFK. I was accepted and sitting in First Class seat 2B but the flight was oversold and I was off-loaded with apologies. Along with 4 other staff passengers the airline paid our night stop costs at the Paradise Beach Hotel. I was getting anxious as I had my complimentary firm booking for a BA Concorde flight on the 14th and this was something I certainly did not want to miss. On Saturday afternoon, 13 August, I got a seat on the American Airlines flight to JFK and stayed overnight at the Airport Hilton.

Holding a free Braniff Airlines ticket I flew on the Sunday morning from JFK to Washington and landed just 2 hours before the scheduled departure time of Concorde. With thousands of flights and many years of flying this was one of the most stressful and worrisome connecting transfers I ever made.

Gleaming in the sunshine on a remote parking stand at Dulles Airport was Concorde G-BOAE. My adrenaline level was rising. I checked in with about 25 other passengers. Before going to the special VIP lounge, where all manner of goodies and champagne were freely available, I went to the ticket desk. With me I had brought the 25 commemorative Post Office first day covers which had previously been carried aloft in the balloon 'Concorde' at Balleroy. The BA receptionist applied the IATA date-stamp franking with its unique cachet to the envelopes. The date was 14 August 1977. During flight Captain Eric Morley kindly signed the covers on the flight deck.

30 minutes before departure of BA 578 we boarded the Mobile Lounge which carried us across the tarmac to the aircraft. My first impression was that of the narrow cabin but I was more than delighted to be aboard. Exactly on time at 1245 the plane taxied away to the runway holding point whilst the crew explained in some detail the acceleration and sensations we would experience. The powerful thrust and speed as we lifted off was gripping to say the least. My elation was almost total. Noise avoidance procedures restricted our speed and climb until we were clear of the land. Then with re-heat applied and another period of thrust the plane got faster and higher. The flight deck crew alerted us to the slight jolt we would feel as Concorde became supersonic. Later the speed increased to a maximum of Mach 2.02 and the plane slowly reached its maximum height of 56,200 feet. The curvature of the Earth was clearly noticeable through the deep blue sky. As I was a staff member Captain Morley allowed me a few minutes in the cockpit and briefly explained some of the instruments. This was a real bonus. I was told that it was the first East bound Atlantic crossing of this newly delivered aircraft which had previously made only one commercial round trip to Bahrain.

Meanwhile the cabin staff were serving lunch, which consisted of a set menu without choice, but some very fine wines. Knowing I had to drive myself home I had to refuse the generous offers of liqueurs. All too soon G-BOAE started its descent toward the Irish coast and reduced speed as the plane had to be subsonic before approaching Wales. My log shows that we landed at LHR at 2135 London time. We had been airborne for 3 hours 35 minutes.

Before getting to Mass and receive Holy Communion in my parish church in Kew, I made a mistake when in Dominica on Wednesday 10 August. Directly opposite the Fort Young Hotel where I was staying I heard church bells and walked out to investigate. The notice board said 'Mass and Communion: 7.00 pm'. I walked in as the service was starting. Together with about 20 local people I duly went up and received Communion. Although there were slight differences from the Mass as I remembered it, nothing alerted me to the fact that this was not Roman Catholic. As I left the church the minister then told me that few visitors ever attended his High Anglican services. Inwardly I cringed and quickly tried to bluff my way around the barrage of questions. As soon as I returned to the hotel I ordered a double rum punch.

On Sunday 21 August I got it right and went to St Winefride's in Kew for the 0800 Mass and received Holy Communion. The priest was understanding of my error and gave me an up-to-date Missal. In the years to date I have attended many services in non-Catholic churches but not repeated the Communion mistake made in Dominica.

Ballooning in Helsinki was next. With 3 Dante group members I travelled there on 25 August for a 2 day International Air Fair. Despite much persistent rain we did manage to tether the balloon, G-BEND, on both Saturday and Sunday 27 and 28 August. The highlights for us were the various foods and eating places. On Friday it was the organisers lunch with a good steak dinner. On Saturday our lunch was in the airport staff canteen. David Sloper, as Manager Finland, had a magnificent house complete with basement sauna. He invited us for drinks before dinner. We ate at the Water Tower Restaurant, although the reindeer steak was tough. I was either nominated or volunteered to drive the transit van and therefore could drink no alcohol. On the Sunday we went to a Russian restaurant and chose bear steaks. My diary records no more. On Monday the 29th another Trident returned us to LHR.

World Hot Air Balloon Championships are held every 2 years. I attended the first two at Albuquerque in 1973 and 1975. The third event was held at Castle Howard, Yorkshire from 10 to 17 September. I was on the organising committee but because of my unstable walking and uncertain health I had just three jobs to do at the event. Firstly I was the 'Signals Officer' which entailed raising coloured flags to advise pilots on their readiness to fly. Secondly I did the public commentary from a mobile van plus I also arranged for balloon post covers to be carried by all the pilots.

There were 50 competitors from 22 countries around the world who during the week flew 6 tasks sometimes in less than perfect weather conditions. Most pilots, crews and officials were accommodated at Derwent College in York. This meant that we had to rise by 0345 for the drive to Castle Howard to attend the briefing sessions which were held at 0500. I found it all great fun but very tiring and at times my energy was drained to almost zero.

Very few pilots had a night flying rating - but then not many wanted to fly in the dark. On several mornings we drove underneath an airborne balloon on our way to the Slingsby Field. I thought it was a foolish way to establish the upper wind speeds. The other abiding memories of the World Championships were the lunch time hospitality get-togethers arranged by the overseas teams, the wonderful camaraderie of most pilots and crews, plus the dedication and hard work of all the officials.

Many American citizens had come to support their pilots and were intrigued to see the city and historic surroundings of the 'old' York. Paul Woessner of USA was declared World Champion Pilot with Bruce Comstock also of USA just 37 points behind in second place. David Bareford at number 10 was the highest placed British contestant. (20 years later David was declared the 1997 World Champion in the contest held in Japan.)

Neil Robertson of Bath had 3 advertising balloons to promote the Robertsons Jam Company. They were named 'Golly' and included the world's first large special shape balloon. He persuaded the firm to sponsor the Castle Howard event. The final evening Awards Banquet was held in Terry's Ballroom in York City on 17 September. It was a night I am sure none of the 250 guests will ever forget. The food was good, the wine was wonderful and the relaxation was almost total. My diary describes it as 'a wild and feastive occasion'.

During November I had two duty visits. The first was to Zambia and the new office in the Copperbelt town of Kitwe which had moved from Ndola. I left Gatwick at 2145 on 06 November for a 9 hour 40 minute non-stop flight on a B Cal B707 to Lusaka. District Sales Manager John Bird met and drove me to the Intercontinental Hotel. I carried out an inspection visit before flying on a Zambia Airways HS 748, 9J-ADM, to Kitwe on 09 November. A former London based reservations inspector Ian MacRae had been posted there for one year and my visit was more of a routine nature. On 12 November I boarded another B Cal plane for a 10 hour 35 minute non-stop flight to Gatwick travelling in First Class.

Exactly 14 days later I was on my way to Africa again. However BA 121 took just 4 hours 50 minutes from LHR to Cairo. After one night at the Nile Hilton Hotel I moved to the quieter more secluded Jolie Ville Hotel on 28 November. After an inspection visit and report to the local management I was on my way back to London. I had been out of the country for just over three and a half days. Life at work had intense bursts of activity, and there were rarely many long dull periods.

Again I flew to Scotland to spend 5 days with my mother and family over Christmas. For some now forgotten reason my diary records my weight according to the scales in Woolworths as 64 kgs (10 st 11 lb).

The official logo of the 3rd World Hot Air Balloon Championships held in York, England, in September 1977.

A studio photo taken in June 1977, requested by the organisers of the Chateau de Balleroy Balloon Meet. It was wanted for inclusion in the official programme.

18

AUSTRALIA AND YUGOSLAVIA-PLUS MANY OTHERS

Some ballooning history was made at the 6th International Icicle Balloon Meet held on 7th and 8th January 1978. 85 different balloons made a total of 179 free flights. This constituted a record at that time for the largest number ever at any meet outside of the USA. Again I gave the pilots the met briefing on both days, but the conditions were near perfect. I flew in the balloon Dante. Mike Thorne who was one of the European Superintendents at work also had a flight. Later he became my manager and was promoted through the ranks to a very senior position.

Australia and New Zealand were on my short list of 'places to visit'. My free firm concessional airline tickets were also available to my brother. On the 4th of February we left LHR on G-AWNC for Hong Kong via Frankfurt and Delhi. After a 15 hour 30 minute flight Gordon and I were both pleased to get to the Sheraton Hotel. There was a big buzz of excitement in the Colony as we landed on the eve of the Chinese New Year. This was planned deliberately. We did all the usual sightseeing and marvelled at their local celebrations. Balloonist Geoff Green (a B747 Captain for Cathay Pacific) and his wife Sheena invited us for tea and dinner on the 6th. By chance Neil and Diana Robertson, British balloonists, were in Hong Kong and also at dinner. On Wednesday the 8th we flew to Auckland with a transit stop at Melbourne.

The Rotorura hot springs area was only a few hours drive from Auckland. Two New Zealand friends, Joan and Arthur, took us to a holiday bungalow that afternoon. It was a beautiful setting beside a lake. Early the next morning, the 10th, we visited some of the many geysers and it was a wonderful experience to see the volcanic activity. We had a late lunch at a Maori camp and later experienced the thermal springs in a radium pool. At the back of my mind I thought there was an outside chance that perhaps this would improve my walking ability. Regrettably it did not. Late that evening we drove to a motel in Hamilton for a short overnight stay. After another early rise we continued on to Auckland to see a little of the city before going to the airport to catch BA 865 for Melbourne.

Publicity material for Sydney was better presented than that for Melbourne. On arrival I changed plans by cancelling the overnight stay in Melbourne and Gordon and I caught a connecting Ansett B727 to Sydney. The temperature earlier that day, 11 February, had been 37 degrees Celsius but from the clear blue sky the scenery below looked interesting. It was late Saturday afternoon when we checked into the Crest Hotel in the Kings Cross area - comparable at that time to Soho in London. There was much to see but we did not stray too far from the main bus routes. Early the next morning I went to Mass and was at first rather shocked by the very casual clothes worn by many of the congregation, both young and old. We spent the rest of the day exploring the sights of Sydney. On the Monday we went to Bondi Beach for the obligatory swim, but I was not impressed with it or the surrounding area. On Tuesday morning we took an organised tour around the city before heading to the airport for the evening flight to Singapore.

Money is an important commodity on holiday. Either I had under budgeted or we had overspent. Thankfully plastic credit cards go a long way and during our shopping spree in Singapore I felt we had bargained wisely. Again the weather was hot and the fatigue factor was affecting me. Too much to do and see with not enough time and rest intervals. Shortly before 2300 on 15 February the B747 left for LHR via Bahrain. The London weather was just 1 degree Celsius when we landed at 0725 the next morning.

Khartoum was my next duty visit when I left LHR on 06 March. The trip started with a mini drama. Whilst waiting to board the aircraft in the departure lounge of Terminal 3 a fire developed in the basement of the duty free shop and all passengers were evacuated from the danger area. The aircraft, G-AXXZ, left only an hour late for the 7 hour 25 minute flight via Cairo. It was a 3 day fact finding and inspection visit after complaints of irregular passenger service. Regrettably there was little time for much sightseeing before going to the airport at 0115 on 10 March. The plane, G-AGSP, was late with a technical fault and then made an unscheduled stop at Cairo for air traffic control reasons. We landed at LHR at 1220. That was a duty tour I could well have done without. Few things went right and I got very little enjoyment from it.

To walk with the aid of a stick almost immediately brands you as disabled. I had been doing so for the past year but on 21 April I finally had to use it in the office. In all my working life there was only one boss with whom I could not easily work. He was small in stature but big in moodiness. For about a year there had been underlying tension which at times gave rise to almost total silence and non-communication.

An ambulance journey is rarely a pleasure. On Sunday morning 23 April when getting up to go to church my left leg collapsed and I fell heavily. After enduring the pain for some while a doctor was called and I was taken to St Marys Hospital in Roehampton for an x-ray. There was no obvious fracture, but I remained in pain. The following day the doctor prescribed a 15 day course of ACTH injections. To recuperate better, and get some TLC, I flew to Scotland and stayed with my mother for 2 weeks. On 22 May I returned to the office.

A full medical examination at work can be a daunting experience. On 12 June I was apprehensive when Dr Dunlop, a BA Medical Officer, gave me a full check. He was sympathetic to my unstable walking conditions but to my relief gave me full clearance to visit overseas stations world-wide.

Buying a new house can be exciting. I decided to move to a mid-terrace 3 bedroom house on a new estate at Thatcham near Newbury in Berkshire. It was near the ballooning field at Marsh Benham and the price was right. On 17 June I viewed the still unfinished building and 2 days later paid a £100 deposit on number 58 Derwent Road. On the fourth of July the Woolwich Building Society agreed the mortgage. The estimated completion date for both mortgage and building was December.

South Africa for a 14 day duty visit was next. On 12 August I was upgraded to First Class on BA 051 from LHR and was enjoying a pre-dinner drink as we passed overhead Frankfurt. I heard a muffled bang. Soon afterwards the Captain announced that number 3 engine on B747 G-BDXB had failed and we were returning to London. In more than two and a half thousand jet flights this was the only time I ever experienced an engine shut-down in flight. After landing the cabin crew served dinner before we were taken to an airport hotel for the night.

At 11.30 the following morning the delayed service left LHR, operated by G-BDXF. I retained my First Class seat and at that time the upper deck on Jumbo Jets was a spacious lounge for First Class passengers. As the plane droned across the Sahara that Sunday afternoon I became fidgety. Using my ID card I asked the cabin crew if I could visit the cockpit. When I entered, to my astonishment the Captain was Stuart Robertson, a friend I had not seen since his RAF days more than 16 years earlier. We had much to talk about and I sat on the 'jump seat' (extra pilot's seat) for an interesting dusk landing at Nairobi. It was of extra relevance to me because the sophisticated instruments clearly showed there was considerable wind shear on the approach (a problem we had been investigating with ballooning). Stuart Robertson was an accomplished pilot and later became a Captain on Concorde aircraft.

Finally we landed at Johannesburg Airport at 0130 local time on 14 August. After just 4 hours sleep at a nearby hotel I was preparing to board a South African Airways (SAA) Airbus aircraft for Durban. Ken Lubbe, the local Reservations Officer, accompanied me on this tour of inspection to assess the staffing levels and quality control. Two days later we flew to Port Elizabeth, via East London, to be met by the vibrant District Sales Manager Tertius van Zyl. It was a busy day and a half before Ken and I then flew to Cape Town. There was rain on Saturday the 19th which gave me time to write the basic points of my reports. To complete a very busy week I flew on an SAA B747 - SP variant, ZS-SPC, for a 1 hour 45 minute journey to Johannesburg. It was 20 August and I very wearily got a taxi to the Carlton Hotel. For a change I went to bed early that Sunday night.

Pretoria was an attractive city which I had visited on my previous tours to South Africa. Jacaranda trees lined the wide avenues and the flower gardens were a delight. Just outside the city was the famous Voortrekker Monument. BA had opened a small off-street sales shop in the city and there were doubts as to its cost effectiveness. On 21 August I made a day visit to get an outsider's perspective. After that it was three days examining the procedures in the Johannesburg resevations unit and sales shop with the CRO Jean Jones. It was a financially important Sales Area and I had discussions with some of the British-based managers, Jim Kutas, Les Robertson and Laurie O'Toole. I was booked to return home on my birthday, 24 August, but the southbound Jumbo was delayed 24 hours at Nairobi with a technical fault. It was 0935 on Saturday 26 August when the flight, via Nairobi, landed at LHR.

Nine days later I was back at Heathrow boarding a BAC 1-11, G-AYMV, for Belgrade via Zagreb. The Dante group was short of volunteers to take the balloon to inflate at the first major pop concert to be held in Yugoslavia. David Liddiard with Celia Redhead and I spent the evening of 05 September in a corner of the city sports stadium trying to impress the crowd with the tethered balloon, G-BEND. The music fans did not appreciate our presence at 'their' event and after 50 minutes we quickly packed the balloon away and left the arena. After a sightseeing tour of the city the next day we returned, again via Zagreb, to LHR on another little BAC 1-11.

Cairo was my next duty tour when I left LHR on 09 October aboard a beautiful Super VC10, G-ASGD, at 1750. The flight arrived just before midnight local time and I got to the Hilton Hotel at 0115 to be told there was no room available. I was angry. A complimentary meal in the coffee shop did little to placate me. Eventually a hotel room was found for me at 0420. John Hanlon, Regional Manager Egypt, Sudan and Libya thought the reservations unit was overstaffed. My near-impossible task was to convince him otherwise. John Bird was the District Manager and Adib Gabra was the CRO with whom I had talks. Maybe as a sweetener to my poor arrival reception I was given a First Class seat back to London on Friday the 13th.

Manager Western Caribbean, Dick Muir, wanted advice from Head Office on a proposed reservations re-organisation in Jamaica. It was Sunday 29 October when I flew to Kingston with transit stops at Bermuda and Nassau giving a flying time of 11 hours 45 minutes. As a result of a fog delay at LHR it was almost midnight Jamaica time when I got to the Pegasus Hotel. With District Sales Manager Garland Thompson I also interviewed staff for the impending vacancy of the Chief Reservations Officer. Whilst on these overseas visits I not infrequently found myself being used as an ambassador for the airline in various ways. During this trip I spoke on the Cayman Islands Radio. On 02 November I left Kingston on BA 266 for LHR with a stop at Bermuda. The B747 arrived at Heathrow at 0935.

For something completely different on a Sunday I went to a Seminary. It was called St Johns at Wornesh near Guildford, Surrey. I visited a distant relative, Brother Cyril Tuttle who in his declining years helped arrange the linen for the students who were studying for the priesthood. I enjoyed the day and stayed for the evening service. The date was 19 November.

There was upheaval at work the next day. After more than 15 years of individual offices for the area reservations units on the 4th floor at Victoria Air Terminal we were uprooted to open plan accomodation on the 2nd floor of C Block. It was also the time when the Longhaul and Shorthaul (in reality the BOAC and BEA) Reservations Route structures were amalgamated. The five Superintendents were: Graham Humphries (UK & Ireland), John Kirk (Western), George Pleece (Eastern), Mike Thorne (N & E Europe plus Caribbean and Latin America) and John Ward (S & W Europe plus Africa). Despite months of planning and previews there were the expected gremlins and some groaners. Luckily Christmas was only 5 weeks away to distract the malcontents.

Thunder Balloons, the other British manufacturer, wanted to expand quickly. On 25 November selected balloonists were invited to a press conference at Southampton to announce a partnership with Bruce Bank Sails Ltd. During the drinks and nibbles session a demonstration of a one fifth scale model of a pressurised airship went wrong. The thing caught fire. It was a sorry sight. I was there as the British correspondent for the Balloon Federation of America journal 'Ballooning'.

Fog at Heathrow on 22 and 23 December caused chaos with airline schedules. I had to use a Glasgow Trident Shuttle flight and then trains to Inverkeithing (Fife) changing at Edinburgh to reach my mother's house for Christmas.

On 27 December I flew back to LHR and spent the first night in my new home at Thatcham. The carpet had been laid and the furniture installed. Local balloonists John and Shelagh Green called and visited with groceries. They were most helpful in many ways including tweaking into action the troublesome utilities of a new house. Heavy snow fell overnight on the 29th and 30th. The weather was especially cold and it was the first New Year I spent alone.

Opposite: In January 1979 the annual Icicle Balloon Meet at Newbury lived up to its name. The launch site was covered with a layer of snow. It did not stop some balloons flying as this photo from the British Balloon Museum and Library shows.

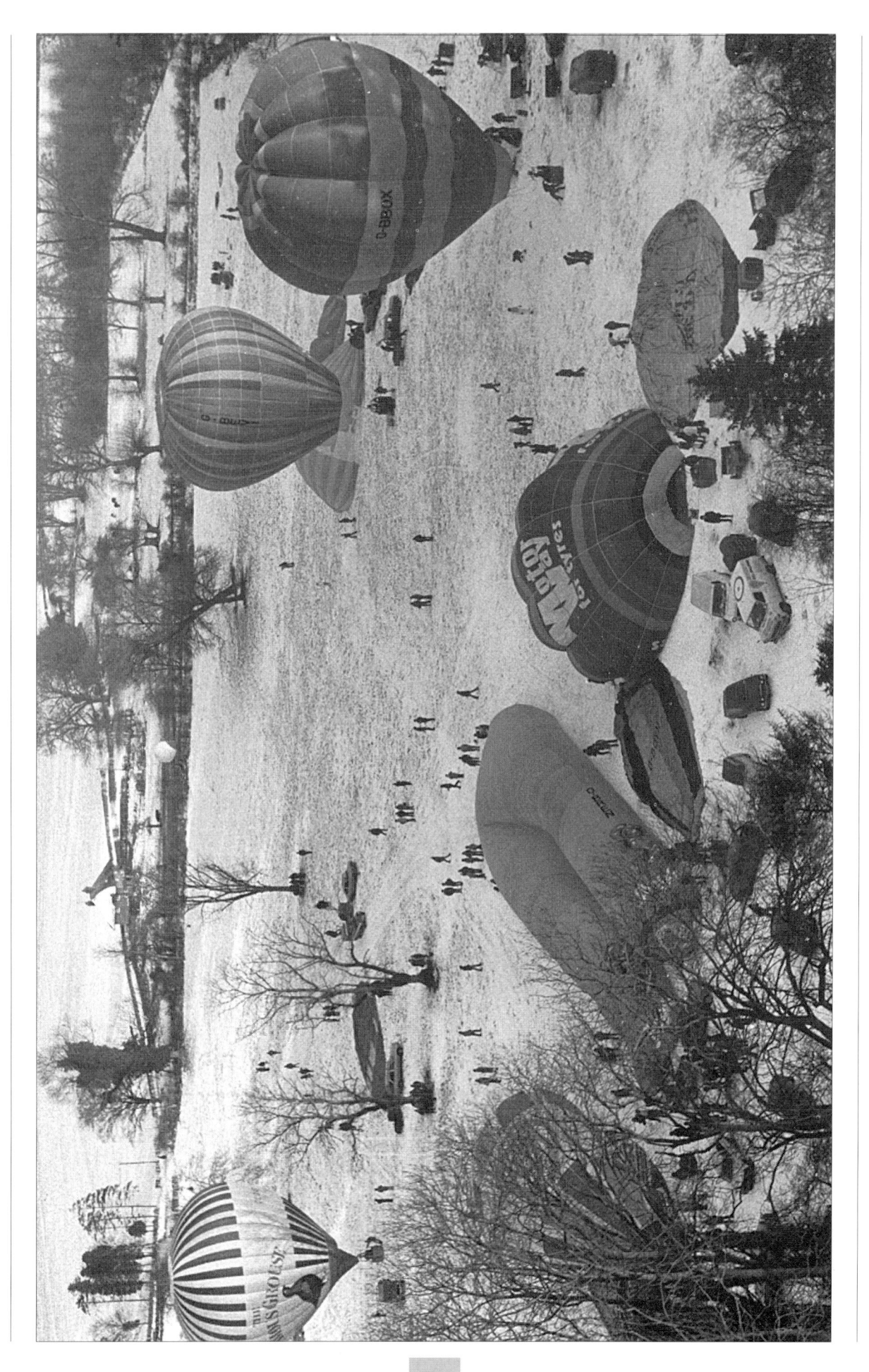

19
11 OVERSEAS TRIPS PLUS THE BRISTOL BALLOON FIESTA

Travel to work by car was a 112 miles a day round trip. With two colleagues, Peter Welek and Peter Sargeant, I formed a car pool but this meant the journey was via Yateley (Hants) and Camberley (Surrey) to Victoria in Central London. I left home at 0545 to be ahead of the rush hour and we arrived in the office before 0800. We tried to get away by 1530 which with luck got me home by 1800.

New Year started with snow and severe frosts. On Saturday 06 January 1979 the balloon field still had a lovely hard white covering. 66 balloons flew and made 101 flights at the Icicle Meet. An inconsiderate warm front on the Sunday with strong winds and rain prevented any flying.

Jamaica in January was a great escape from the cold winter in England. On 31 January a B747 flew me via Bermuda to Kingston. On the following morning I interviewed a former BOAC overseas trainee, whose home was in Jamaica, for the post of Chief Reservations Officer. The main purpose of my visit however was, along with a team of five, to 'cutover' the reservations units to the BABS computer system. With help from some local staff we completed the task in 9 hours on Saturday the 3rd. Our treat of the week was when 4 of us hired a car and drove to Ocho Rios (on the North of the island) for a swim and a barbecue. We returned before dark via the much visited local waterfall. The next day Monday the 5th a Boeing 707 routing via Nassau and Bermuda carried us to London. The plane arrived at LHR 30 minutes early due to the seasonal Atlantic jet streams, so much sought after, even in the late 1990's, by balloonists eager to cross the Atlantic and others to achieve speed records. (In 1996 a Concorde aircraft G-BOAD was airborne for 2 hours 52 minutes and 59 seconds making a record crossing from JFK to LHR on BA 004 on 07 February).

Sea shells on the sea shore in the Seychelles. This is not true. I enjoyed a swim on the fine sandy beach on Sunday 25 February after an overnight flight via Zurich and Nairobi on a B747. The 4 day visit was a fact-finding mission to check the efficiency of our handling agency managed by Brian Cannandine, an old friend from my BEA days. The Seychelle islands were still unspoilt and not overrun by tourists and I greatly enjoyed the facilities. On 01 March I left the Coral Strand Hotel to fly to Nairobi on a VC10. After reporting my findings the next day to the Regional Manager Peter Baker and with Mike McDonald I returned to the UK that evening. A B747-136 series aircraft was rarely able to operate non-stop to London with a full payload. G-BBPU stopped at Rome to uplift fuel and arrived at LHR on 03 March.

Together with many ballooning enthusiasts I was at Marsh Benham on 31 March to see a partial inflation of a 10 year old home-built balloon, G-AXXP named Ignis Volens. Sadly it started to disintegrate despite our careful handling. Other old balloons were present but this was the real 'goodie'. Many memories were recounted during our pub lunch at the Red House.

South American cities of Rio de Janerio, Sao Paulo and Buenos Aires were next due for a visit. I left Gatwick on 05 May on a BCAL DC10 aircraft, G-BFBL, at 2200. During the night flight as we passed abeam the Azores I asked to visit the flight deck and during a prolonged stay was most impressed with the methodical way the captain had prepared a contingency list of alternate airfields in the event of an emergency. In the late 1970's there were fewer computer aided guides on the plane and we were heading toward an area of poorly controlled air space with the ocean bellow us. After 8 hours 45 mins the plane stopped at Recife for fuel. Another two and a half flying hours later and I was on Brazilian soil for the first time.

Three days in Rio is not long enough for sightseeing when I had a job to do. My principal task was to assess the workload against the direct revenue from an off-line country. The local staff were very pleasant and keen to impress. Jack Maso, Regional Sales Manager based in Buenos Aires, accompanied me. On 09 May I flew on a Varig Electra aircraft from the Rio downtown airport to the Sao Paulo downtown airport. Despite a hectic work schedule I found time to visit a well known Brazilian balloonist Victorio Truffi. On 11 May I flew on LH 508 from Viracopos airport (which was almost new) for the two and a half hour flight to Buenos Aires.

Again my enemy was shortage of time. When visiting a new country I wanted to see as much as possible and yet accomplish my set mission. The Claridge Hotel, where I stayed, was plush and almost over-luxurious.

It had a colonial style ambience and from memory was probably in the super de luxe category. The beef steak meals were succulent in the extreme. Meanwhile back at the office many of the procedures were old fashioned but it did generate just enough revenue to warrant its existence. (The political presence was another consideration.) On 13 May I boarded another DC10 of BCAL for Gatwick with a stop at Rio. The flying time was 14 hours 5 minutes.

Another Sunday and another flight. Six days after arriving home a VC10 flew me from LHR to Cairo. The purpose of this tour was to visit Alexandria to size up the suitability of the Reservations Officer with a view to promoting him to be in charge of the office in Cairo. The morning after my arrival, 22 May, the CRO Adib Gabra and I travelled by train for the two and a half hour journey to Alexandria. My timetable allowed just one day in the city which regrettably was nowhere near enough to form a work appraisal and see the sights of what was an historic and yet cosmopolitan city. The blend of Arabic and (French) Christian cultures fascinated me. At 0730 the next morning we boarded a coach for a journey across the desert to Cairo. After meetings with the management teams I did a rapid inspection of the Cairo Reservations office and found many irregularities. The subject of putting the computer into Cairo was also examined. On 25 May BA 150 took just over 5 hours to fly me back to Heathrow.

Staff training is an easy item for any manager to write on an annual review. I was nominated for a week's residential course at the Staff Training College at Burnham Beeches, Buckinghamshire. It started on 04 June and was called Airline Appreciation. Over several years I attended six residential training courses at various staff colleges. Some were good and some were not so good. Some I enjoyed and learned from while others were almost a sheer waste of time.

Sudeley Castle near Cheltenham had a balloon meet on 16 and 17 June. My job was to do the public commentary. It was intended that someone help me but without a relief my voice was almost hoarse by the Sunday evening.

Philadelphia was my next overseas balloon event. On 27 June four of us, with G-BEND, travelled on a B707, G-AWHU. Whilst waiting to reclaim our baggage David Liddiard boasted to a young customs officer that all we had to declare was the importation of an aircraft! The officials decided that a form had to be completed. David volunteered me to do the paperwork. On page 4 of this form there is a single line entry for the official export detail of the aircraft (or balloon). On 01 July the balloon returned to LHR with 3 of the 4 Dante members on board. Due to over booking of the flight I was left behind. I did not remember the form had to be completed. One year later the same balloon attended the same event in Philadelphia and passed in and out of customs without problem. Then 18 months after the original form filling I received a letter, sent by sea mail, stating the importation tax was overdue and would I pay the $650 within 14 days. I ignored this request but 3 weeks later another letter arrived, more strongly worded, with an invoice clearly stamped 'Delinquent'. It took umpteen phone calls to both BA and Customs at Philadelphia Airport to clear the matter, although in the end the Dante Group agreed to pay a fine of about £100.

The good news to this story is that David was the winner of the Hare and Hounds event on 30 June. In unfavourable weather 15 experienced pilots took off from a downtown Philadelphia Avenue. With a great deal of luck David found himself almost overhead the Hare balloon and abruptly landed about 20 feet away. At the Press Reception that evening the Mayor presented David together with Mike Drye, Pete Hornfeck and myself with a replica Liberty Bell trophy.

Five days after returning from Philadelphia I tripped on the floor of my garage. By midday on 07 July my knee had started to swell and I called a doctor. I was taken by ambulance to Battle Hospital in Reading and an x-ray showed I had a fracture of the patella (kneecap) on my right leg. I was an in-patient for 5 days. Recovery treatment including physiotherapy lasted much longer. I returned to work on 06 August.

Next day I left LHR for Nassau via Bermuda. At that time my life seemed to be in perpetual motion punctuated only by occasional enforced rests such as the knee fracture. The trip to Nassau was at the request of Manager Kevin Hatton who wanted a survey of the reservations activities. By staying at the Nassau Beach Hotel I was able to continue my physio by swimming frequently in the warm sea water. The three full days passed quickly and another B707 flew me back via Bermuda to LHR to arrive at 1510 on Saturday 11 August.

It may sound hard to believe but the next day I left LHR via Rome and Nairobi for Johannesburg. The total time spent in my house between these two trips was exactly 22 hours.

BA 051 operated by G-BDXD had a planned 5 hour delay, reason unknown, and we were given dinner at the Tavern in the Sky Restaurant at LHR. The flight left at 0140 on 13 August and we landed in J'burg at 1710 local time. My baggage was not on board. After a few hours sleep at the Carlton Hotel it was back to the airport by 0700 to catch an Air Malawi BAC1-11, 7Q-YKF for the 2 hour flight to Blantyre. I took a taxi into town to buy some clothes. At 1630 I was boarding QM 222, an HS 748 registered 7Q-YKB for a 50 minute flight to Lilongwe, which was soon to become the capital city of Malawi. The purpose of this journey was to be the BA Head Office representative at the IATA African Area Reservations Conference. All 14 delegates were accommodated at the new Capital Hotel.

Air Malawi treated us well and on the afternoon of 16th August we were taken on a coach tour around the shell of the new International airport. The supporting literature read like an over-ambitious project for a small country. The dirt for the runway was still being levelled and space was left for expansion. Today (in 1999) the runway is 3540 meters long which is more than ample even at an altitude of 4035 feet.

To return I travelled on 7Q-YKA to Blantyre the next afternoon which connected with BA 058, G-ASGJ to LHR via Dar es Salaam and Larnaca. The flight arrived at Heathrow shortly after 0600 on the 18th.

Woolaton Park in Nottingham was the venue for the first British National Balloon Championships. 22 pilots entered and there were 8 competitive tasks. The event was held from 25 August until 01 September. My job was to do the public commentary from a mobile vehicle. It was a week I did not enjoy very much.

Seven days later I was again doing the public commentary at the first Bristol International Balloon Fiesta. Early on Friday morning 07 September in calm conditions 26 balloons flew free. Later the weather deteriorated and the strong winds continued until the Saturday afternoon when only one balloon managed to get airborne. The event was sponsored by the Bristol Junior Chamber of Commerce and Shipping. Don Cameron was the Meet Director and Vic Thorne was the balloon Liaison Officer. Many parents and children became separated in Ashton Court Park and I made frequent tedious announcements to re-unite them. At the Survivors Dinner held at the Dragonora Hotel on Saturday evening the Mayor of Bristol presented me with a special loving cup for talking - or more accurately, for keeping the crowd entertained during non-flying periods. There were no restraining ropes around the launch site and from my caravan position I was alarmed that children or parents pushing prams might be injured by some of the tethered balloons. By 0630 on Sunday the 9th with a surprisingly large crowd of spectators 26 balloons took off in calm conditions. I enjoyed doing the balloon commentary as I knew most of the pilots and there was little commercial pressure on me to plug any product or balloon. 21 years later the Bristol Fiesta continues but as a hugely commercial enterprise.

Hanover weekend with balloon G-BEND was next. On Friday 21 September David Liddiard, Ian Culley and I flew on G-ARPX and stayed at the Holiday Inn. The next day we did a tethered display in a local park. The main event was on Sunday when the balloon was tethered for 2 hours in the morning and another short display in the afternoon. By early evening we were flying back to LHR on another Trident aircraft.

Dual purpose visits to different countries were always more exciting. A 15 day tour to Central and South America started badly when I was offloaded from BA 279 at LHR on 14 October. The early series of the B747 aircraft had a weight problem when the Captain needed extra fuel to reach Miami due to Atlantic headwinds. I was re-booked to travel later but via New York on the evening Super VC10. The Captain was happy for me to have an extended stay on the flight deck and explained the extreme northerly routing over Canada. It was interesting to see how often the NATO radar stations interrogated our aircraft. It was 2100 New York time when we landed and I went to the near-by Riveria Hotel for a short nightstop.

By 0900 the next day I was sitting on an Eastern Airlines Tristar waiting for ATC take-off clearance for Miami. The Captain sounded quite excited on the PA system as he explained we had to wait for the BA Concorde to land after its morning supersonic flight from London. Inwardly I felt quite proud that the British Concorde deserved such a mention by the Captain. At Miami Airport I needed a wheelchair to move me to the Mexicana check-in area for flight MX 308. The B727 aircraft, XA-CUB, took just 75 minutes to land at Cancun on the Yucatan Peninsula, Mexico.

To attend the IATA Caribbean Interline Reservations Conference was the purpose of this visit. There were 28 delegates and we all stayed at the hotel El Presidente. The resort of Cancun

At the First British National Balloon Championships which were held at Nottingham in the last week of August 1979 I did the commentary from a mobile van. Photo shows the organising team. I am 3rd from the right, still able to walk with the aid of one stick.

was still being developed although there were a few plush hotels operating. Mexicana Airlines, the host, had gone to great lengths to promote themselves and the area. The conference almost seemed like a bi-product when related to the generosity of the meals and sightseeing. As an example on 18 October we had a full day coach tour to Tulum and Akumal to see the Mayan ruins. On the following morning I had a swim in the Caribbean. Because of my instability in walking and the lack of balance this turned out to be the last time I ever swam in the open sea (although I have been in some hotel pools since). Later that day I flew on another Mexicana B727 from Cancun to Miami where I stayed for two nights at the Fointenbleau Hotel on Miami Beach.

Part 2 of this duty tour was to visit Santiago in Chile. On Sunday 21 October I boarded a Braniff DC8 aircraft for the 10 hour 40 minute journey which routed via Panama City. The plane, N129NA, had a yaw damper fault and although I was sitting in First Class it was an uncomfortable ride as the aircraft was unstable all afternoon. It was good to get back on the ground. At 2300 local time I got a taxi to the Hotel Carrera in Santiago. During the next two days I visited the BA General Sales Agency, Reseco, plus the Lan Chile Airline Headquarters and saw a few of the city sights. Lunch on the 22nd was at the palatial British-style Navy Club where the food and surroundings were akin to what I imagined a London Gentleman's Club would have been like. Later the next afternoon, together with the Sales Rep, we flew across the Andes on an AeroPeru Tristar aircraft for the 1 hour 40 minute journey from Santiago to Buenos Aires.

Hotel Libertador was used on this trip as it was closer to the BA office. My duty was to again inspect the reservations unit and visit selected travel agents. There was also a management meeting at which the GSA Manager from La Paz, Bolivia was present on 25 October. Another Sunday and another flight. It was 28 October and I boarded an Aerolineas Argentinas B747, LV-MLP, for an 18 and a half hour journey to LHR with stops at Madrid and Paris Orly. Although a very interesting tour it was good to be back in England.

Dar es Salaam in Tanzania was my next duty trip. The VC10 left LHR at 1940 on 27 November. and routed via Khartoum and Addis Ababa to arrive at Dar 12 hours 10 minutes later. This was another job to review the office staff numbers and procedures. The ungenerous manager had booked me into the non-salubrious Agip Motel. On 30 November. I flew back to LHR with an en-route stop at Larnaca.

Christmas lunch with wine was served in the staff canteen at Victoria Air Terminal on 19 December. This was the last such occasion where wine was allowed at meal times on BA premises. A group of 16 of us from Reservations Services and a few from the Systems Unit made the most of the occasion.

To complete the year I spent one week staying with my mother in Scotland and then celebrated Christmas in the traditional way with the family.

Bruce King

Governor of New Mexico

To all to whom these Presents shall come, Greetings: I hereby confer the Honor of

Colonel, Aide-de-Camp,

on the Staff of the Governor of the State of New Mexico

To

Alec Jenkinson

Who is therefore to discharge carefully and diligently the duties of said office, by doing and performing all manner of things thereunto belonging in compliance with law, the orders of his superior officers and the usage and discipline of the United States Army.

In testimony whereof, I have hereunto set my hand and caused to be affixed the Great Seal of the State of New Mexico.

Done at Santa Fe, this 14th day of May in the year of Our Lord, One Thousand, Nine Hundred and Seventy Nine.

Bruce King
GOVERNOR AND COMMANDER IN CHIEF

Shirley Hooper
SECRETARY OF STATE

Franklin E. Miles
THE ADJUTANT GENERAL

In May 1979 the Governor of New Mexico, USA, honoured me with this certificate for helping to promote Anglo/American ballooning connections between Albuquerque and the UK. Tom Rutherford, Assistant Governor, arranged the presentation after one of my many visits.

20
UGANDA AND 12 COUNTRIES YET FEWER FLYING HOURS

Marsh Benham, Newbury and the Icicle Balloon Meet was the traditional way for many balloonists and followers to start the New Year. On Saturday 05 January 1980 the weather was just above marginal so only 29 balloons flew free. Once again I gave the met forecasts at the pilot briefings. Sunday morning was better and before evening a total of 94 balloon flights had taken place. The Dante group first flew its 4th balloon and named it 'Antonia' after Dante's 4th child. The balloon was registered G-BGAY.

An extended tour to the BA offices in Nairobi started on 18 January. My diary does not make it clear the precise nature of my talks with the BA managers or the review of the reservations functions. On 29 January the regular BA 050 operated by G-BDXC flew me back to LHR in 8 hours 55 minutes.

One of the side effects of MS can often be troubles with eyesight. A problem of fairly frequent viewing of computer screens can also produce eye strain. For whatever reason I got my first pair of reading glasses on 17 March. It was almost exactly 2 years later when the strength had to be slightly increased. As this is being written in 1999 it is 19 years since I have been to an optician. Maybe a visit is due?

Uganda was my next overseas trip. On 19 March I flew LHR - Nairobi on a newly delivered B747 - 236 aircraft, G-BDXI. The plane landed at 0810 next morning where I was met by Tony Cruickshank, the BA Cargo Sales Manager Kenya, who was to accompany me to Uganda. The purpose of this visit was to explore the possibility of BA resuming flights to Entebbe Airport. We travelled on an Air Uganda Fokker Friendship, 5X-UAP, and the flight on QU 345 took 1 hour 45 minutes. Michael Isak, the local BA representative, met and drove us to the BA Manager's lakeside house. Later that afternoon we drove the 30 miles to the BA office in Kampala where much to my amazement not a lot had changed. The three BA reservations staff accepted only foreign currency or the like from passengers but their monthly sales figures were often staggeringly high at tens of thousands of UK pounds. Michael Isak was quietly treated like royalty when he sometimes arrived at the accounts department in London with a suitcase packed with fully convertible bank drafts and cash.

With extra security guards around the house, Tony Cruickshank and I spent the night at the Manager's luxury home. On 21 March we spent the day meeting important businessmen and visiting the Air Uganda offices. We did not divulge the true reason for our tour, preferring to say we were on a goodwill visit. Shortly before noon the next day we were on a Kenya Airways plane, 5Y-AAB, returning to Nairobi.

Work colleague Peter Welek and his wife Eileen were on a Kenyan holiday and I met them at the Norfolk Hotel. On Sunday the 23rd we left early for a day out at Lake Nakuru and other places in the Rift Valley. It was all very relaxing. They left for London just after midnight.

Early the next morning I had a meeting with Peter Baker, Regional Manager East Africa and Tony Cruickshank, where we discussed our findings on Uganda. Subject to political considerations it seemed the time was ripe to resume BA flights there. After a cursory look over the reservations unit I left Nairobi that evening (the 24th) for London.

Being interviewed for a job can be a bit stressful. On 09 April just two of us, my colleague Martin Rhoades and I, sat before a panel of three managers for the job of our previous boss, Mike Thorne. It was a considerate gesture to interview me since my state of health would have made it impossible for me to have met the demands of the position. The title was Reservations Superintendent Caribbean and Latin America plus Northern Europe - which included France, Germany, Benelux, USSR and Scandinavia.

For his generosity and kindness in allowing all balloonists to use the Marsh Benham farm for ballooning the BBAC decided to honour David Liddiard with the title of Vice President. He was unaware of the impending award. On 19 April I drove David to the AGM of the Club which was held at the Charing Cross Hotel in London.

Mexico had sporadic labour-union difficulties with many national companies in the city. BA was next to be selected by the airport handling agents. However I was assured the strike had been settled and left LHR on 21 April aboard a B707. Whilst talking to the Captain on the flight deck during the Bermuda to Nassau sector I mentioned that we would be the first BA flight to land in Mexico for more than a fortnight. The Captain was annoyed that he had not been briefed. When the plane landed at Nassau the Manager Kevin Hatton told us the strike had been reinstated and the flight had to terminate. The best available alternative to Mexico City for me was a Lufthansa flight on 23 April. I travelled on a DC10 and we landed at 1615 local time. By coincidence the strike was officially called off at 1630. The CRO and Supervisor Sergio Bustos met me and we got to the downtown office just in time to remove the last of the union 'flags' and stickers.

To catch up on the backlog of messages took most of the day on the 24th. Late the next afternoon Manager Dick Muir arranged a staff party to celebrate which happily went on for hours - as far as I can remember. At 1220 on the 26th I was sitting in First Class when G-AVPB left Mexico via Nassau and Bermuda for London to arrive at 1005 on Sunday the 27th. The flight was overbooked from Bermuda and I had to travel in the cockpit for the last 7 hours of the 13 hour 5 minute flight.

Frankfurt by Tristar aircraft, G-BBAJ, took just 1 hour 20 minutes by comparison. My first duty visit to Europe was on 29 April, just 55 hours after returning from Mexico. Freddie Buchner, the German Reservations Officer, introduced me to the local staff supervisors at their meeting on 30 April. By early evening I was back at LHR via a Lufthansa Airbus. Apart from the greater collection of duty-free goods it took me a while to decide whether I liked these one night stopovers in Europe. With my unstable walking and need for a wheelchair at every airport the verdict was against 'quickie trips'.

Long Air Traffic Control delays were not common. On 20 May Martin Rhoades and I boarded a Trident 3 at LHR for Zurich. When the Captain announced a delay of at least an hour, Martin was not prepared to wait and disembarked to cancel his trip. I sat, waited and eventually G-AZGW arrived in Zurich at lunchtime. The reservations office was not the most modern, or maybe I could write 'was struggling to keep up with the times'. My visit was to assess the alleged extra work caused by handling Cyprus Airways bookings. My conclusion: case not proven. 48 hours later I boarded a Swissair DC9 for the 100 minute flight to LHR.

Bogota in Colombia and Panama City were on the visiting list. On 31 May I left Gatwick at 10 minutes to midnight and the BCAL DC10 stopped at Caracas before terminating at Bogota just over 12 hours later. The altitude of the city was 8400 feet and this coupled with the long flight seemed to affect my MS more than usual. Shortage of oxygen in the body triggered bouts of fatigue, instability and extreme stiffness. Therefore I was not unhappy on 03 June flying to Panama aboard a Braniff B727.

An historical flight was made on 05 June when the first BA service from Panama City took off for London. Tristar, G-BFCE, left at 1440 for the 13 hour 5 minute journey. I was on board BA 264 which called at Kingston and Bermuda en route.

Another thorough annual BA overseas medical check was carried out on me on 11 June. Extra care was paid to my slowly deteriorating MS condition, but I was still given full clearance. In the afternoon I spent time in the LHR Air Traffic Control Tower with Ian Culley (of the Dante Group) and greatly enjoyed seeing the enhanced facilities and procedures since my previous visit. My interest in Air Traffic Control did not wane for almost 30 years although the opportunities to visit these centres and to listen to aircraft on VHF frequencies had decreased with so many overseas duties.

Staging a public ballooning event in British summer weather is a risky venture. The weekend of 14 and 15 June was earmarked for the Woburn Balloon Meet in conjunction with the BBAC. Gales and much rain prevented any flying on the 14th. Anne Lewis-Smith and I were judges and we arrived on site at 0430 on Sunday 15th along with a few other optimists in murky weather. There was a second briefing at 1045 when 31 balloons flew into a low cloud base with drizzle. A lot of us put much time and effort into organising such an event which ended up as almost best forgotten.

BA 780 a BAC 1-11 with me on board, left LHR at 0825 for Berlin - Tegel Airport on 25 June. Dietrich Linz, Reservations Officer Berlin, drove me to Tempelhof Airport where I met the telephone sales staff. The purpose of the visit was to introduce new computer equipment (BABS) to Germany using Berlin as the focal point. The 'Works Council' (trade union) had to be consulted on such matters and on the following day this was done. After more talks and demonstrations with staff the idea was accepted on 27 June and I had a brief meeting with Willie McKie, Manager Germany, to report my findings before catching the evening flight to LHR.

Scandinavia was part of the 'parish' administered on a reservations basis by Martin Rhoades and I. On 07 July I left LHR on a DC9 of SAS, LN-RLA, for Gothenburg, Sweden. The afternoon was spent investigating office procedures. Early the next morning I was on another DC9 of SAS, SE-DBR, for the 45 minute flight to Arlanda, Stockholm. It was a routine inspection of the office heavily disguised as a familiarisation visit. We had to be circumspect to avoid the local trade union organisation getting involved. On 09 July I had a meeting with David Sloper, Manager Scandinavia, before catching the afternoon Trident 2 aircraft to LHR.

After work on 11 July I went to the field at Marsh Benham where Pete Bish with Steve and Celia Hall were 'playing' with balloons. It was a lovely summer evening with virtually no wind. My log book records that I did a 2 minute solo flight in G-WETI, a Cameron N-31. How this happened is a mystery! Maybe I was updating my flying knowledge since I had to attend a carnival at Basingstoke on the next afternoon to do the commentary on the public address system.

Next I made a second two day visit to Gothenburg this time mainly to visit the BA travel agents in the city. I flew up on the mid-morning SAS flight on 12 August and returned the next evening on the BA service operated by a B737, G-BGDO, when I spent much time on the flight deck. This was my first experience of flying on a B737 aircraft, which had entered service earlier that year.

Sunday lunch at the Liddiard home was a ritual. David selected a huge joint of meat and his wife Jo cooked it with a variety of fresh vegetables. They invited me to join them on several occasions along together with their son James and daughter Kate, who later married Anthony Robinson. With a good bottle of wine and good conversation, the meals not infrequently lasted more than 3 hours. David was also a generous host when it came to barbecue time. On 16 August Dante Group members with wives and children enjoyed an extra-super evening at the Mill House. The occasion was almost spoilt when some pilots wanted to fly balloons!

Stories about the Bermuda Triangle were to me just stories and I never feared the area. On 25 August a Tristar, G-BFCD, took 7 hours 25 minutes to reach Bermuda. I visited the flight deck and Captain Swain gave me a fascinating and detailed explanation of the many new computer aids available on this type of plane. My trip to the colony was to visit the travel agents who were showing interest in American computer systems. I had to extol the virtues of BA and BABS. The CRO, Nat Chambers, drove me around parts of the island, including the now almost decaying dockyard, to again revive memories of the places I knew as a youth. On 28 August I boarded a late in-coming Tristar for the flight to LHR.

Bristol Balloon Fiesta Number 2 was held from 05 - 07 September. Again I was asked to do the public commentary. On the Friday morning there was heavy steady rain but no wind. At about 0900 somebody whispered "HTV" and one commercial pilot and his balloon immediately tethered for the television cameras. Other pilots with advertising balloons were not best pleased with this act of bravado. 13 balloons flew in the afternoon. On Saturday morning 20 balloons got airborne and 21 others tethered. That afternoon 41 balloons took off on a mass ascent in 23 minutes. The Survivors Dinner was held at the Grand Hotel and the Lord Mayor of Bristol presented me with a mug in recognition for my efforts in the commentary caravan.

On Sunday morning there was a strong wind but 3 balloons flew. The afternoon was sunny, hot and windy but 7 balloons were just able to fly after 1900. With an estimated crowd of 40,000 in a wide-open park and many static displays it was an ideal place for families to become separated. This was almost a repeat of the previous year and I became more than frustrated in using the PA system to try and unite wayward children and parents. This was not helped by Don Cameron writing in the official programme "The public will be allowed to pass freely onto the launch site to meet the balloonists and see the balloons at close quarters." The Civil Aviation Authority then invoked a rule that made the public stay off the launch site at a safe distance and behind a rope, which later became a fenced barrier, for all future Fiestas.

Exhausted by the long hours and bustle of the event I used a Trident 3 shuttle flight to Edinburgh for a weeks holiday at my mother's house in Fife from 08 September.

Gerry Turnbull, a retired Wing Commander, during the war had given cursory training on gas balloon flights to volunteer secret agents to fly solo across the North Sea with the intention of landing in the Nazi occupied Low Countries. On 23 August 1966 Gerry first flew in the hot air balloon 'Red Dragon' and by the time 'Bristol Belle' first flew on 09 July 1967 he was also training others to fly. Although I never flew with him he was helpful to me during ground training sessions. Gerry attended the 5th World Gas Balloon Championships held at St Niklaas, Belgium, and on 10 September 1980 he had scored the greatest number of marks. But as a result of a 'misunderstanding' and / or 'objection' he was not officially declared the winner at the Awards Ceremony. After following the lengthy appeals procedure Gerry was recognised as the highest placed contestant.

Yugoslavia was the first East European country to have the BABS computer system installed. On 19 September I flew to Belgrade via Zagreb and was met by Manager Brian Burgess. For the next 3 days my job was to teach the 4 staff how to use the equipment. A little bit of history was made at 1000 GMT on 23 September when the computer finally became 'live' and on-line to London. When satisfied that all was working well I left the country on a Yugoslav B727 aircraft (YU-AKE) via Zagreb for LHR on 25 September.

From a remote country region there was a special type of honey which was recommended as a possible cure (or help) for MS. I brought home a 3 Kilo jar together with some herbal tea. I persisted with a prescribed course for several months but like other apparent remedies tried before it gave no benefit to me.

Hungary was next on the list of countries for possible computerisation. On 15 October I flew on BA 700 to Budapest on a fact-finding mission. After talks with the local Manager Imre Bencze, the Reservations Officer Charlie Potsa and Airport Manager John Juarez my conclusion was positive. In the time available I was impressed with the twin-city layout of Buda on one side of the Danube and Pest on the other. Two days later another Trident 2 returned me to LHR.

Hot air ballooning was a subject that often occurred in conversation. On that Hungarian trip I gave copies of my book 'Balloons Around the World' to the staff and to my surprise discovered there was a local balloon club. Soon afterwards the Dante Group was invited to fly in Budapest on a sales promotion visit and this cemented a friendship with the Hungarian club which still exists now in 1999. The BA balloon has been to their country on umpteen occasions and the home-built Hungarian balloons have been to Britain many times.

Zagreb, Yugoslavia, also needed a feasibility study to justify the BABS computer. On 11 November I visited the city and had talks with the BA Manager and the local Communications Officials. My conclusion was favourable but of lower priority than that of Belgrade. The next day I flew to the capital to report my findings and assist with some advanced staff training. On 14 November I returned to London on JU 200 routing from Belgrade via Lublijana.

Thirty hours in Denmark in cold November weather is not pleasant. On 18th I flew to Copenhagen for a quick inspection of an unsettled office. There were gale force winds with horizontal snow and rain the next morning as I left the hotel Kong Frederick. At 1830 I boarded Tristar G-BEAK for a 2 hour 20 minute flight to London. The extended flying time was due to an unusual en-route ATC holding delay. I was upgraded and this was the last time I flew in First Class on BA European routes as the service was replaced by Club Class three months later.

Longhaul flights to the Caribbean and beyond in daylight were tolerable to me, but the return night flights were often tedious and boring. On 14 December G-BFCB left LHR at 1220 bound for Mexico City via Bermuda and Nassau. I was on board when the plane landed at 2210 Mexican time - but 0410 GMT. My diary does not make it clear exactly why I made this trip for just 2 days. However Manager Paul Fisher and his staff made me very welcome and I greatly enjoyed their Christmas awards party. By lunch time on the 17th I was sitting in First Class on an American Airlines DC10 for the 4 hour sector to Chicago. My baggage did not arrive with me. After a 3 hour transit I boarded G-AWND for LHR.

Christmas as usual was spent in Scotland with the family–and I was still on the honey diet. By New Years Eve my missing baggage had still not arrived and I made a claim against American Airlines. 48 hours later the somewhat battered suitcases arrived at Thatcham.

To satisfy my need to keep statistics: In 1980 I accumulated just 171 hours 10 minutes flying time on 53 sectors. My car in comparison logged 26,500 miles.

Above: BA had 3 types of Lockheed Tristar aircraft. Shown on a training flight in 1985 near Stansted Airport is a long-range L1011-500 version, G-BLUS. (BA)

Below: One of BOAC's first B747s (G-AWNA) on a training flight at Prestwick, Scotland, during late 1970. It entered service in the spring of 1971 and remained flying with BA for 28 years. It was withdrawn from use early in 1999. (BA)

Above: Concorde G-BOAE, wearing the new BA colour scheme, seen landing at Chateauroux, France, in the autumn of 1998. On this aircraft I had my first supersonic flight from Washington to Heathrow on 14 August 1977. (BA)

Below: A cover flown by me on the 'Concorde' balloon (G-BDSE) at Chateau de Balleroy, France, on 12 June 1977. It was then carried two months later on the Concorde aircraft and signed by Captain Chris Morley during my first supersonic flight.

Above left: During one of many postings to Zambia I crossed the border into Rhodesia. The country was in a state of UDI from Britain. This photo taken in May 1968 shows me on the frontier at the Kariba Dam.

Above right: Another crossing into Rhodesia, but this time at Victoria Falls. There was often a lot of spray so a raincoat was necessary when using the footbridge. Taken in June 1968.

Right: On a visit to Kathmandu I took the once-weekly Royal Nepal Airlines F27 excursion flight above the Himalayas to see Mount Everest. This photo from a passenger window shows both Everest and K9. Photo taken on 23 January 1969.

Taken on the same flight, but a slightly different view shot from a cockpit window. The Nepalese Captain said that the peak to the left was Everest.

Left: 30 April 1969 was the date of the last BOAC aircraft to use Ndola Airport, Zambia. A view showing the portside of the Standard VC-10, G-ARVL, with me in the foreground.

Right: G-BKYF, a B737-236, seen at Seattle, USA, prior to delivery in November 1984. By early 1999 this aircraft, in common with some others of the 200 Series, was withdrawn from BA service. (BA)

Left: When 'Victor Lima' had roared down the runway, Manager Chris Preece, Reservations Assistant Jenny Pickering and myself drank a toast to happy memories.

Right: G-DOCF, a B737 of the 400 Series, at LHR in late 1992 awaiting its routine nighttime check. (BA)

A commemorative flown cover of the first BOAC Boeing 747 to Nairobi and Johannesburg on 10 December 1971. (Eight months earlier the first B747 from LHR to JFK was on 14 April 1971).

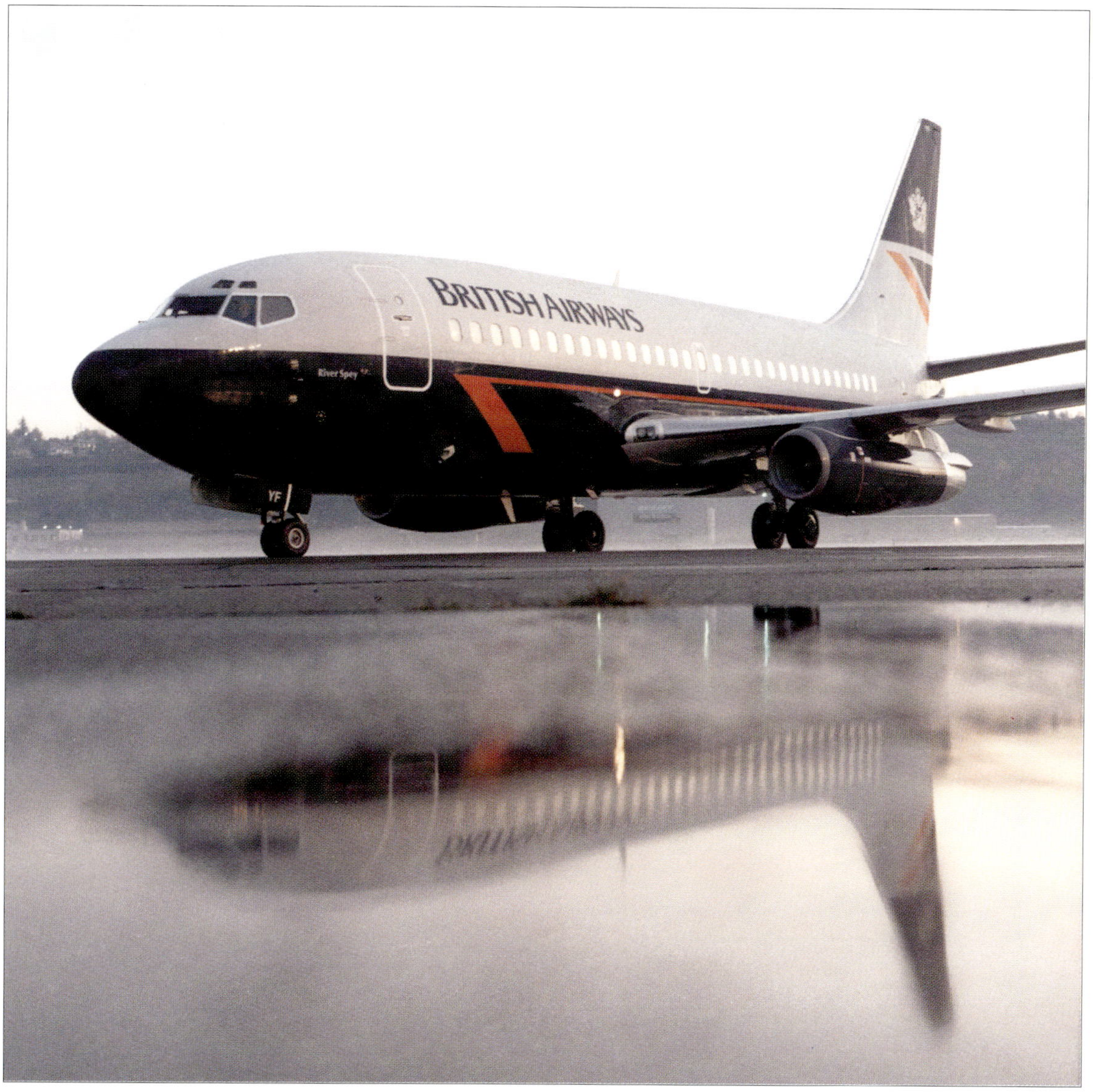
BRITISH AIRWAYS
River Spey

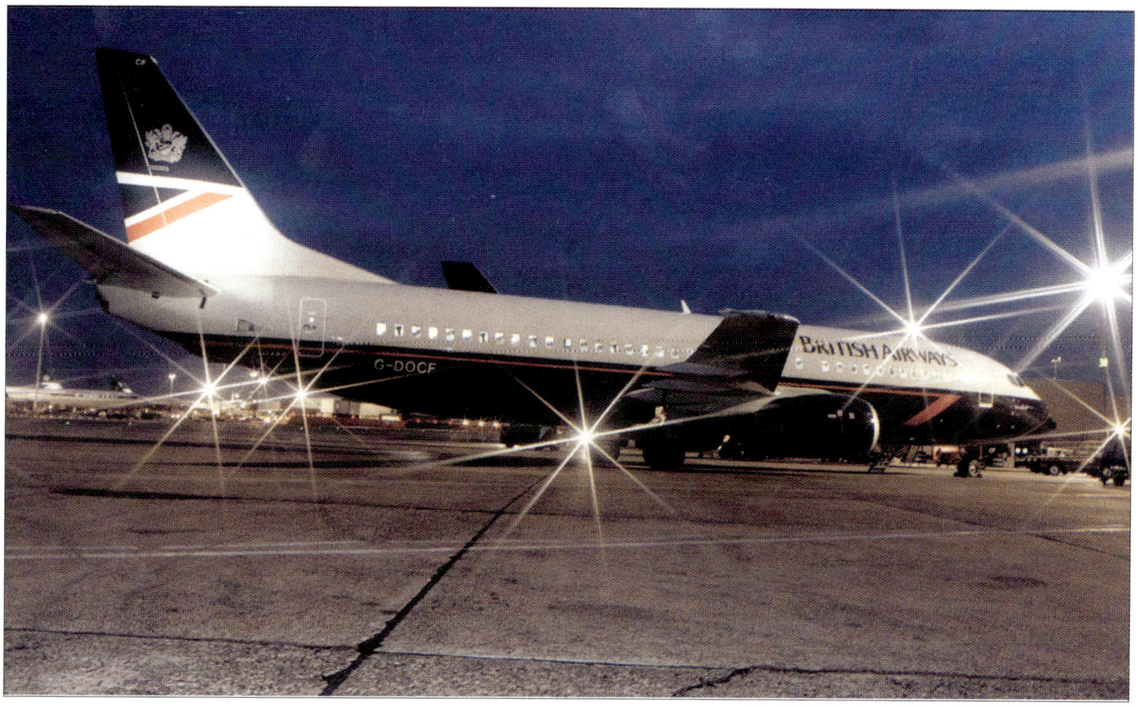
G-DOCF
BRITISH AIRWAYS

Left: On 30 January 1972 the first balloon flight was made from Marsh Benham, Newbury. The balloon 'Dante' was inflated by me (my first such experience) for only my second balloon flight. Peter Langford, the pilot, gave me instruction during the 90-minute flight.

Above: 'Dante' photographed at Markham, Ontario, Canada, on 19 June 1973. I made a short flight over waste ground in company with a local 'Export A' balloon.

When BEA heard that BOAC was advertising on a balloon at an event near Munster, Germany, it too wanted to get publicity. This photo, taken on 21 May 1972, at my first European Balloon Meet, shows both airline balloons.

Above: 'Carousel' was one of the 4 British entries at the First World Hot Air Balloon Championships held at Albuquerque, New Mexico, USA in February 1973. I attended as a spectator.

Above right: A relaxed-looking me giving an American a training flight near Indainola, Iowa. It was 5 August 1974, the day after I was granted an American Balloon Pilot's Licence.

Right: The Dante Group took delivery of a new BA balloon to reflect its new colour scheme. Here G-BBAC is being inflated soon after its delivery in September 1973.

In the early 1970s velcro panels were pulled apart by the red cord to release the hot air for landing. This photo shows a partially opened panel.

Taken at the February 1973 World Hot Air Balloon Championships at Albuquerque, New Mexico. The launch site was the State Fairground. In the background are the Sandia Mountains. Two British entries seen are: airborne on the left hand side is 'London Pride II' and at the rear of the photo, 'Dream Machine', in blue with the white zigzag at the base. I was a spectator.

Right: A diploma given to me by the British Balloon and Airship Club in recognition of 20 years service. 22 March 1992.

Diploma

The British Balloon and Airship Club

congratulates

Alec Jenkinson

upon

his

20 Years of Ballooning
on **22nd March 1992**

PRESIDENT OF THE BBAC

CHAIRMAN OF THE BBAC

THE BRITISH BALLOON AND AIRSHIP CLUB KIMBERLEY HOUSE VAUGHAN WAY LEICESTER LE1 4SG

Above: July 1985, the 7th World Hot Air Balloon Championships. Lift off started in almost flat calm conditions.

Below: Competitors at the July 1985 7th World Hot Air Balloon Championships at Battle Creek, Michigan, USA.

The sky became peppered with balloons above Kellogg's Airfield, which was used as the base for the Championships.

Special shaped balloons were originated by Cameron Balloons of Bristol, England. This one for Walt Disney, based in the USA, is named 'Mickey' and appropriately registered G-MIKY.

Two more special shaped balloons, both made in England, and a hot air airship preparing to land at dusk. These were part of the fun flying exhibitions to entertain the crowd as part of the 1985 World Championships.

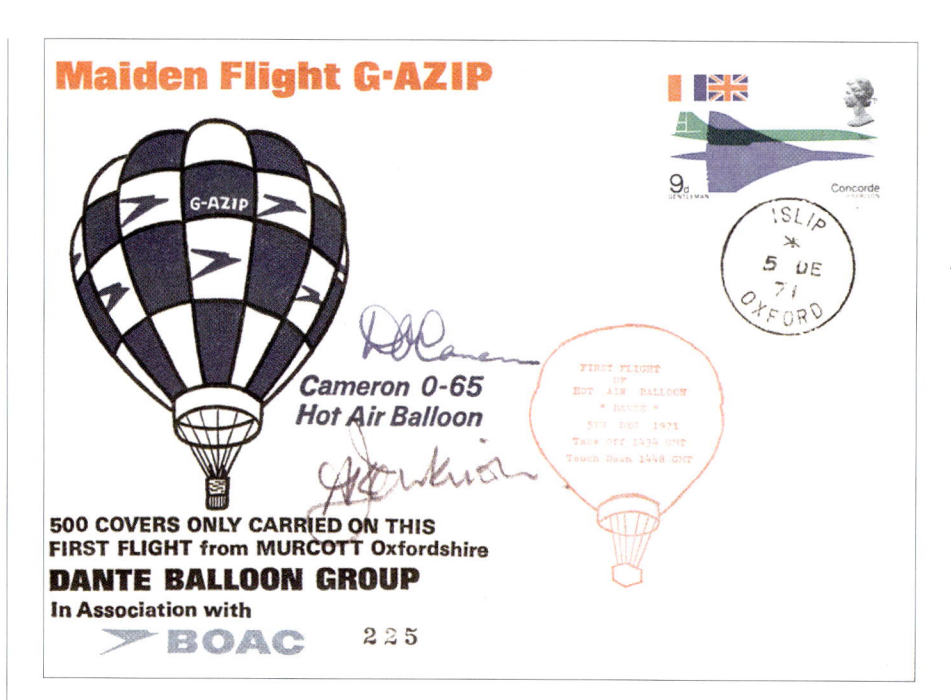

This cover was flown to commemorate the beginnings of the Dante Hot Air Group, 5 December 1971. I was lucky enough to be aboard the first flight.

Flown in both of the Dante Balloons by different pilots at the first Icicle Meet.

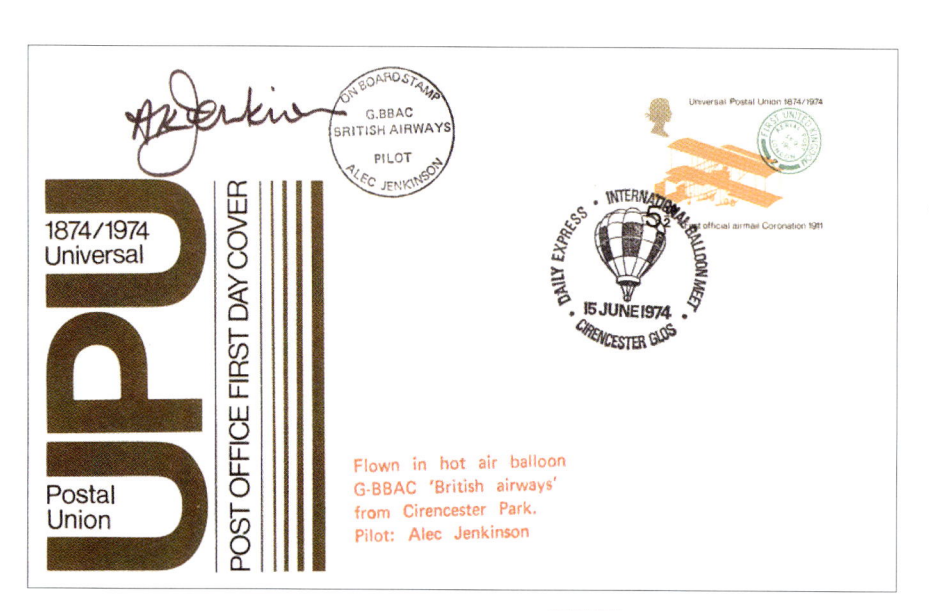

The Post Office again provided a special hand stamp cancellation. I carried this cover in my favourite balloon, G-BBAC.

Many 'Firsts' for this cover, which I carried aboard Comet G-ARJN. Scotsman Captain David Jack signed some covers during flight.

The Albuquerque Post Office specially overprinted a number of aerogrammes. I flew this one at the 1974 Balloon Fiesta.

The 3rd World Hot Air Balloon Championships were held in Yorkshire. Most of the 50 competitors carried covers (organised by me) but this one was flown by the winner, Paul Woessner.

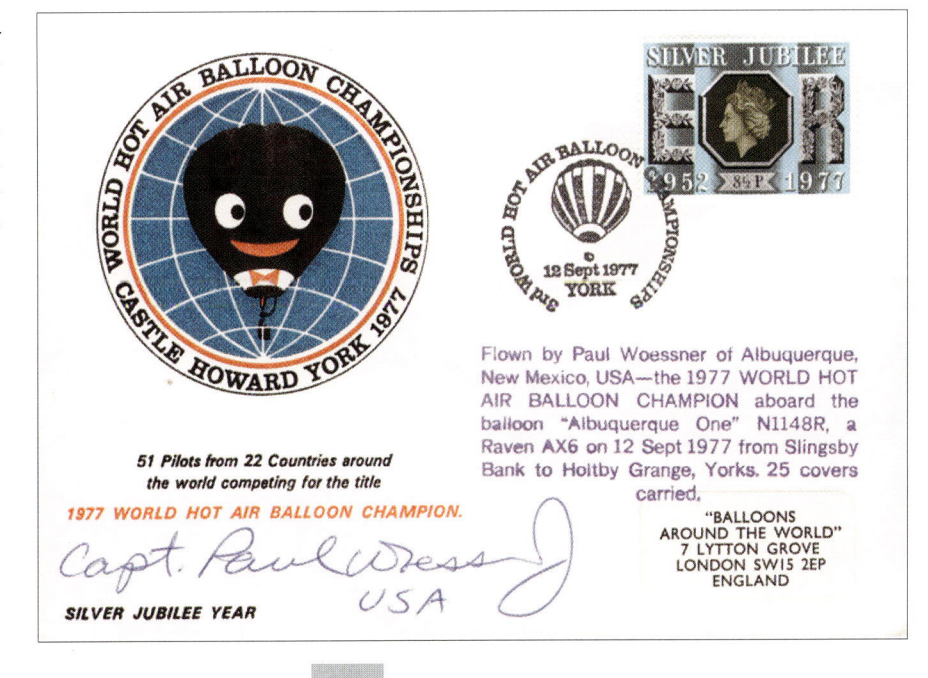

Above: Waiting for a flight at Malmesbury 2 July 1987. I was in a wheelchair as my right leg had been amputated six months earlier.

Below: The pilot, Karen Coombs, was a bubbly girl from Bath University. Sitting in a balloon basket restricts the view but I greatly enjoyed the flight.

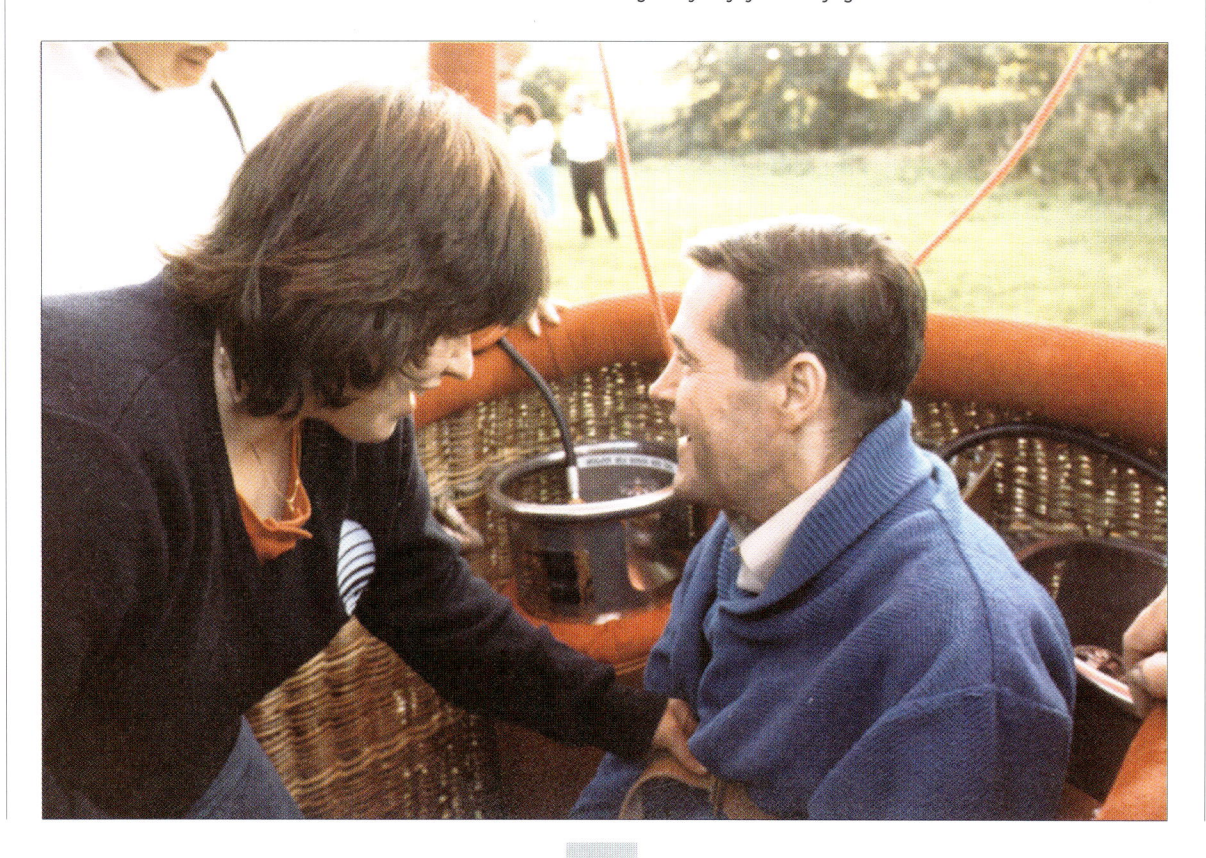

Photo taken of me flying using hand controls from y wheelchair in December 1980, watched by pilot David Boxall. In February 1988 I flew in a similar balloon but with a TV crew on board and part of the flight was shown on the BBC news that evening.

Preparing to take off with three friends on a cold and frosty morning from Malmesbury. It was a glorious flightand we travelled just 4 miles in 80 minutes. The date was 25 October 1997.

British competitor, Martin Moroney and I cooking a mini English breakfast on the balloon burner pilot flame. The place was the 2nd World Championships, Albuquerque in October 1975.

BBC TV cameraman, David Saunders, took me in June 1988 for a flight in his private aircraft from Old Sarum Airfield, Salisbury.

21
VISITS TO EASTERN EUROPE PLUS USA WORLD CHAMPIONSHIPS

Saturday 03 January 1981 was very stormy. There were no balloon flights to start the 9th Icicle Meet. Again I gave the met briefing for the pilots but they did not like to hear that the surface wind was at least 15 knots with gusts of 30 knots. Inside one of David Liddiard's barns 14 model sized balloons were inflated mostly to entertain a coach load of aircraft 'reggie spotters' who had travelled through the night from Manchester in the hope of seeing the full-sized balloons. The Sunday briefing was brought forward to 0700 on the half-promise of early flyable weather. Local balloonist David Smith was airborne at first light - 0727 - followed quickly by 36 other balloons.

After three meetings at Victoria and LHR, the latter with Ken Virgo on European Reservations strategy, I caught the evening flight to Geneva on 07 January. Almost the entire next day was taken up with more dreaded meetings followed by yet more discussions at Geneva Airport on the following morning. After lunch with Manager Laurie O'Toole I boarded a B737 for LHR.

Denmark and Sweden office managers wanted a fact-finding survey. On 09 February I flew on the morning Trident 3 to Copenhagen. The weather seemed to sense that this was not my favourite city and for the next two days there were periods of snow. On 11 February I flew on an SAS Airbus, OY-KAA, to Stockholm. Local reservations staff were often wary when someone from London arrived and asked questions but here the staff were relatively relaxed. On Friday the 13th, after discussions with the local manager, I caught the afternoon SAS DC9 flight for the 2 hours 25 minute flight to London.

Balloon trip to Vienna - but without a balloon. On 28 March with two Dante members I flew on a B737 from LHR to Vienna with the intention of doing a balloon promotion for BA. Due to volumetric problems in the aircraft hold the balloon 'Concorde' did not travel. We spent a happy Saturday evening at the Hotel Intercontinental and flew back to LHR on the next afternoon. On 29 March the clocks changed, the summer schedules began and the new Club Class was introduced on BA flights. We sampled the Club Class service on the first day of its introduction during our return to London.

Monday morning to Moscow. A routine visit to the small reservations unit was requested by Hank Appleyard, Manager USSR and I travelled out on a Trident 2, G-AVFO, on 06 April. It was an experience I had been looking forward to but because of my walking difficulties I was restricted to what I could see and do. At that time Intourist, the official government travel agency, provided all visitors with a chauffeur driven car for a few hours every day. I used this for tours of the city and one visit to the Moscow State Circus. Regrettably I could not access the metro system or other places where steps were involved. The Hotel National was very basic although the food for tourists paying in hard currency was quite good. One evening in the hotel I insisted on joining a queue to sit in the rouble paying section, where the locals ate. With some language problems I had a meal which was tasty and different, but I could not vouch for its contents. The BA office did limited business and could not issue BA tickets. The 4 days passed quickly and on 10 April the same Trident flew me to LHR in 4 hours 10 minutes.

With 90,000 miles on my Renault car it was beginning to reach its 'throw away date'. From 21 April for 3 weeks I used a National coach from Thatcham to London Victoria as a trial. Road traffic delays frequently made me late for the office and the boredom sometimes left me fractious.

Using a Lufthansa B727 I flew to Hannover on 28 April for talks with Manager Monika Schade and architects concerning the re-location and refurbishment of the reservations unit. On 29 April I hosted a small celebration lunch to commemorate the 25th anniversary of my joining the airline. The following evening I returned to LHR.

Warsaw was the next East European country to get the BA computer. (Yugoslavia was theoretically the first 'East European' country.) On 18 May I flew to Warsaw with almost 100 kilos of food including 200 fresh lemons. The food items had all been requested by the Manager as there were food shortages in the country. Being in a wheelchair I did not see Customs on arrival but the food was 'nodded' through for the BA staff in the town office. However later that evening in the hotel Orbis

Forum I overheard a bar tender boast to a customer that they had just received a supply of fresh lemons. Were they mine I wondered?

Staff training on the computer started immediately with 7 hours on the first day and 11 hours on the second. I had little time to see anything of the city. On 20 May I spent the morning helping the airport staff with the computer before catching BA 691 back to London that afternoon. I found it a tiring trip, but the staff seemed to enjoy the goodies.

Frankfurt was the headquarters for BA in Germany. On 26 May I visited the city for 27 hours to attend two meetings connected with staff utilisation and the expansion of computer equipment. I got little pleasure from these short sharp meetings.

More food, but no lemons, travelled with me to Warsaw on 10 June. The local Sales Manager Jurek had been queuing half the night to get petrol for his car in order to meet me at the airport. This was planned as an 8 day visit to get the BA computer working and all the staff fully trained. On the day I arrived many of us stayed in the office until after 2000 to prepare for an early 'cutover' the next morning. For the record books the BABS computer came on line at Warsaw at 0920 GMT on 11 June.

For the next two days staff training continued from 0830 until 2000. At times the line to London gave slow responses with occasional 'outages'. On Sunday the 14th I went to Mass and was surprised to see a line of Russian cars sporting the red flag parked outside the church. Inside were some uniformed Communist officials who seemingly attended weekly as a duty. Jurek drove me around parts of the city on a sight-seeing tour of non-sensitive areas. Martial Law was in effect at that time. On 15 June the office was officially opened with BABS to customers and we had a lunchtime celebration with cakes and pastries. Two days later I flew home on a Trident 3.

An Air Traffic Control dispute, or some upset, at LHR on 18 June caused much congestion and many delayed flights. I was booked to travel on BA 277 to Detroit via Washington. We boarded G-AWNP for a scheduled departure of 1145 but did not leave the ramp until 1400. Consequently the plane did not land until 2355 or 1855 local time. Tucker Comstock met and drove several of us to Battle Creek where we arrived at our hotel at 2200.

Purpose of this trip was to be a minor official i.e. scorer at the 5th World Hot Air Balloon Championships at Battle Creek, Michigan. Tom Sheppard, the Meet Director, had invited several Britons including Anne Lewis-Smith and myself to assist.

A brief summary of the next 9 days reads as:

19 June Almost 30 helpers met in the morning to collect their briefing sheets. Met Gary Britton, chief de-briefer, at a restaurant supper party in the evening.

20 June We all visited the launch site which was the Kellogg regional airport at Battle Creek. After lunch everyone connected with the event attended the first full briefing.

21 June The morning task was cancelled due wind and rain. Despite unfavourable thundery weather task number 1 was flown in the early evening. A huge Military Lockheed Galaxy aircraft roared down the runway whilst the balloonists were getting airborne. Dick Wirth wrote that 'It was lucky that 1) No one was struck by lightning 2) No one was drowned in the basket 3) No one got injured in the wake of the Galaxy taking off'. I too was amazed at the events that evening. We did not finish the scoring until 0200.

22 June The morning flights were cancelled. Tasks 2 and 3 were flown in the evening and along with the other helpers it took us all night to do the scoring.

23 June Watched the balloons take off on the morning task (number 4).Then I got to bed at 0915.

24 June Due to fatigue I was late and missed the only task before rain arrived in the morning. That evening I enjoyed a good dinner at the Lobster Pot Restaurant.

25 June Most of the scorers and helpers drove about 12 miles out of town to see the balloons fly over the 'marker drop zone' for tasks 6 and 7. It was a great sight to see the balloons swoop down as the pilots threw their marker at the target - a large white 'X' in a corner of a field.

26 June The pilots flew solo on the last task of the Championships. There was an almighty sigh of relief when we had completed the final scoring just after lunch time. There were Fiesta balloon fun flights in the afternoon before a Rum Party that evening.

27 June Many of us were glad that it was windy and with no fixed programme we could relax. However in the evening there was the formal Awards Banquet. Bruce Comstock of USA was the declared Champion with David Bareford of Britain second and Janne Balkedal of Sweden in third place.

The people of Battle Creek were friendly and hospitable to balloonists and I truly enjoyed being there and helping with the event. There were 82 competitors from 23 countries and it was good to meet many of the pilots in the leisure time available. On Sunday 28 June Tucker, Anne and I drove to Ann Arbor for tea and then on to Detroit Airport for the evening BA flight via Washington to LHR. At 0940 the next morning I was back in Britain.

BA Sales Manager Dusseldorf, Lothan Kegelmann, wanted an appraisal of the Essen reservations office. On 22 July I made a 48 hour visit to the area but the result was inconclusive. Later however the Essen unit was closed.

On 31 July I went to help Pete Bish and John Baker with the finishing touches to their book 'British Balloons', a register of all British built balloons. This comprehensive guide was finally launched in January 1982.

Five days holiday in Wales went all too quickly from 03 to 07 August. Peter and Anne Lewis-Smith had moved to a hillside house overlooking Newport, near Fishguard, in Pembrokeshire (or Dyfed to be correct). I travelled from London to Carmarthen by coach and onward by car. It was a most relaxing time with good meals, warm sunny weather and I felt very content and 'rounded'.

Berlin was my next duty visit on 10 August. For the next two days with Reservations Officer Dietrich Linz I had meetings on a telephone call survey and with the Office Works Council (trade union) on a possible re-organisation. On the afternoon of the 13th I caught another BAC1-11, via Hannover, to LHR.

Twenty eight hours in Oslo started on 26 August. The local manager was Chris Preece, whom I had previously worked with in Zambia. The local trade union was not satisfied that BA was ergonomically friendly with the recently acquired computer furniture. I was not qualified to voice a professional opinion but my presence there, if only for a few hours, helped to temporarily quieten their misgivings. Rather than use a hotel Chris and Ann Preece invited me to stay overnight with them. It was a very pleasant evening and superb meal followed by stories remembered from years ago. The next morning Chris drove me to a ferry terminal for a scenic trip across Oslo harbour. The sea was like a millpond and the city looked majestic in the bright sunshine. I could easily have done another round trip! After a short meeting in the office, to reassure the staff, it was time for the 50km drive to Fornebu Airport. Chris arranged my pre-boarding on OY-KGH, a SAS DC9 for LHR where I arrived at 1715.

Less than 24 hours later I was sitting on board a Dan-Air plane, G-AWWX, at Gatwick Airport en route to Lourdes in France. It was a 7 day religious pilgrimage arranged by my local parish priest. This was my first visit to the shrine of Our Lady of Lourdes and a wheelchair had been arranged for me to attend the various services. During the week different parishioners pushed me to many gatherings including the huge International Mass on the Sunday, the St Bernadette Chapel and the evening torchlight processions. Situated high in the French Pyranees the Lourdes weather is known to be fickle and we were blessed (or maybe unblessed) with a share of severe thunderstorms. I enjoyed the occasion and even allowed myself to be immersed in the ice-cold holy waters. I could hardly have expected a cure but the experience certainly gave my system a shock! On 04 September another Dan-Air plane, G-BDAT, returned us to Gatwick at 2120.

Bristol Balloon Fiesta number 3 was held from 11 to 13 September. Once again I was asked to do the public commentary. Some balloons flew on the Friday morning but rain cancelled the planned mass ascent. On Saturday the 12th it was a cold, calm morning when 37 balloons flew free. Rain prevented any afternoon flights. The next morning started with a thunderstorm and flying was abandoned. When leaving Clifton Cathedral after Mass at 1130 my walking sticks slipped on some wet leaves and I fell badly. With difficulty I drove back to the launch site at Ashton Court Park and then returned home feeling distinctly unwell.

After lunch the next day (the 14th) I found myself immobile downstairs and phoned the doctor for help. He visited then called an ambulance and by 1730 I was an in-patient at Battle Hospital in Reading with a high temperature. An x-ray showed no broken bones but suffering from some viral infection. By the 17th the antibiotics were helping and I was able to stand briefly. In the week that followed many welcome visitors helped my recovery in the dull surroundings of Castle Ward. On 23 September I left hospital. Good neighbours are a blessing and I was fortunate to have many. After some tedious physiotherapy I returned to work after 5 weeks absence on 19 October.

Goodbye Renault–Welcome Ford Fiesta. On 20 October the Renault 5 was sold for just a few pounds with 99,974 miles on the clock. On the same day I collected my new car using the Motorbility purchase system. One week later the car was fitted with hand controls by a specialist firm in North London.

Another foundation meeting of the British Balloon Museum and Library was held at Mike Allen's home near Newbury attended by 7 of the core members. It was Sunday 15 November. The concept was established but our various ideas needed to be consolidated. It took longer than a year and many meetings before we could agree on a workable project..

Ticket printer problems in Helsinki gave me the chance for another quick trip to my favourite country. With a computer engineer we fixed the fault in the 24 hour visit and returned to London on the evening B737 on 02 December. There was an unfavourable exchange rate but I did some Christmas shopping in the delightful Stockmanns department store.

Almost exactly 10 years to the minute since my first ever balloon flight I had a one minute commemorative trip in the same balloon, Dante G-AZIP, with the same pilot, Don Cameron, from the same field at Murcott in Oxfordshire. It was a windy afternoon but for me it was a great way to celebrate the 10th Anniversary. Other members of the Group also had brief flights on 05 December.

Snow and very icy conditions almost delayed the official opening of the British Balloon Museum and Library's first exhibition on 12 December. It was held at the Newbury Library with many local dignitaries present. Later 33 members and guests attended a lunch at the Chequers Hotel in Newbury.

Short one or two day visits to European offices became a feature of my life. On 14 December I flew to Dusseldorf to officially cutover the office ticket printer and give the staff additional training. The following afternoon another B737 flew me back to LHR in 75 minutes.

Christmas dinner in the staff canteen at the Victoria Air Terminal was always a merry occasion. On 16 December with wine unofficially available it was.

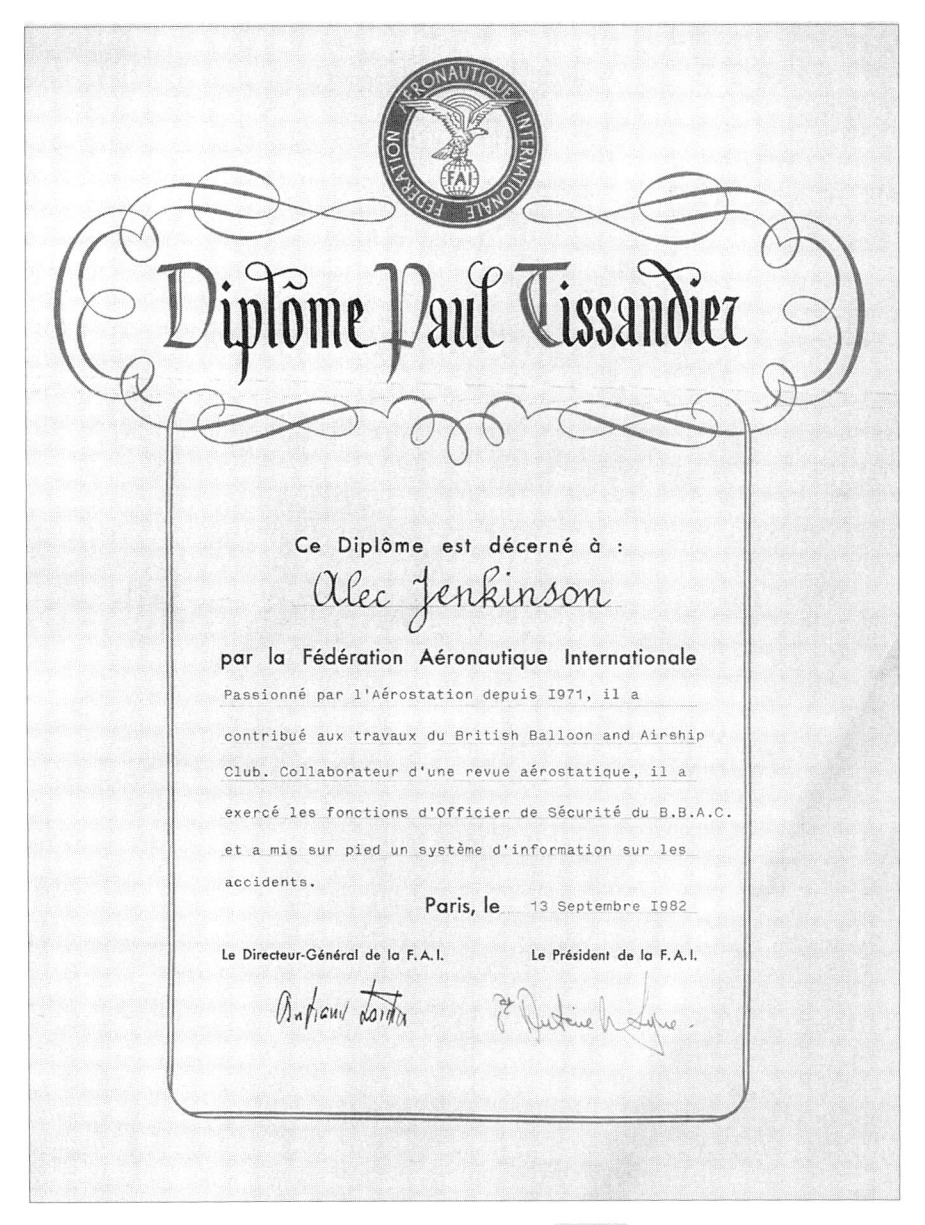

The Paul Tissandier Diploma is awarded by the FAI in Paris(on the recommendation of the local Royal Aero Club) to members of the aviation fraternity who contribute to activities. My award was for the introduction and implementation of the Balloon Incident Report form. Prince Andrew made the presentation to me at an award ceremony on 9 December 1982.

22
SEVENTEEN TRIPS TO EUROPE

January the 1st 1982 was a Friday and a public holiday. The 10th Icicle Meet, for the first and only time, was held over 3 days. That was a fortuitous decision since only the Friday weather was good enough to allow any flying. During the afternoon 16 balloons got airborne in low stratus conditions. I gave the pilots the met briefings on both the Saturday and Sunday but no flying on either day was possible due to winds and rain.

There was a need to computerise every reservation sales office in Europe. On 18 January I flew to Budapest for discussions with the SITA communications people on the availability of computer lines. Talks continued next day and the result was favourable. The Hungarian staff were quite excited at the prospect of a reliable link to the outside world. On 20 January I was on the flight deck of BA 701, G-AVFR, for the landing at LHR runway 28 Right. I asked the Captain to check with ATC if Pete Bish was on duty. He was and briefly talked to the aircraft on VHF frequency of 119.2. I got some pleasure from small incidents like this.

Dante Group 10th Anniversary dinner and dance was held at the Castle Coombe Hotel, Wiltshire. When celebrations go on until after 0200 then it was a great event. After a late breakfast the next morning, 31 January, two Group balloons flew.

Unstable walking, even with the aid of two sticks, plus some tension had made it difficult for me to keep my balance in January. I saw Dr Perkin at Charing Cross Hospital on 03 February and he prescribed another course of Prednisolone. The condition of my MS fluctuated within a fairly narrow band but it was on a slow downward trend.

Another ticket printer became active ('cut-over') at Hamburg on 09 February the day after my arrival. Then followed talks with Manager Monika Schade before I left the next afternoon on a Lufthansa B737 for LHR.

Three weeks later I flew to Frankfurt Airport on a Lufthansa Airbus to cut-over the airport ticket printers. I stayed overnight on 01 March for extra staff training before returning to LHR.

Luxair was the only airline that flew from London to Luxembourg. On 23 March I flew there on LX-LGH for talks with Manager Belgium and Luxembourg and the local representatives. It was to consider a feasibility study on BA opening a mechanised reservations office in the country and maybe later resuming an air service to London. The following morning the same B737 diverted to Gatwick due to fog at LHR and I along with the other passengers used a British Rail train to London Victoria.

Problems with the Frankfurt Airport ticket printer and additional staff training meant I had to make a day trip there. Flight timings on 30 March made it easier for me to use Lufthansa in both directions, an Airbus out and a B727 back.

31 March is the end of the airline financial year and often a time used for staff retirements and re-organisations. My manager, Alan Collier, retired along with Bob Bouteloupt, Chief of Space Control, and Bob Tarrant of Reservation Systems. On 01 April there was a formal presentation and party in their honour. Very many past and present colleagues attended and I was just one that felt a tinge of sadness at their going.

Bordeaux was the first office in France that I visited. The thought of tasting the local wines 'sur la table' was really only part of the reason that my visit was planned to last for three days. On arrival, Local Manager Terry Hines, met and showed me some of the city sights. Later, on 21 April, I was inspecting the cramped reservations and ticket office before an evening meeting. The following morning I looked at some prospective premises to re-house the reservations unit. French red tape was enough to drive you to French red wine! No firm decision was possible but I did enjoy some outstanding meals. When I checked in for the London flight on 23 April my hand baggage was somewhat heavier and of a fragile nature!

Two for the price of one journey was achieved 3 days later. Early on 26 April I flew to Stuttgart and by lunchtime had cut-over the airport ticket printer. Then a taxi took me to the town office where I tweaked its ticket printer into action. The next morning I rose at 0500 to catch the 0705 Lufthansa flight to LHR which arrived at 0725 BST. With a colleague waiting the car journey to Victoria got us to the office by 0850.

Czechoslovakia was slowly relaxing its travel restrictions which encouraged BA to broaden its sales scope under Manager Roger Woof. On 17 May I flew to Prague and was impressed by the three helpful and friendly reservations girls in the town office. When I checked into the Intercontinental Hotel I was even more impressed with its plush surroundings and high standards. After a quick morning tour of the city the next day I met the local SITA Communications Manager and was pleased to learn that computer quality lines were available to London. On the 19th I did a quality control check on the reservations office before catching the Trident 3 flight back to London. I asked the Captain and he allowed me to sit in the cockpit for the 1 hour 55 minute journey.

The Falklands War ended on 14 June and totally unrelated to this I started a 3 day course on a new word processor at work. As mobile or roving reservations officers we had to keep ourselves one step ahead of the computer developments in order to train overseas staff.

Monday morning of the next week, 21 June, I flew to Budapest. A taxi took me to the reservations office and within 90 minutes of my arrival the BABS computer was on line to London. The time was 1420 GMT. After Belgrade and Warsaw this was the 3rd East European country to have the computer system. With occasional outages on 22 June and during the morning of the 23rd the old sales record cards were 'meshed' into BABS. The weather was very hot and reached 34 degrees Celsius at lunchtime on 23rd. The following day staff training was interrupted when many visitors from numerous companies and organisations came to view the computer. On 25 June I returned to LHR via Prague on BA 701.

On 05 July a letter arrived from the Royal Aero Club in London advising that I was to receive the Paul Tissandier Diploma. This was in recognition of my being the first Safety Officer of the British Balloon and Airship Club and for initiating an Incident Report Form which was later adopted by most countries with balloons.

Some final staff training needed to be done at Zurich Airport ticket desk before the ticket printer could be cut-over on 15 July. I travelled out that morning and left the following afternoon.

Holiday time for me was a 5 day visit to Wales staying with Peter and Anne Lewis-Smith. On 19 July we arrived in time for afternoon tea on the lawn. After lunch the next day we went to the local beach and saw a partial eclipse of the sun. During the following days I enjoyed a variety of experiences including Gaelic coffee at a nearby pub, feeding ponies on the hills, over-eating afternoon cream teas, a picnic on the beach and evening dinner parties. It was all so relaxing and enjoyable.

Flying on a Tristar 100 series I made a 2 day visit to Paris at the request of Manager Jim Kutas. It was a busy working trip and included an appraisal of the ticket office on the Champs Elysee. On Friday the 13th August I returned to London.

4th Bristol International Balloon Fiesta was held from 20 to 22 August. The dates were brought forward from the previous year in the hope of getting better weather, but the elements conspired to defeat that decision. On Friday morning the 20th soon after 0630 before the winds arrived 28 balloons flew and that was it for the day. Solicitor Roger Harper helped me with the commentary for the next 6 years and we were the only ones spouting hot air - and trying to keep the crowds informed. Early the next morning another clutch of hot air balloons flew before wind and rain arrived to disappoint the Saturday spectators. I enjoyed talking on the public address system but at times it could be taxing to find fresh information without being repetitive. Despite a lengthy lunch hour it was a long day from 0630 until after 2030. This was especially so on the Sunday when there were no balloon flights.

Using an airline concessionary travel ticket I flew on the morning Luxair B737 to be a minor honorary official at the European Balloon Championships. Pierre Stoors, a policeman, met me at the airport on 26 August and was assigned to be my 'guide' for the next 5 days. After an informal reception and lunch we visited the launch site near the north end of this tiny country of Luxembourg surrounded by three major countries.

After an early rise at 0500 I attended the first pilot's briefing for Task 1 on 27 August. In between the flying events there was a good feeling of camaraderie and the Chairman of the FAI (Federation Aeronautique Internationale) made a positive effort to seek out and speak with all helpers at the Championships. After the evening flying the competitors and helpers enjoyed a grand dinner at the Cactus Restaurant.

Saturday lunchtime 28 August was billed as a barbecue and National costume spectacular at the Castle Bourscheid. In all my ballooning years this function stands out as the most memorable for so many reasons. More than 200 of us associated with the event were treated to a gourmet feast of plain and luxurious dishes accompanied by a huge selection of wines, beers and more besides. The ancient Castle was decorated for the occasion and there was a strong emphasis on the proud historic background to the Royal Duchy of Luxembourg. In the bright sunshine the views from the Castle across the mountains far outweighed anything Hollywood could have staged. After three hours we all left reluctantly, fully satisfied at the marvel of the experience.

When we returned to the launch site British balloonist Phil Hutchins was giving a tethered display in his special shaped J & B Rare Whisky balloon. Just after he had finished he untied the restraining harness from the seat on his balloon when a rogue thermic gust of wind lifted the still tethered balloon into the air. At about 50 feet the tether yanked the balloon violently and Phil fell from the seat to the ground below. The impact caused instant death. Many of us watched in horror and disbelief.

Most of the spectators were unaware that it was a fatality. At 1830 the next Championship task took place. The pilots and crews were in a sombre and reflective mood that evening at the loss of a well liked colleague. Pit Thibo, the Meet Director and Organiser, used his skills and influence to give the press as little information as possible.

There was very little wind on the Sunday morning and I was at the marker drop-zone when some balloons drifted gently overhead including Englishman David Bareford. A First Officer on a BA aircraft flying nearby called on the balloonists VHF radio frequency for news of the event. I replied using a mobile transmitter and told him of Phil's death. Later that day there was a buffet lunch on site and it was an occasion where I met some old friends including Nina Boesman from Holland and Jean Costa de Beauregard from France. In the evening, when feeling tired and very stiff, I stumbled on some steps and was grateful for the help given to me by Hans Akerstedt and his wife. Fortunately the only damage was a bruised knee. Hans was an early Swedish balloon pilot who got his licence in 1972 whom I first met ten years earlier at the Stanford Hall Meet. I have kept in contact with him ever since. He was an airline pilot for SAS and is now in 1999 an official of the world governing body of ballooning, the FAI formerly based in Paris but now in Lausanne, Switzerland.

On 30 August there was the traditional Awards Banquet to end the Championships. Much very good food and champagne was consumed from 1930 until after midnight. It had been both a happy and yet sad competition but the overriding memory for most of us was of friendship.

By 0530 the next morning I was on my way to Luxembourg airport for the Luxair plane which arrived at LHR at 0715 BST. My carpool colleagues met me and we got to the office in London by 0830.

Next aircraft journey was to Gothenburg on 07 September for a Sandanavian Area Reservations meeting and workshop. This started with a working breakfast the following morning with the five regional office supervisors and continued until tea-time. I flew back to London on the evening BAC 1-11, G-AVMY.

As an interim measure whilst seeking a new permanent home following separation from her husband, Kim Cameron with her 2 children, Hannah and James (plus their dog), moved into the vacant rooms in my house on 09 September. The youngsters were at school in Oxford and Kim drove them the 50 mile round trip from Thatcham whilst she spent many days looking for suitable accomodation. 13 weeks later on 15 December Kim and family moved into their new home in Southmoor Road, Oxford.

During their stay at Thatcham we enjoyed a great variety of home made and take-away foods and Kim was very kind and helpful to me when I had a major problem with my car.

No matter what they say, a motorway accident in fog is probably a driver's worst experience. At 0530 on 16 September whilst driving to work on the M4 near Reading in fluctuating visibility due to fog I ran over a tyre in lane 3 of the motorway at about 50 mph. I had about 3 seconds of total fear. The 2 inner lanes were occupied by lorries and I could not avoid hitting the tyre. Parts of the engine and underside of my Fiesta were badly damaged but I got to the hard shoulder just ahead of at least 10 other cars which had also hit the obstacle. I was relieved to be unhurt and more so when the AA towed the car to a garage and took me home. Hassle with the insurance company and slow garage repairs meant I was without a car for almost a month. It was finally fixed by 11 October.

To hire a car with hand controls, which was what I needed, was not possible. I found a small bed and breakfast hotel, the Arden House, near the office in Victoria and stayed there from Sundays to Fridays for the next few weeks. Kim kindly drove me to the hotel or to LHR when I had to make overseas trips.

There was a pleasant surprise on 21 September when flying to Marseilles on a BAC 1-11. The Captain was John Hervieu, a former Jersey flight clerk, whom I knew well but had not seen for 23 years. I was in the cockpit for the landing when the ILS (Instrument Landing System) cut off during the final approach and he had to land visually in unfavourable conditions. Maybe it is strange but I enjoyed being part of minor incidents such as this.

District Manager Noel de Marque and Reservations Officer Jacques Fidani met me and we had talks at the airport concerning some booking/seating irregularities. The following day was spent inspecting the town office procedures before going for a superb late lunch which was generously seasoned with garlic, a real favourite with me. The location of the restaurant in the hills above the city and the local wine made it an afternoon I cannot easily forget (or should I say cannot easily remember!). Quite early the next morning Noel drove me around Marseilles which included a non-stop tour of the port area where the variety of local girls on street duty almost shocked me. After collecting some bottles of wine to take home we drove to the airport for another meeting during lunch. BA 349 on 23 September flew me back to LHR by 1610 where Kim met me.

Heard of the death of well known British balloonist Dick Wirth on 04 October. He was a co-founder of Thunder Balloons in London and was a cheerful character who was widely respected. He died in a tragic manner on a balloon flight at Albuquerque, USA, the day before. I was one of many who crowded into the church of St Martin in the Fields in London on 05 November to attend his memorial service.

Another country to add to my list was Austria when I made a 2 day visit to Vienna from 11 November. The purpose of the trip was a quality control inspection of the reservations unit at the request of Manager, Peter Fieldhouse. When the office closed I was taken for a drive around the city to see some of the interesting landmarks but darkness does not give a visitor a chance to appreciate the real beauty of the city's features. Later Sales Rep Ekka drove me to a village bistro which offered traditional food and wine in a lovely setting overlooking the city. The following morning I met Geoff Bridges (at that time Regional Manager Europe) by chance as he was also reviewing the organisation in Austria. In the late afternoon an Austrian Airlines DC9 carried me back to LHR.

Two day visits to reservations/sales offices were in my view less useful than many managers believed. In the six to eight hours available to inspect and review local working practices it was not too difficult for staff to hide or gloss over their weaknesses. Although I was experienced at looking 'in the corners' I was also aware that diversionary tactics were sometimes used. The above statements do not necessarily refer to my next visit to Copenhagen on 25 and 26 November.

During my stay at the Victoria hotel I frequently worked late in the office. This gave me a chance to use the WANG computer to update the Balloon Museum and Library inventory. On 06 December I had armfuls of paperwork to distribute at the AGM held at a Binfield pub near Bracknell, Berkshire.

For security reasons in London the Royal Aero Club decided to use the RAF Museum at Hendon for its annual presentation and awards ceremony. On 09 December I received the Paul Tissandier Diploma from Prince Andrew. This was the honour nominated for me by the British Balloon and Airship Club in recognition of my work as Safety Officer and the Incident Reporting system. Later followed an informal reception where guests and recipients mingled freely.

To get some French wine for Christmas was not the true purpose of my visit to Bordeaux on 13 December. There were difficulties with the BA airport handling agency and a 3 hour meeting with the local managers tried to resolve the problems. A satisfactory outcome achieved for both parties. I wrote my report before enjoying a good evening meal at a downtown restaurant. The next morning I arose at 0500 to be at the airport at 0635. Fog conditions at LHR disrupted airline schedules but I managed to re-route onto a TAT (French airline) which stopped at Nantes en route to LHR and arrived at 1235. The plane was an F28, Fokker Fellowship (a new aircraft type for me) registered F-GBBX. A colleague met me at LHR and I was in the office by 1400. Looking back now I am sure I was doing my health no good in taking on so many of these brief concentrated assignments.

However in the next 10 days my diary records six pre-Christmas lunch or dinner parties either in London or the Newbury area. As usual I spent 4 days over Christmas in Scotland with my mother and family.

23
TRANSFERRED TO GROUND DUTIES

Saturday 8 January 1983 started as a frosty morning and I again gave the pilots the weather briefing for the 11th International Icicle Balloon Meet. 72 different balloons flew that day and made a total of 90 free flights. Local pilot John Green flew his balloon 'Gemini' on 4 separate fights from Marsh Benham. There was a wide and varied social programme at the Elcot Park Hotel and in its adjoining marquee that evening. On the Sunday strong winds caused the meet to be abandoned.

Studley Priory Manor Hotel at Horton-cum-Studley was the venue for the 11th Annual Dante Dinner and Disco held on 22 January. This was the last I attended mainly due to access difficulties with my wheelchair. Dave Munson and family invited us to Sunday lunch at his home at Brill in Buckinghamshire to round off a good weekend.

Manager Eamonn Mulaney wanted a reservations transaction timings exercise in the Dusseldorf office and I travelled there on 08 February. The survey continued next day in a pre-lenten carnival atmosphere in the city. The following morning a sales rep drove me to Essen for a workload assessment at that office. After an overnight stop at the Sheraton Hotel on the 10th there was a generous covering of snow on the ground. On my way to the Essen office the walking sticks skidded and I fell, but luckily only suffered bruises. That afternoon BA 749 was overbooked and I was offloaded (a rare occurrence) but travelled to London on a later flight.

With computer engineer Len King I travelled to Helsinki on 02 March to finalise the move of the BA Sales Shop to new premises and to assess the suitability of the new airport offices. 25 hours later I was flying on another B737 back to LHR.

Another two day trip was made on 14 March but to Gothenburg. The purpose was for talks with the District Manager and London architect concerning proposed changes to the reservations premises. My northbound flight was on the morning SAS DC9 and I returned the next evening on a BA B737.

Copenhagen reservations unit did not always function smoothly. At the request of Manager John Wood (by 1999 his title was Director Pacific and North East Asia) I flew there on 11 April. The purpose of the two day visit was to conduct a survey on the alleged high work load. This was not really enough time to accurately assess the complexities of all the tasks allegedly undertaken by the staff. However my overall assessment and recommendations were accepted by the Manager. My return to LHR was on G-BIKA which was my first flight on a B757 aircraft.

Back to Bordeaux on 25 April. Within hours of arriving at the town office I had activated the ticket printer. After an uncomfortable night at the economy Frantel Hotel staff training on the ticket printer continued until noon on the 26th. There was a French aircraft called a Mercure (a limited edition of 10 passenger jets) and I wanted to fly on it from Bordeaux to Paris and then onward by BA to LHR. My ticket was changed for this routing. The Mercure went 'sick' in Paris and as the BA plane had left I was compelled to travel on an Air Inter B727 to Charles de Gaulle where it was necessary to have an uncomfortable coach ride to change airport terminals and catch the BA Tristar for London. That was the hassle I endured to try and fly on an obscure aeroplane. I learned a lesson and never again tried chasing odd aeroplanes.

Air France had the first flight of the day to Marseille so on 09 May I flew there on AF 1827 and was driven straight to the BA town office to 'cutover' the ticket printer. As with most of these jobs the staff stayed on for several hours after office closing to continue training on the machine(s). At noon the next day the Manager, Noel de Marque, organised a Champagne celebration to get local publicity for this 'new' technology. After a good lunch at the airport I flew home on a BAC 1-11 and I enjoyed a bumpy approach to runway 23 at LHR.

'Pocket Rocket' was the nick-name given to the small BA fleet of BAC 1-11, 539 variant aircraft. My first ride on one was to Lyon aboard G-BBKE. It was 19 May and another town office ticket printer 'cutover'. The local staff were 'jolie' and next day District Manager Clive Raymond gave me an early morning tour of the city. Both the ticket printer and automatic Ticket Sales Return systems worked perfectly. After collecting some good local wine I boarded another 'Pocket Rocket' for the 1 hour 20 minute flight to LHR.

Six days later I was flying again, this time to Vienna for a follow-up visit with Reservations Officer Elfi. The flight on 26 May did not arrive until 1325 local time hence discussions continued until early evening. Sales Rep Ekki and his wife then invited me to a local restaurant and park area for a good meal and Czech beer. The next morning I had a meeting with the Manager and visiting computer engineer Eric Nolan before catching the afternoon B737 back to London.

Election Day was 09 June and using sticks I found it difficult to stagger to the Polling booth. After that registered myself for a postal ballot.

Stavanger in west Norway was a new place to see when I visited on 16 June. The reservations office was at the airport and my job was to activate the ticket printer. It was a compact unit with friendly multi-functional staff. After work District Manager Clive Davis gave me a guided tour of the city in the long evening sunshine. Early the next morning the local sales rep showed me more of the surrounding area including the harbour and the local fish market where I bought several kilos of freshly landed prawns. By mid afternoon I was flying back to LHR.

As part of another internal BA re-organisation our reservations services unit was brought under a new manager. Peter Horder had the job of bringing 4 sections together and did well to reassure us at our first meeting on 22 June.

Was there a magnet in Copenhagen that attracted me to the place? The next day I flew to Kastrup Airport to 'cutover' the ticket printer. By 1930 all was well and I left for the Kong Frederick Hotel in the city. It was mid-summer day celebrations in Denmark and from the roof of the hotel I could clearly see the Tivoli Gardens and the giant fireworks display which lasted until midnight. As expected there was much merriment everywhere. However the next morning I was less amused when I waited 40 minutes for a (sober) taxi driver to return me to the airport. I flew back to London on BA 635 on 24 June.

Flying east to Istanbul was my next assignment on Sunday 03 July. The 3 hour 30 minute flight in Club Class had an expanded breakfast service which I rated highly. No one met me on arrival and I got a taxi to the Sheraton Hotel. The purpose of this trip was to assess the staffing levels and efficiency in the town reservations units. Manager Les Robertson showed me around the rambling offices and I found this tiresome with my unsteady walk. He had planned a day trip to the BA Ankara office on 05 July and assumed that I would accompany him. I declined his offer using as an excuse that my medical clearance was only for Europe and technically Ankara was in Asia. He went alone.

That decision was fortunate. Firstly I was able to see more of the reservations activities and secondly I would have missed an experience. A funny thing happened to me on my way from lunch ..... At 1430 an earth tremor jolted Istanbul as I was walking with the aid of sticks along an uneven pavement with alcohol in me. I did not feel a thing! Other pedestrians however, gave out wailing noises or screams. The office supervisor and I continued to the BA premises where the electricity had just failed. The earthquake was small and there was little structural damage. Fear was evident for the next few hours.

To leave Istanbul without many packets of local Turkish Delight would have been almost a sin. The choice selected for me was first class. It was a four hour flight home and we landed between heavy thunderstorms on 06 July.

Greenham Common Air Base was only a few miles from my Thatcham home but I rarely went near the area where the protesters against nuclear weapons had set up camp. On 22 July the RAF held an Air Tattoo which was noisy and I could see a lot of the display from my back garden.

BA had an 'implant' office inside the Ministry of Defence Brigade Headquarters in Berlin for ticketing the servicemen and families travelling on BA flights. On 01 August I flew to the city for talks with the airport supervisor and prepare the procedures to attend the Headquarters the following morning. Shortly after midday on 02 August I had initiated the ticket printers and auto sales report systems in a busy MOD office. After further talks at Tegel Airport with supervisor and staff I returned to London the next morning.

An upset stomach delayed my arrival at the 5th annual Bristol Balloon Fiesta on 12 August. There were many spectators for the Friday evening mass balloon ascent and I did the public address commentary. The Unicorn Hotel was chosen for me since the multi-story car park gave direct wheelchair access to the corridor leading to my bedroom.

Saturday the 13th was very hot and sunny. There was a mass ascent of balloons which started just before 0700 with some tethered commercial displays later in the morning. The evening mass ascent was delayed until after 1800 due to unstable and thermic wind conditions. The last flights did not take off until almost 2000. With a big crowd to witness the event this gave severe road traffic congestion from the site and I got caught in it. With the delay and fatigue factor I was too late, too tired and not in the mood to attend the Survivors Dinner. A fish and chip take-away and then to bed was more satisfactory to me. The next morning I arose at 0445 to be at the launch site an hour later, before the crowds, and start the commentary in time for the first ascents at 0630 in very calm conditions. Before midday weariness had overtaken me and I left Ashton Court to return home.

Longleat House in Wiltshire was the site for a BBAC balloon event on 21 August. I attended to see some of the people and not the balloons. The weather was truly dreadful with torrential rain. After some lunch in the crowded marquee I drove home.

Another chance to fly in Concorde became available to staff on the return sector after a charter flight. On 05 September I flew on the evening B747 from LHR at 1835 and arrived at JFK at 2125 local time. The flying time was 7 hours 50 minutes. I spent the night at a nearby hotel. Full of excitement I checked in at 1000 and was allocated seat 10B on Concorde G-BOAF. With Captain Brian Titchener in command the plane was airborne at 1545 GMT. During the 3 hours 21 minute flight the aircraft reached a maximum speed of Mach 2.01. This was my second flight on Concorde and was equally as exciting as the first. Most of the staff passengers who asked, visited the cockpit but unfortunately I was too stiff and unsteady on my feet that day. To compensate the flight deck and cabin crew kindly presented me with a signed Concorde certificate after we landed. Such an experience can never be forgotten.

Norwegians seemed to like the new science of ergonomics and staff in the BA office were a dedicated follower of this fashion. On 08 September I flew to Oslo for a rather high powered meeting on the subject in the BA office with the local manager, personnel department staff from London plus a local trades union official and an office staff member. The afternoon meeting dragged on and by evening my knowledge on the subject had improved. The next morning there was another meeting with some junior Norwegian Government officials and five of us from BA. It was amicably agreed to 'investigate' the problems. Without time for lunch a taxi sped me to Oslo Airport for the 1445 SAS flight to LHR.

Sometimes one month can be a long time. During the next 4 weeks my life changed direction several times. The salient points were:

a) On 12 September I was moved from my long held job in Reservation Services to the desk bound Reservations Procedures Unit under Gary Lovell.

b) 27 September I had a medical check at West London Air Terminal and discussions with personnel reference emergency evacuation from the building.

c) 30 September was our last day at the Victoria Air Terminal before our move to West London Air Terminal. There was a lot of sadness at the upheaval.

d) 03 October was the first day at WLAT and I was refused entry to the building until 0815 as the fire drill procedures certificate had not yet been signed. Medical Sister Shirley Grubb persuaded me to use a wheelchair to and from the basement canteen.

e) On 10 October I was due to have my last overseas duty trip. I had been looking forward to revisiting Budapest, which was a favourite city of mine. For some inexplicable reason, both physically and mentally, I could not leave the house at 0750 due to a sore hip and had to cancel the visit. It was a day of sadness as I started a week of sick leave due to extreme stiffness.

Another sad decision was made on 11 November when I attended the routine Dante Group meeting. Since I was able to contribute so little to the group balloon activities I felt it necessary to resign to allow a more active member to join. The past 12 years had given me hundreds of hours of joy, excitement, travel and most of all friendship with balloonists both in and outside the Dante Group.

Mans First Ever Flight was in a Montgolfiere hot air balloon across Paris on 21 November 1783. Two Frenchmen were airborne for 25 minutes and travelled about 5 and a half miles. Hundreds of spectators witnessed this event. To commemorate the 200th Anniversary the BBAC arranged to inflate the first British built balloon named 'Bristol Belle', G-AVTL, just minutes after midnight on the 21st. This was preceded by a banquet at Trentham Gardens, Stoke-on-Trent. It was rare to see so many balloon pilots from the youngest to the oldest at the dinner and enjoying themselves during the fireworks display following the tethered balloon ascent.

After only a few hours sleep I was one of the many spectators to see a sky-full of balloons take off from nearby fields to commemorate Montgolfiere Day. I had a late breakfast, then drove to Bristol and visited the Cameron Balloon factory. That evening the Western Region of the BBAC held its annual Dinner and I was honoured to be the guest speaker on this special day.

Gliding had interested me but I became very excited when Roger Barrett arranged for Tim Godfrey, also a balloon pilot, to give me a flight on 03 December. It was 1223 at the Dunstable Gliding Club when a light aircraft gave us an airtow in glider ECM. There was moderate thermal activity which carried us up to almost 3000 feet and I was enthralled as we sailed through the air. Tim then suggested he demonstrate how to stall a glider. At less than 30 knots it dutifully slid sidewards and earthwards. I was in an undemonstrative but happy frame of mind and when asked if I enjoyed that, replied "Yes, very good.". Tim then offered to repeat the experience and let the air speed fall even lower to give a shuddering stall. Again I enjoyed the thrill but said nothing. Tim was the one who uttered expletives as he frightened himself. Soon afterwards the 23 minute flight ended with a good landing near the club house. Without saying too much Tim was quickly in the bar for a large drink.

Strong winds persisted over Britain for more than 10 days from 21 December. On the 23rd I travelled on the Trident 3 shuttle, G-AWZF, from LHR to Edinburgh and because of the winds the plane flew at the unusually low level of 14000 feet. The Trident was the only modern jet liner that could put its engines into reverse thrust before landing. This allowed a faster approach speed in unstable or cross winds and to me was an added excitement to a flight. After 4 days with my mother and family over Christmas I returned to London.

1984

Five balloons made free flights on Saturday 08 January and six balloons on the Sunday of the 12th annual Icicle Meet. The low numbers were due to gusty surface winds and this was the last year that I gave the pilots the official met briefing. There was some interest for all with the social programme at the Elcot Park Hotel, which included an increasingly large Sales display, Club meetings and buffet supper.

Larnica in Cyprus was to be my last overseas holiday, unconnected to ballooning. On 19 February my brother Gordon and I flew on my free firm airline tickets for a six day break. During the 4 hour 15 minute flight on Tristar G-BBAF there was time for me to visit the flight deck after the Club Class lunch. The Karpasiana Beach Hotel was only a short distance from the airport and offered good facilities. I had wisely chosen the full package which gave us priority at the superb buffet, barbecue and local 4-course dinner evenings. Mostly the weather was warm or hot and sunny and the hotel pool was easier for me than the nearby beach. Gordon hired a car and we drove to Nicosia crossing part of the Troudos Mountains with their excellent views. Other excursions included driving up to the United Nations peace line of the Turkish sector and visiting a local market and then a supermarket for some good local fruit and wines. On one afternoon I met by chance some ex-colleagues from my BEA days. Despite my disability it was a wonderful holiday, with a choice of great foods, good hotel service and an interesting variety of guests. On 25 February the same Tristar aircraft flew us back to LHR.

Meetings were never a favourite with me. The AGM of the BBAC was held on St Patrick's Day (17 March) and there was enough blarney around to make this the last such event I ever attended. It was held at the Holiday Inn near Slough which allowed some of the Dante members and I to escape quickly to an Indian Curry House at Windsor.

Sore throat and infections rarely affected me. From mid-March for a month I was troubled by a series of minor illnesses. On a routine visit to Dr Perkins at Charing Cross Hospital he recommended I try a relatively 'new cure' for MS. This involved HBO - hyperbaric oxygen treatment - in a diving chamber. There were only 3 or 4 multiple person chambers available in the UK at that time. Quickly I phoned all the centres and by luck got a vacancy at the MS research station at Dundee in Scotland. On 29 April I drove the 445 miles from Thatcham to my mother's house at Rosyth and stayed there for the next 24 nights.

Monday 30 April I started the 20 day HBO course in the diving bell with 3 other patients. For the first week the pressure in the chamber was set at 17 feet and thereafter at 24 feet. Apart from the extra oxygen in the compartment we wore masks to give extra oxygen to the body. The principle was to saturate the blood and hopefully this would dissolve or break up any fatty substances which were affecting the central nervous system. Each session lasted for one hour and the cost of the course was £250. The car journey time from Dundee to Rosyth took just over an hour via the Tay Road Bridge and then I had the choice of several scenic or motorway routes.

Very high protein foods were recommended and I seemed to over-eat on venison steaks, red meats, eggs, fish plus nuts. We were advised there would be almost daily fluctuations in our condition during the course but overall there should be an improvement if we continued with 'top-up' sessions every fortnight for the next 3 to 6 months. I followed this recommendation with the one hour 'top-ups' in a single person chamber at Basingstoke. As there was no apparent change in my condition I stopped the sessions after four months.

Rising at 0430 I was able to leave Thatcham before 0530 to be at the WLAT in Cromwell Road London just after 0700. I would leave the office at 1530 and was usually home by 1700. This was my regular routine from 24 May until February

1985. There was a farewell party for our Manager Peter Horder on 31 May. The following morning we met our new Manager Stan Mason who was very sympathetic to our individual needs and later allowed me to work a staggered pattern which included the then uncommon practice of preparing job assignments at home. In mid-July Chris May joined the Reservations Procedures Unit and he helped Mike Wickins with the extended work load on the hotel and car booking activities. John Eagan was our contact on the Reservations Systems side and on the development of Timatic.

Holiday time was again spent in Wales when Kim and I had five relaxing days at the home of Anne and Peter Lewis-Smith from 22 July. Although high season the area north of Fishguard in West Wales did not seem crowded and the local trades-folk were friendly and seemed happy in their own slower way of life.

Three weeks later it was the annual Bristol Balloon Fiesta. Again I did the public commentary for the 3 days from 17 to 19 August, assisted by Roger Harper. That year fog and low stratus was the weather problem but balloons flew every day. The excitement of the Meet was the appearance of a Smoke Balloon from America. I had seen a smoke balloon flight ten years earlier in August 1974 at Indianola, Iowa and its operation is described in that year.

Shepperton Studios, west of London, made an interesting site to visit on 06 September when I saw many of the pseudo-locations used in film making. My purpose for visiting was to do the voice-over for the audio visual to be used at the Newbury Museum in its balloon section. The first attempt was not a total success so I had another session there on 04 October.

Nuneham Park near Oxford was the venue for a two day charity Balloon Event from 08 September. The organisers wanted a public commentator and I volunteered. Sadly for the spectators only one free balloon flight took place due to strong winds.

An ambition was realised on 12 September when I took a pre-arranged return trip to Milan on the flight deck of a Boeing 757 with Dave Munson as the Senior First Officer and Captain Joel. Flights BA 510 and 511 were operated by G-BIKB and we left LHR at 0830 and arrived at Linate Airport at 1015. The plane had a scheduled 1 hour 45 minute turn round time and the ground staff helped me into the building and kindly presented me with 3 bottles of local wine. It was a fine clear day and the views were exciting as we passed overhead Geneva and close to the Alps. The Captain did a manual landing at Milan and Dave set the aircraft up for a fully automatic (category 3B) landing at LHR. This ranks as one of the more satisfying flights.

Malmesbury in Wiltshire is a small town but I heard through a friend that there was a development under construction which might have a suitable early retirement home for me. After an initial viewing of the flats I visited Orchard Court on 26 September. Almost instantly and intuitively I said "Yes" to Flat number 9. This was a decision I was not to regret. Two days later I contacted my solicitor and started the process to buy the property by sending a £200 deposit to the builders based in Cirencester. The timetable of events went like this:

02 Oct   Speedy action threw me into a wobble as the Thatcham estate agent called and put 57 Derwent Road on the market.

04 Oct   Spoke to the Woolwich Building Society reference my mortgage.

07 Oct   Two prospective buyers viewed my house and I heard the next day that one had said yes.

08 Oct   Completed Building Society mortgage application form.

20 Nov   Woolwich mortgage offer arrived.

21 Nov   Was told by the builders that my flat would be available by early February.

Next came the 200th anniversary of the first balloon flight by an Englishman. The date was 06 October and the balloonist was James Sadler who flew from Oxford. To commemorate this many of us paid tribute at his gravestone in St Edmunds College before a festive lunch. BBAC President Anthony Smith gave an enlightening speech. By late afternoon we went to a balloon field but due to strong winds only 6 balloons were able to fly free.

British Airways had become a Public Limited Company in April but an extravagant display of the new Corporate Livery did not take place until 06 December. I attended one of the sessions in a hanger at LHR where a change of paint and design lifted our spirits in the airline.

One of the best Reservations Services parties I attended was a Christmas lunch held in a Chinese Restaurant in London's Soho on 21 December. George Pleece, Reservations Services Superintendent Eastern Region, arranged the event and my diary description simply says 'Good beyond description.'.

The following day I maintained the tradition of flying to Scotland where my mother cooked the family Christmas dinner. Four mornings later a Trident 3 Shuttle flew me back to LHR.

24

NEW HOUSE, NEW WORKPLACE AND BA COMPUTER AT HOME

Most of the previous years in my life had been full of excitement and adventure. 1985 also had periods of elation and enjoyment but ended a little less happily with a circulation problem on one foot.

As I was no longer involved in the organisation of the annual Icicle Balloon Meets I watched the 13th event as a spectator. On Saturday the 5th of January I attended the expanded trade display which had moved location to the Newbury College Centre.

From 08 January for almost 3 weeks there was a period of very cold weather with almost continuous sub-zero temperatures and at times heavy snow falls. On 16 January Central London had its coldest day for 21 years with a daytime temperature of minus 4 degrees Celsius. This cold snap coincided with my feeling unwell and needing antibiotics. The bad road conditions for the 2 weeks from 14 to 27 January would probably have prevented me from driving to London anyway.

Without ever seeing my solicitor, Mrs Hammond of Camberley, I signed the title deeds and other documents for Orchard Court on 29 January. The date to move in was confirmed as 08 February.

Next followed the horrible task of sorting out years of accumulated rubbish and packing in preparation for the move to the smaller flat. My brother flew from Scotland on 05 February and I had difficulty in curbing his enthusiasm to 'chuck it out'.

Friday 08 February was moving day. As Gordon and I drove west along the M4 it started to sleet and by the time we got to Malmesbury there was an inch of lying snow. The removal van had unloaded my goods by 1400. The tedious task of unpacking then started. It continued until late evening and again from early morning on the Saturday. Overnight there had been much snow and with a level 3 inches on the ground my brother wanted to return to Scotland lest he be marooned in Malmesbury. I drove him to LHR along the only single lane open on the M4 to Heathrow where he caught a Shuttle flight to Edinburgh. Without even a rest stop at the airport I drove as quickly as I dared and arrived home shortly after darkness. There were sub-zero temperatures for the next 2 days whilst I continued unpacking. Apart from the warden, Judith, there were only 4 other residents on the estate as houses were still being built.

The St Valentine's Day surprise for me was a phone call from my boss saying there was a chance that the BA computer, BABS, might be installed in my new house. This meant I would be one of the first to have this facility at home. The few other sets were all with senior managers.

A daily motorway drive, of 170 miles round trip, to and from London put some strain on my health. Less than a mile from the WLAT there was the Tara Hotel which had a number of rooms adapted for the disabled. By negotiation I got a special rate which enabled me to stay overnight on Wednesdays. From 27 February my new work routine was to arrive in the office by 1000 and remain until 1930 before going to the hotel. On the following morning (Thursday) I would be in the office by 0830 and leave at 1530. My manager, Stan Mason, was very considerate and I always had enough 'home-work' to keep me busy for the other three days.

During March and April Kim often visited from Oxford to arrange and organise my furniture and fittings. My mother also wanted to help and flew down from Scotland and 'encouraged' me to visit the shops in Bristol. Buying household items is not my idea of a happy day out.

RAF Hullavington, just 3 miles from Malmesbury, was a non-operational flying station except for a semi-military gliding club and the occasional visit of a barrage balloon for cadet training. A motorised glider manned by RAF staff sometimes flew from there and through a charity took disabled people for a short flight. On 04 May I flew in this plane, registered G-BSEL, and was airborne for 22 minutes and took the controls for part of this time. It was an interesting but relatively 'tame' experience. One year later I had another flight in this aircraft which was more exciting as the pilot did some aerobatics overhead Minchinhampton Common near Stroud in Gloucestershire and the flight lasted for 70 minutes.

30 May we had a farewell party at West London Air Terminal as we were about to move to Comet House at Heathrow. WLAT had been

our work place for just 20 months and as the building was up for sale all BA staff were being relocated.

Wednesday, 12 June, I started yet another routine by leaving Malmesbury at 0545 to arrive at LHR by 0700 and working through until 1900. I then drove a few miles to the Holiday Inn to spend the night. The following morning I would be at the office by 0730 and remain until 1530.

Tom Sheppard, Meet Director, of the 7th World Hot Air Balloon Championships again invited me to be an official of the organising team. My job was listed as official scorer coordinator working in the computer room. On 11 July I flew from LHR on G-BBPU for Detroit with a transfer connection to a US Air Casa 210 aircraft for Battle Creek, Michigan, with an intermediate stop at Kalamazoo. It was 2045 local time when I got to the Stofeffar Hotel which was the same headquarters used for the 6th World event 2 years previously.

At lunch time the next day there was the official registration procedure for pilots and crews and a chance to meet many friends including the 12 British pilots. On Saturday the 13th there was a press reception and interviews at the Kellogg's airfield hanger. Being in the company of World Champion Bruce Comstock and being a Brit and being a minor official and being disabled I was nobbled by a reporter from a local Sunday newspaper. I made just one big mistake. I opened my mouth and talked. What appeared in print (with a photo) the next day was almost pulp fiction. When I read the article the next morning I wanted to buy all the copies from the hotel newstand to prevent anyone else from seeing it.

Violent thunderstorms woke most of us before 0530 on Sunday the 14th and continued for more than 2 hours, hence no flying. Local liquor laws precluded drinking before noon on Sundays but we all enjoyed a brunch party in mid-morning. The first official task took off after the 1800 briefing and we were kept busy in the computer room until 0300 collating the scores.

Shortly after 0900 I was awakened with a request to address the Battle Creek Rotarians on the subject of ballooning. Without any preparation the 30 minute talk was well received - I always found it easier to make an impromptu speech. By 1800 that Monday along with several other officials I was at the 'drop-zone' to watch some of the balloons fly in windy conditions. Then back to the computer room to check and enter the scores which took us until almost day-break.

After attending pre-flight briefings on 16 July, I was at work in the computer room all afternoon before being driven to the launch site to see several hydrogen gas balloons take off. Two competitors collided in mid-air and the American balloon pilot was badly injured after a very heavy landing. It caused an upset in the flying programme and amongst some pilots but our work in the computer unit continued until well after 0200.

It was hot and sunny on 17 July when we attended a huge lunchtime picnic on an island site. The heat affected my mobility and I did not enjoy the gathering. The air-conditioned hotel computer room kept us busy from 2200 until almost 0500 the next morning. Even after that stint we were still not fully up to date with an accurate score list. Pilot protests at the deduction of penalty points for flying infringements were causing delays.

The next day we were still working on results from task number 9 whilst the pilots were flying task number 11. The paperwork involved and the double scrutiny was slowly overwhelming the system before it even reached the two professional computer operators, Cheryl and Robin.

19 July was the last official championship day and Meet Director Tom wanted to get in the maximum number of tasks (a record at 13). By lunchtime the paperwork was mounting and some of it remained unscrutinised. The Japanese hosted a midday reception which gave a premature end-of-term atmosphere to some officials. Debbie Spaeth, a member of the Organising Team, was especially kind to me when help was needed with a variety of difficulties such as transport. There was the compulsory group photo session at the airport in late afternoon before almost everyone went out to parties. From 1930 until 2330 Cheryl and I were the lone 'workers' in the computer room but with very little to do until the others returned from dinner.

Starting before 1130 the next day there was the Official Awards Ceremony with brunch. Here the results of the Competition were announced. An American, David Levin, was the declared Champion with British pilot Crispin Williams in second place. A protest had not been fully resolved. Months later after a forthright appeal through the BBAC, Royal Aero Club and FAI the correct number of penalty points were adjusted which gave Crispin the highest number. In reality he was the World Champion. However the Championship rules state that the name of the winner announced at the Official Ceremony cannot be changed.

Kalamazoo Airport to Detroit was to be my last US domestic flight when I left at 1750 on 20 July. For the record the plane was a Convair 500 registered N968N. I did not realise it then but I was about to have my last trans-Atlantic flight. This was on BA 074 from Detroit to LHR on a B747 registered G-AWNA. The flight landed at 0840 BST on 21 July and I drove home, very tired. (That aircraft, G-AWNA, along with five other old B747-136 series was withdrawn from BA service at the end of 1998.)

Bristol Balloon Fiesta weekend was from 16 to 18 August. Friday morning flying was curtailed by some wind and rain but in the evening 35 balloons either tethered or took off at 'pilot's discretion'. The Red Arrows gave a full display to the crowd at 1700. Probably the most interesting sight was to see 3 hydrogen gas balloons take off in a gusty wind shortly after midday. The smallest of these, size A2 at just 250 cubic metres capacity, was first away and radioed back that he had crossed the M4 near Swindon in just 35 minutes! The French pilot, Vincent Leys, had flown solo. Another French balloon was next followed by Gerry Turnbull and his son Richard piloting Omega III, G-BDTU, with Fiesta secretary Angela Smith as passenger. My job as usual was to do the commentary. The less flying often meant the most talking .....

Saturday 17 August was an historic date in British Ballooning history. In the 1 hour from 0645 there were 94 hot air balloon take-offs and 3 hot air airships flying from Ashton Court. That was a record for any single mass-ascent of LTA (Lighter Than Air) craft anywhere ever in the UK or Europe. This the 7th Bristol International Balloon Fiesta made yet another record. Chief sponsor, London Life, agreed to have 11 hydrogen filled gas balloons at the Meet. This was also a new British record, certainly since World War II. The previous number of 10 gas balloons was at Stanton Harcourt in 1965. Jonathan Harris was the balloonmeister and Nick Bosanquet was the co-ordinator. The average time taken to fill a hydrogen balloon and get airborne was more than 2 hours and the first of these took off just after 1100.

Maybe as a reward for manning the public address system over the years I had my first (and only) flight in a gas balloon. I was given space in the French balloon, named Pierre Ladeveze with Michel Dubernard and two other pilots from L'Association Aerostatique du Nord de la France. We took off a few minutes after noon when there was not much wind but quite a lot of thermal activity and I was fascinated to see how the balloon reacted in such conditions. F-GCXB drifted slowly towards Bath at almost 4000 feet then with a mind of its own flew around the city a second time as we plotted the movements of inter-city trains below. Near Bradford-on-Avon we approached a deep valley where the cool air caused the balloon to descend quite rapidly. The crew responded by shovelling trowel-fulls of sand (the ballast) overboard. The response by the balloon was slow and almost a bag full was released before the balloon started to climb. I was sitting on a stool in a corner of the basket but beginning to feel uncomfortable and asked the pilot if we could land when a suitable field appeared. Shortly afterwards with judicious use of the venting system some hydrogen was released and the balloon started its descent. By dragging the trail rope through two small hedges the flight ended in a stand-up landing after 3 hours and 35 minutes. This will remain as another of my most memorable flights.

By 0600 on Sunday the 18th I was at Ashton Court where many pilots were keen to fly. Again the weather was frustrating them with drizzle and low cloud. A few balloons did fly in marginal conditions.

That year a total of 115 different balloons attended the Fiesta. The Bristol Junior Chamber had skilfully developed the Meet into the principle public event in the City of Bristol. It was also profitable with an estimated revenue to Bristol of more than £1 million.

After work on 11 September, and before going to the Holiday Inn for my weekly night stop, I visited the West Drayton Air Traffic Control Centre from 1830 until 2200. This security conscious building houses the main civil and military ATC movements for the UK. Dante Group members Ian Culley and John Baker showed me several 'sectors' and as always I was fascinated to see the radar blips and the skilful integration of these along the various airways.

Belmont Abbey in Hereford was the Benedictine Abbey where my second cousin, Philip Smith, was ordained to the priesthood on 14 September. I attended the early evening Ordination Mass. Before the ceremony there was a reception and tea at which I met a number of distant relatives, many for the first time. I stayed overnight in an annex and attended Philip's first Mass at 0930 on the Sunday morning.

By midday I was driving to the Nuneham Park (Oxford) Balloon and Parachute event. As in the previous year my job was to do the commentary on the ballooning but the wind speeds were above the limits and even tethered displays proved impossible.

An important event in my life was the installation of the BABS, the BA computer, in my home on 01 October. The engineer, Ted Darnell, had no problems and the system was working by 1130. It gave me great satisfaction to be able to do my computer work at home.

Amstrad had just brought out an improved personal computer and demand exceeded the initial supply. With luck and after many phone calls I reserved a set at Dixons in Bristol. On 05 October I collected the equipment and with help from a neighbour installed the machine by mid-afternoon. This item is recorded as it was the start of a general trend in many British homes towards the acquisition of a personal computer.

There were many annoying breakdowns with my car on the motorway during October. On 01 November I ordered a new Escort 1.6 automatic from Fords of Bristol. The vehicle needed hand controls to be fitted and I did not take delivery until January 1986.

Celebrations for the 20th anniversary of the formation of the British Balloon and Airship Club (BBAC) were organised by me for 30 November. It was a low-key event with President Anthony Smith, Anne Lewis-Smith, David and Jo Liddiard and Pete and Elaine Bish at the Five Bells Public House at Wickham near Newbury. There was no flying but we all enjoyed a happy lunch.

With my walking becoming more unstable I found it necessary to use the wheelchair more often. This affected my circulation and a pressure sore developed on the small toe of my right foot. During December the problem got worse and I saw two of the local doctors. The day after I returned from Christmas in Scotland another GP diagnosed gangrene. At the time I did not appreciate the significance of this, and celebrated New Year's Eve without any anxiety.

With my love of statistics, a list of the countries I visited either on BA duty or for pleasure follows. (Some have since changed their names.)

This list of 86 excludes the places in which I was in transit on an aircraft such as Angola, Ecuador, Ghana, the Gulf States and Iraq.

To complete this list of statistics, the furthest North / South / East and West points I visited were:

North: Reykjavik, Iceland at 64.09N.
South: Rotorua, New Zealand at 38.07S
East: Rotorua, New Zealand at 176.17E
West: San Francisco, USA at 122.27W

Western Hemisphere		Africa & Near East	Asia & Pacific	Europe
Antigua	St Kitts	Egypt	Australia	Austria
Argentina	St Maarten	Ethiopia	Ceylon	Belgium
Bahamas	St Vincent	Kenya	Hong Kong	Canary Islands
Barbados	Tobago	Lebanon	India	Cyprus
Bermuda	Trinidad	Libya	Japan	Czechoslovakia
Brazil	USA	Malawi	Nepal	Denmark
British Virgin Islands	US Virgin Islands	Mauritius	New Zealand	Finland
Canada	Venezuela	Nigeria	Singapore	France
Cayman Islands		Rhodesia	Thailand	Germany
Chile		Seychelles		Gibraltar
Colombia		South Africa		Greece
Costa Rica		Sudan		Hungary
Dominica		Tanzania		Iceland
Dominican Republic		Zambia		Italy
El Salvador		Zanzibar		Luxembourg
Grenada				Malta
Guadeloupe				Monaco
Guatemala				Netherlands
Guyana				Norway
Jamaica				Poland
Martinique				Portugal
Mexico				Spain
Montserrat				Sweden
Nevis				Switzerland
Panama				Turkey
Peru				USSR
Puerto Rico				Yugoslavia

25
THE YEARS 1986-1999

This chapter for the next 13 years has been truncated. As well as aviation experiences it includes some details of my health problems.

Consultant Surgeon Andrew Turnbull of the Royal United Hospital (RUH) in Bath arranged my admission on 06 January 1986. The purpose was to amputate the little toe infected with gangrene. During my 9 day stay other tests and minor surgery (angiogrames and angioplasty) were done to improve the arterial blood supply to my right leg.

Shortly before Easter I returned to the routine of a once-a-week visit to the BA office at LHR and over-night stay at the Holiday Inn. Having taken delivery of my new car in January it made travelling on the motorway more tolerable.

On 09 August I was re-admitted to the RUH with a gangrene sore which had developed on my right foot. Three days later part of the foot was amputated but the ankle fluid joint was damaged and would not heal. Because of uncontrolled spasms in my leg it was not possible to repair the leaking joint. Many valiant attempts failed and I remained in hospital for the next 7 months. In December Mr Turnbull said there was no alternative but to amputate the right leg. I asked for and got a second opinion from an independent consultant. After giving me some kind and comforting words his prognosis was 'the leg must go'.

Christmas and New Year in hospital was as happy as it could be. I had many friends from Malmesbury, some colleagues from work and a good number of balloonists visit me in the Aubrey Bateman Ward.

On 13 January 1987 my right leg was amputated at the 'through-knee' joint. I recovered easily from the general anaesthetic and the wound also healed quickly. There was just one small weeping sore that persisted for more than a fortnight. The physiotherapists then had me hobbling along on my good leg.

An Occupational Therapist arranged for an overhead hoist to be fitted in my bedroom at home to allow me to transfer to and from the wheelchair. After what seemed like ages, I finally left hospital on 16 March to re-adjust my life. With help from a home carer, provided by Social Services but paid for by me, I was able to do most things as before.

My arms were unaffected and I was able to tranfer from bed to wheelchair. With the aid of a 'slide board' I could get across the passenger seat of my car and drive without any problem. The biggest impediment was in fact my 'good leg', which had to be dragged everywhere I moved.

By early April I returned to work when I did a once-weekly day trip to the office to keep informed on new developments. British Airways was going through a period of expansion and I needed the knowledge for my contributions when updating the computer at home.

Karen Coombes was a lively and bubbly commercial balloon pilot whom I had met when in hospital and she kindly took me out for lunchtime excursions after my operation. On 02 July Karen, with her crew from Bath University, brought a balloon to nearby Burton Hill School at Malmesbury to give me a flight. It was a perfect summer evening and I had a happy 20 minute flight in G-BNBR a Cameron N-90. We landed on Malmesbury Common and then went to The Vine Tree pub to enjoy celebratory drinks and a meal.

Bristol International Balloon Fiesta number 9 was held from 14 to 16 August 1987 and I gave the public address commentary. It was an event where many records were made. For our club magazine 'Aerostat' I wrote an article entitled 'Almost 700 up at the 9th'. This heading was inspired by the breaking of some European Records.

1) 129 hot air balloons took off in a mass ascent, within 65 minutes, on the Saturday morning (August 15th).

2) 127 balloons flew on the Saturday evening mass ascent to make the total for the day of 256.

3) Maximum density - 76 balloons got airborne in 30 minutes on the Saturday evening.

4) The weekend total was 659 free flights plus 34 tethered displays during the 3 days. This gave a grand total of 693 airships and balloons.

Other highlights from this Fiesta included:

a) A World Record of 45 people flew together in the same big balloon of 850,000 cubic feet capacity for 70 minutes on Sunday morning the 16th. The balloon was PH-EEN piloted by Dutch owner Henk Brink.

b) Local estimates put the total number of spectators during the three days at Ashton Court at three quarters of a million. The local press reckoned that at least double that number of people had seen the balloons in the sky over Bristol.

c) The British Airways balloon, G-BHOT, flew on five occasions and attracted quite a lot of attention..

d) With very light winds a number of balloons flew within feet of the Clifton Suspension Bridge and drifted down the Gorge. The TV and press got some excellent photos of this spectacle.

Despite my immobility I flew to Scotland on an Edinburgh Shuttle to spend Christmas with my mother and family. I stayed at a nursing home 12 miles outside Dumfermline. It was maybe one of the most sober Christmas times of my life as the anti-spasm tablets had a label on the bottle with the dreadful words 'Avoid Alcohol'.

Savernake Forest, Marlborough in Wiltshire was the take-off site for the first flight of a wheelchair accessible balloon basket fitted with hand controls for the burner. Colin Wolstenholme had brought along a Colt AX8-90A balloon registered G-BOBU on 19 February 1988. A BBC News West TV team had come along to film the flight and I was the passenger to operate the controls with Colin as pilot. At 0830 on a perfect morning for flying, the balloon took off with a cameraman aboard to record the event. After a brief intermediate landing the flight continued until 0921. Naturally I was pleased at being part of this the world's first such flight.

We all enjoyed a glass of champagne at the landing place, near a Roman Road at Scot's Poor. Then we returned to the launch area at Warren Farm, home of David's son, James Liddiard. He and his wife Fiona prepared and served a huge farmhouse breakfast for ten of us involved with the flight. Pilot Colin then signed the 50 commemorative balloon post covers carried on the flight which the Post Office later hand-franked. An unrepeatable morning!

That evening the BBC TV News transmitted the story with an in-flight sequence and the cameraman, David Saunders, falling over during the landing. My broadcast comment described it as "a positive landing". Four months later David Saunders took a friend and I for a flight in his private aircraft from Old Sarum airstrip near Salisbury, Wiltshire.

In May 1989 with just 2 weeks prior notice, accompanied by Ann Ryan, I joined the Knights of Malta on a pilgrimage to the shrine of Our Lady of Lourdes in France. We flew from Luton Airport on a Ryan Air BAC 1-11.

After breakfast on the first morning, while sitting at the table with a Union Jack in front of me, a gentle voiced Irish girl asked me if I was ready. I replied, "yes" and was wheeled away to join a line of pilgrims waiting to attend Mass. Not recognising any others around me I queried where we were going. There was an indistinct reply as we moved off to the underground chapel. With Irish flags on the altar I again asked if this was the British group. The lovely girl replied, "No, but you can't get out now". I then realised I had been hijacked by the Irish! After the one hour service I was re-united with the British contingent who had been searching for me.

With a variety of religious and secular activities the remaining six days were all interesting. The candlelight processions, lasting about two hours, were facinating as prayers and singing were recited alternatively in at least five languages. I stayed at the St Bernadette Hospital and had numerous helpers for assistance. One in particular, Justin Shaw, was I felt allocated to keep an eye on me from getting lost. He became a good friend and even now, ten years later, calls at Malmesbury for a meal and a drive to various nearby historic and scenic places.

Less than 10 miles from here is the Arboretum at Westonburt. On many visits there, sometimes with Justin, I have always marvelled at the beauty and variety of trees. In quiet moments when amongst them I could appreciate that their purpose in living was to grow as strong, preferably as straight and as tall as possible to attract maximum daylight. If I was in contemplative mode I could liken the singular life of a tree to that of a straightforward human.

John Wilkinson, whom I first met 15 years earlier at a Cirencester Balloon Meet, had been editor of the BBAC Club journal Aerostat from February 1987 until June 1989. I was sorry to see him leave for Australia. He had been helpful to me for a number of years especially during my move from London to Thatcham.

For my 15th birthday in Bermuda (1948) my parents bought me a typewriter mainly to prepare lists for my father. I used it also to submit scripts and reports for various small publications. That trait became a habit and throughout my life I have written many hundreds of reports, both for work and my leisure pursuits. British, American and foreign balloon publications carried my reports and I continued writing for the new editor of Aerostat, John Christopher, from August 1989 onwards.

As usual I did the commentary at the 11th Bristol Balloon Fiesta in August 1989, organised by Bristol Balloon Fiestas Ltd. Don Cameron was Meet Director with Jonathan Harris as Technical Director. Saturday morning 169 different balloons took off including 4 hot air airships and 12 special shapes. Almost 900 people attended the Survivors dinner in the marquee erected on the site. On Sunday, starting before the official 0600 briefing time, 123 balloons flew free and 17 others tethered. Soon afterwards strong winds arrived and the Meet was abandoned. There was heavy commercial sponsorship.

On 31 January 1990 I officially took early retirement from BA but attended the office once a month until mid Summer. I was on a consultancy contract to work at home when required, using the BA computer. This arrangement continued until September 1993 when the BA contract was farmed out to Morgan and Banks, a subsidary firm of consultants with the name Speedwing. This has continued as an annual renewal, the last being in January 1999.

22nd March was the day of the Big Storm in Southern England. By early afternoon the wind at Heathrow was 55 knots gusting to 68 knots. My mother flew from Edinburgh to land at LHR on the cross-wind runway 23 in a B757 but described the approach as "not too bad".

Flown on the maiden flight of the World's First Hot Air Balloon Basket certified to carry a wheelchair passenger and fitted with hand-held controls to an automatic pilot. I was the passenger and Colin Wolstenholme was the pilot. A BBC TV newsman filmed the on-board experience and it appeared as an item on the evening news. The date was 19 February 1988.

What was very bad was our six hour road journey to Malmesbury on the M4 which was partly closed in places due to overturned vehicles.

Attended the 12th Bristol Balloon Fiesta in mid August and helped with the public address system. It was the biggest event yet with a wide variety of attractions and 756 hot air balloon flights plus airships and hydrogen balloons. The intense commercial aspect, including the interjection of snazzy music during my commentary, did not appeal to me. This was the last Bristol Fiesta I attended.

Using a special wheelchair-accessible basket I enjoyed a 55 minute flight from Great Shefford, Berkshire on 02 December. David Boxall was the pilot and Kim Cameron was also on board. There were hand controls available so I was able to 'fly' the balloon across the M4 (above the legal minimum of 1500 feet of course!). We landed not far from the A34 near Newbury. The retrieve crew met us and brought chilled champagne and a selection of delicious home-made sandwiches. A winter open-air picnic (temperature was just 6 degrees C) rounded off an enjoyable Sunday lunchtime.

David Boxall, working for Cameron Balloons, was a design engineer who by computer helped 'manufacture' the complex hybrid envelope for the 'Breitling Orbiter 3' balloon. This craft made the First Non-Stop Round-the-World Balloon Flight from 01 to 20 March 1999.

During late spring 1991 a pressure sore developed on the big toe of my left foot as a result of poor circulation and a badly fitting shoe. I attended Malmesbury Hospital almost daily until August when Consultant Andrew Turnbull suggested he should cut off the bad toe.

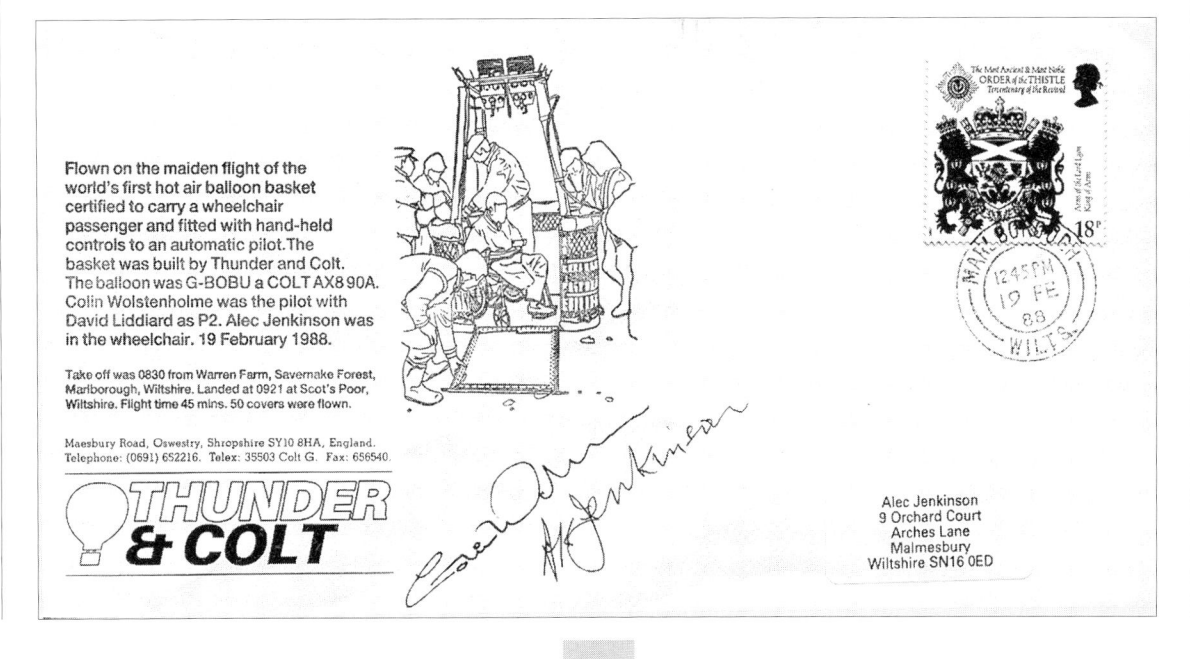

On 3rd September, the day of the proposed operation, whilst surgeon Mr Turnbull was briefing me on the procedure I asked to have the entire left leg amputated. One leg was a useless lump of flesh and bone which hindered my driving and impeded moving to and from the wheelchair. Mr Turnbull was somewhat taken aback when I made this request and I asked that he perform a similar 'through knee' amputation to give me a matching pair! Later that day it was done and it was a decision I have never regretted.

Forty staples were removed from the wound on 11 September and the bruised area healed quickly. I was able to return to Malmesbury Hospital on 15 September to convalesce. Ten days later I was back in my own home, happy but lighter in weight at 55 kilos.

Maria Melborne, the local Occupational Therapist, was extremely helpful and kind and suggested some modifications to my flat. This included a ramp into the kitchen which raised the floor and made the working surfaces more accessible from my wheelchair.

John Christopher, Editor of the BBAC journal Aerostat, produced a book entitled 'Hot - Air', capturing a good cross-section of events of '25 years of hot air ballooning in Great Britain'. This 1991 edition was published by his Skyline Company. The book quoted a number of articles I had written for Aerostat including one that was critical of the way commercial sponsorship was dominating ballooning, which for me was a leisure sport. My thoughts were out of fashion as it seems today most 'sports' are governed by commercialism.

05 December 1991 was the 20th anniversary of my first ever balloon flight. To commemorate the occasion I arranged a celebration flight with permission from the RAF at Hullavington. Don Cameron agreed to pilot the balloon, Colin Wolstenholme brought along the wheelchair accessible basket and many Dante Group members came to help. It was a cold day with a strong gusty wind so only a tethered flight was possible. I was grateful to all who had helped but a little disappointed not to have made a free flight. Afterwards we had a celebration lunch and drinks at the Knoll House Hotel, Malmesbury.

Again my mother flew from Scotland to spend Christmas and New Year with me.

Flying this time from Stansted Airport I joined the annual Knights of Malta pilgrimage to Lourdes during the first week of May 1992. It was a French airline and the plane was a veteran Caravelle. I had met many of the helpers and a few of the pilgrims two years earlier.

For me Lourdes holds happy memories, not only because of the diversity of the people there, but because of the deep sense of 'togetherness' in a religious way. It is thought provoking time to see so many people of different nationalities with the same common goal. Even the sad but realistic sight of seeing sick people try and utter a final prayer before dying made me appreciate how fortunate I was.

During the week whilst I was away my flat had been fully redecorated. I wanted to, and did, write another booklet with the title 'Balloons Around Newbury - Twenty Adventurous Years.' using my Amstrad PC. It was not always easy to get the historical information I wanted in the few months I had set aside for the project. The private publisher was irritatingly slow for my impatient nature but it was finished by early December.

The Government introduced the 'Care in the Community Act' to start from 01 April 1993. As the BBC television units had previously used me as a 'model', they again came to my flat to film me being hoisted from bed to wheelchair and other aspects of the care I received, for screening on the day of its inauguration. Later BBC Radio Bristol also used me for live phone-in programmes.

In July some friends took me to the International Air Tattoo at Fairford, Gloucestershire to see the display. During the Saturday afternoon two Russian aircraft brushed against each other at speed and crashed at the side of the 3047m long runway. Both pilots ejected safely and the incident was well captured on film for TV transmissions.

At the end of August Kim Cameron and John Barrett arranged a joint birthday party for me and James Cameron at Southmoor Road, Oxford. It was a sunny day and we enjoyed a picnic-style lunch in the garden, which led down to the river. It was one of those happy days that is hard to forget.

My two days a week at the BA office, then located at Pegasus House, Hounslow, were full of interest and enjoyment. The girls always seemed full of fun and helpful, not to mention collecting a pile of papers for me to sort and action at home. Martin Smith was involved in the Central Information System (CIS).

In February 1994 I was given the task of putting the BA Reservations Manual into the CIS pages. It was a lengthy job since it involved condensing almost 300 pages of text into a limited number of quick-to-access-and-easy-to-read instructions. Linda Wills, Product Presentation Executive, became my new Head Office contact. Natalie Smith, also a member of

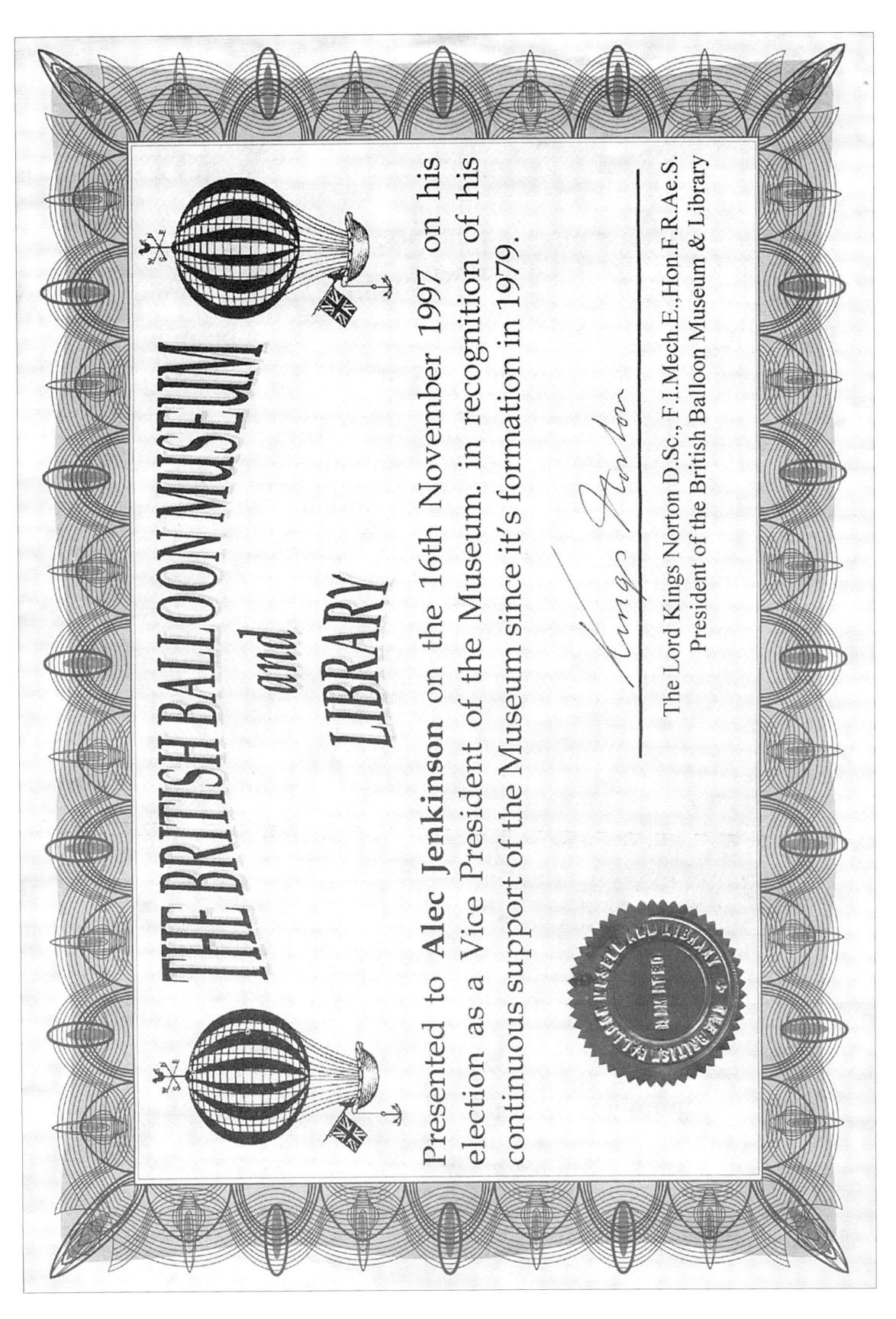

THE BRITISH BALLOON MUSEUM and LIBRARY

Presented to Alec Jenkinson on the 16th November 1997 on his election as a Vice President of the Museum. in recognition of his continuous support of the Museum since it's formation in 1979.

The Lord Kings Norton D.Sc., F.I.Mech.E., Hon.F.R.Ae.S.
President of the British Balloon Museum & Library

As a founder member of the British Balloon Museum and Library in 1979, I was elected a Vice President at a formal lunch in 1997.

the Distribution Support and CIS team, and I had frequent communications relating to new chapters.

Lourdes as a place of pilgrimage was open only in the six summer months due to the harsh winter weather in the French Alps. I travelled in early May on a British World Airways BAC 1-11 aircraft from Stansted. As on previous visits I had moments of great happiness and joy mixed with periods of sadness and frustration at being unable to do many things for myself. Most of my life I have been strongly independent, in fact probably stubbornly so, hence many of the most difficult times now are being reliant on others for even simple tasks.

Balloonist Pete Bish was part owner of a single engined private aircraft and with Roger Kunert flew to Oaksey Park airstrip near Malmesbury on 22 September. I had a 16 minute flight in G-BIAP around the area which was appreciated and enjoyed.

On 15 November I attended a presentation by IBM of the Personal Dictation Computer System. I was most impressed and after discussion with a computer-knowledgeable friend, Anthony Robinson, I decided to buy a package. For me there were many advantages in having a talk-to machine. Sometimes my fingers became stiff and the speed in typing was slower than my brain wanted. There was a five month waiting list for the software.

'Balloons & Airships' magazine of February 1995 carried a feature article by the editor listing many of my ballooning achievements. It was an accurate and well written story.

When the IBM package was installed on 23 May I was pleased although there were gremlins and some tedious commands which for me did not allow the speed of action I wanted. The back-up and 'help desk' did not fully satisfy my needs. Anthony suggested I look at another system coming on the market called 'Dragon Dictate'. To abbreviate the story I changed to the new software eight months later.

Gervase McCabe, a helper I met at Lourdes the previous year, had diligently gained an Instrument Rating to his private pilot's licence to fly a twin engined Navajo aircraft. On 27 July he invited me, another disabled person and four girls for a day trip to France. He hired aircraft G-ONAV to take us from Blackbushe, Hants to Deauville Airport, just south of the Seine near Le Havre. The idea was to visit and have lunch at the picturesque small port of Honfleur. There was a strong unstable northeasterly wind which gave us a 'bumpy' 70 minute flight southbound. This I enjoyed (although the others did not) and for me there was the added bonus of listening to the VHF radio wearing a head-set and holding a portable GPS (Global Positioning System) to follow the aircraft's progress. This was one of the more enjoyable flying day trips of my life.

'Brambles' was the name of an MS respite home near Crawley in Sussex. On 14 October I went for a seven day break from the routine at Malmesbury. The facilities were good and the staff were generally helpful. I enjoyed the opportunity of some excursions but the downside of my stay was seeing so many people in a less able condition than me.

During the year my mother flew from Edinburgh to Bristol for three visits. This included spending Christmas and New Year at Malmesbury. Apart from the inevitable shopping we enjoyed some adventurous pub meals.

Dragon Dictate, the voice activated computer system, was loaded on 14 January 1996. It was well worth the wait and cost. With a colour printer and twin speakers I was now capable of doing almost anything. Some computer-minded friends visited and were fascinated at its capabilities. A few games, especially airline related ones, were played frequently.

Despite the expected frustrations I again went on the May pilgrimage to Lourdes. My disabilities were now more evident and I relied on many willing carers even to feed me. Almost all tried their best to help but many lacked either experience or what to me seemed like common sense. It is an honour to be invited but I think there is more benefit gained from a visit every two or three years.

On a fine summer July afternoon most of the Dante Group members met at a pub near Newbury to celebrate the 25th anniversary of the founding of the Group. More than 20 long-term friends also joined the Saturday afternoon and evening celebrations. I was especially pleased to see Joe and Heather Phelp with their 8 month old son. Many nostalgic stories were told whilst enjoying a lavish barbecue. Five balloonists could not resist flying just before nightfall.

25th Anniversary of my first flight from the Newbury area was celebrated on 30 January 1997. As the original balloon field was no longer available the flight was made from the Folly Dog Leg site just north of the A4 near Hungerford. David Smith had a Cameron O-120 size balloon, registration G-HOTT, and we took off at 1105 to land 20 minutes later at Chilton Foliat. The flight was made in a strong cold unstable north easterly wind but the landing alongside some tall trees was almost perfect. Afterwards ten of us had a celebration lunch and drinks at a nearby pub. Another happy day for me.

At home I was not idle as BA often kept me very busy updating, or creating, parts of the computer system pages in CIS. Additionally I started to prepare the first draft of these memoirs using my Dragon Dictate machine. Rene Chong, a friend in Malmesbury who had made a wonderful recovery from a heart and lung transplant in January 1995, helped me unravel my diaries and notepads for these jottings.

Saturday 25 October was the pre-arranged date for a Bath balloon company with a wheelchair accessible basket to give me and 3 friends a flight from Malmesbury. The morning was perfect - no surface wind, no clouds, kilometres of visibility and a thick white frost. The balloon was a Cameron 0-120 registered G-BURN and the commercial pilot was Paul Spellward. We took off at 0920 and climbed gently to 1000 feet straight above the launch site which was the sheltered garden of Burton Hill School (for children with special needs).

Bath University students brought along their chequered BBC sponsored balloon to fly with us and for a while both balloons played a yo-yo game in the sky before we climbed to nearly 3000 feet. I was just as interested as my friends, Diane Payne, Ann Ryan and Natalie Smith, when we saw a fox being chased by an organised hunt. From the balloon basket the women laughed as the fox escaped in the opposite direction to the hounds.

As we prepared to land we met a shallow boundary layer of warm air above an uncultivated earth and scrubland field. This gave us the fastest forward speed of the flight at about 7 knots. Paul controlled this well with a few gentle bumps before a sapling ended our magnificent flight at 1040 near Easton Grey, a little more than 3 miles from the take-off field. The one hour twenty minute flight had just flown past! Two bottles of champagne arrived with the retrieve crew and we celebrated my friends' first balloon flight.

The British Balloon Museum and Library held its annual lunch at a Newbury hotel on 16 November 1997. I was one of four founder members who were honoured by being made a Vice-President.

On 11 June 1998 I was invited to Heathrow for a 90 minute session in a BA Boing 747 Flight Simulator and thoroughly enjoyed the occasion. The instructor demonstrated two landings and take-offs but avoided any extreme motion exercises in deference to my lack of balance. I would have preferred some 'rough and bumpy' experiences! Nevertheless it was a happy evening.

British Airways moved most of its key non-operational units to a £200 million centre named Waterside in the first six months of the year. I was keen to visit this radically innovative building created in a 240 acre parkland boasting the biggest new public park and nature reserve in the London area this century. On 15 October I went, I saw, I was amazed and marvelled especially with the system of 'hot desking'. How life had changed from the cubby-hole offices of my admin days 30 years ago. Briefly I was able to say 'hello' to some colleagues I had worked with in the 70's and 80's and to meet Alan Hughes, now Distribution Support Manager.

No Ford Fiesta lasts forever but my 13 year old model with just 54000 miles was beginning to rust. On 03 December I bought a Ford 'Chairman' to carry me in the wheelchair with more comfort and ease. Some friends dubbed it the 'Alecmobile'.

1999 started quietly for me, in fact very quietly. A carer had helped me to bed some two hours earlier. I am very fortunate in that many Home-Carers, mostly from Social Services, call at frequent intervals to help and assist me to lead a routine life in my own home. The whole package is not cheap but worth it to keep my independence. I am also most grateful to the District Nurses who call and attend to my medical needs.

Recently I was asked 'Can you think of anything that has not changed since your childhood?' After a lot of thought, the almost silly answer is 'Yes, on some rural roads today during repairs there is still a workman with a large circular Stop and Go sign'.

In the few months before Easter the media found some good news in tracking the balloons trying to circumnavigate the world. A surprising number of friends phoned and asked the question "Do you think they will make it?" When the Swiss registered balloon 'Breitling Orbiter 3' finally crossed the longitude finishing line over Africa it almost seemed anti-climatic. The dates were 01 March to 20 March, although the final landing was next day in the Egyptian desert. So when the FAI finally homologates (a lovely but 'official' word) the last of the ballooning 'firsts' for this century will have been achieved.

Few people have had such a hectic, satisfying and happy life as I have. From childhood through youth to the early flying days and then on to the overseas postings and travels with British Airways followed by the adventures in ballooning–it now all seems like a dream. Naturally there were short bursts of less satisfaction and in the latter years my illness has partly restricted my activities. I met many hundreds of kind and considerate people around the world and was so fortunate at having the opportunity of seeing so many places in 86 countries. These memoirs, I hope, reflect to some degree most of the highlights of a very contented life.

Looking almost like a model aircraft, this is Concorde G-BOAF in the new colour scheme seen in the autumn of 1998.

APPENDIX

Below is a list of aircraft registrations, by fleet, I flew in as an operating Flight Clerk:

PIONAIRS:
G-AGHJ / GHL / GHM / GHS / GIP / GIU / GJV / GJW / GJZ / GNK / GYX / GZB / GZC / GZD / HCV / HCZ / IWD / JIA / JIB / JIC / JDE / JHY / JHZ / KJH / KNB / LCC / LLI / LPN / LXK / LXL / LXM / LYF / MDZ / MFV / MGD / MJX / MJY / MKE.
Total: 1091 flights on 38 aircraft.

PIONAIR/LEOPARDS:
G-AGHP / HCU / HCX / LTT / LXN / MDB / MNV / MNW.
Total: 67 flights on 8 aircraft.

ELIZABETHANS:
G-ALZN / LZO / LZP / LZR / LZT / LZU / LZV / LZX / LZY / LZZ / MAA / MAC / MAD / MAG / MAH.
Total: 45 flights on 15 aircraft.

VISCOUNT 701:
G-ALWF / MNY / MNZ / MOA / MOB / MOC / MOD / MOE / MOF / MOG / MOH / MOI / MOJ / MOK / MOL / MON / MOO / MOP / NHA / NHB / NHC / NHD / NHE / NHF / OFX.

FRED OLSEN VISCOUNT 779D:
G- APZP
Total: 10 flights on 1 aircraft.

VISCOUNT 802:
G-AOJB / OJC / OJD / OJE / OJF / OHG / OHH / OHI / OHJ / OHK / OHL / OHM / OHN / OHO / OHR / OHS / OHT / OHU / OHV / OHW / ORD.
Total: 305 flights on 21 aircraft.

VISCOUNT 806:
G-AOYG / OYH / OYI / OYJ / OYK / OYL / OYM / OYN / OYO / OYP / OYR / OYS / OYT / PEX / PEY / PIM / PJU / PKF / POX.
Total: 189 flights on 19 aircraft.

VANGUARD V951 and V953:
G-APED / PEI.
Total: 4 flights on 2 aircraft.

GRAND TOTALS AS AN OPERATING FLIGHT CLERK
1916 flights on
129 different aircraft
totalling
2102 hours **10** minutes flying hours
carrying
54,873 passengers
with an estimated
331,800 flown miles.
(Excluded are training, positioning or extra crew flights.)

APPENDIX
EXTRACTS FROM MY LOGBOOK NO.1

EXTRACTS FROM MY LOGBOOK NO.1

EXTRACTS FROM MY LOGBOOK NO.1

EXTRACTS FROM MY LOGBOOK NO.1

EXTRACTS FROM MY LOGBOOK NO.1

EXTRACTS FROM MY LOGBOOK NO.1

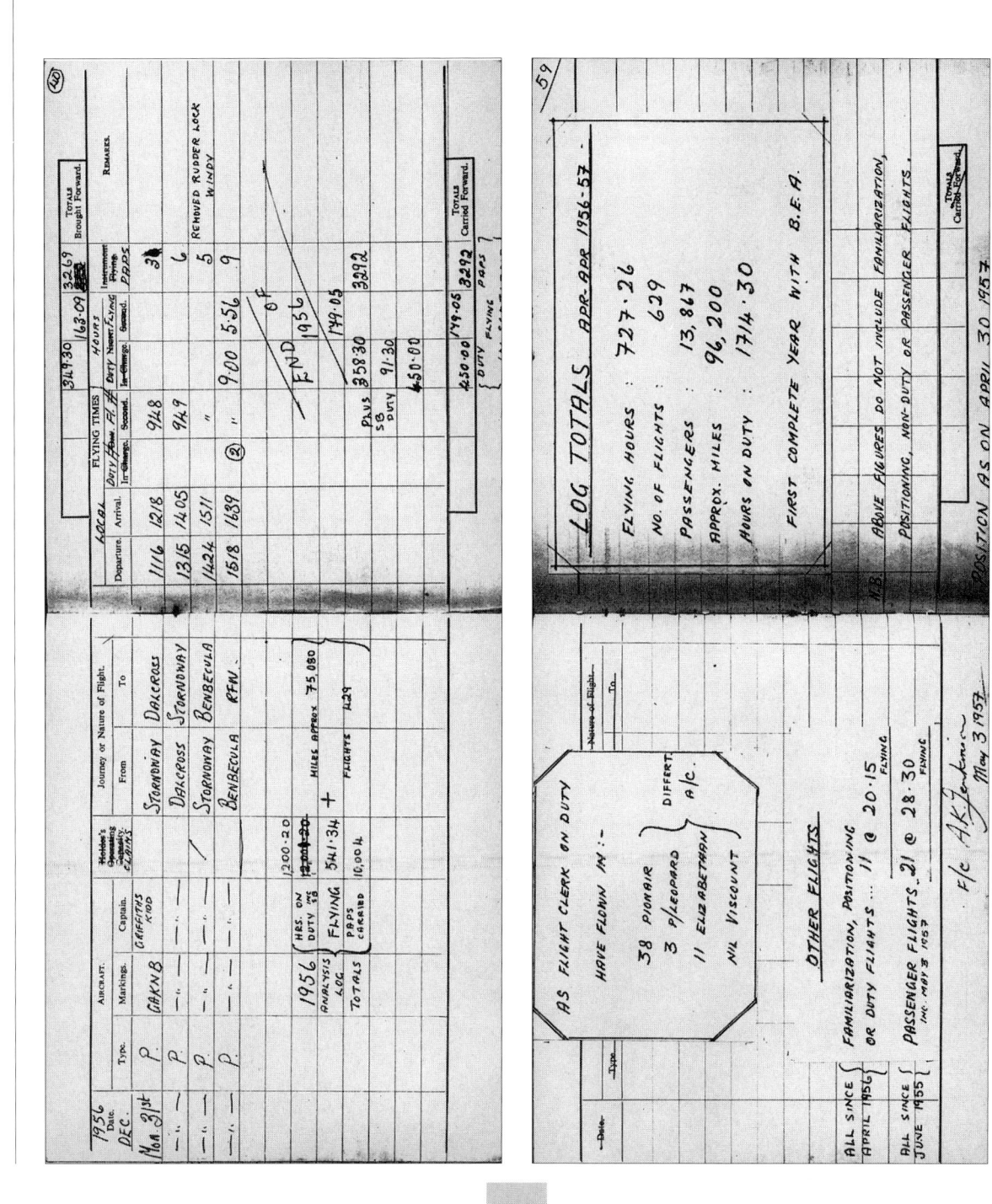

EXTRACTS FROM MY LOGBOOK NO.1

NEW START

1957 Date	Type	Aircraft Markings	Captain	Holder's Operating Capacity	Journey From	To	LOCAL Departure	Arrival	FLYING TIMES Dev F/ In-Charge	Second	DUTY Night/Flying In Charge	Second	Instrument Flying P8PS	REMARKS
MAY SAT 4	P	G.AMJY	REID EBMER		RFW	RFW	1801	1824	940				30	UNDERCARRIAGE FAILED TO RETRACT. RETURNED RFW
"	P	G.AHCZ	"	D	RFW	BFS	1849	1949	940				30	A/C CHANGE TO HCZ
"	P	"	"		BFS	RFW	2016	2118	941				26	
"	P	GAJIB	REID %MASON	INCID	RFW	ABERDEEN	2133	2245	986	6·30	3·37		8	W/E STOPOVER ABZ
SUN 5				INCID						7·30				
MON 6	P	GAJIB	REID %MASON		ABERDEEN	WICK	0923	1029	980				19	SNOW SHOWERS ABZ. STRONG N-NE WIND
"	P	"	"		WICK	KIRKWALL	1034	1100	"				16	
"	P	"	"		KIRKWALL	SHETLAND	1126	1214	952				24	
"	P	"	"	L	SHETLAND	KIRKWALL	1235	1319	953				21	INC. LINKLATER TO RFW
"	P	"	"		KIRKWALL	WICK	1401	1425	"				21	
"	P	"	"		WICK	DALCROSS	1434	1507	"				21	
"	P	"	"		DALCROSS	RFW	1539	1636	(28)	8·45	5·01		14	BUMPY TRIP
										22·45	8·38		230	

END OF RENFREW BASED FLIGHTS.

NEW CHECK FROM HERE

Totals Brought Forward: 83·15 35·51 926

Date MAY	Type	Aircraft Markings	Captain	Holder's Operating Capacity	Journey From	To	LOCAL Departure	Arrival	FLYING TIMES Dev F/ In-Charge	Second	DUTY Night/Flying In-Charge	Second	Instrument Flying P8PS	REMARKS
MON 27	P	GAZXK	McDOWELL CAPT. TAYLOR CAPT. SEVE		ORKNEY	ABERDEEN	1032	1131	981				6	SAW "BRITTANIA" + HON FLEET
"	P	"	"	INCID	ABERDEEN	SHETLAND	1259	1428	984				31	LOW FLYING OVER FAIR
"	P	"	"		SHETLAND	ABERDEEN	1522	1640	985	10·30	6·19		10	PADDLE OT SUMBURG
"	P	"	"		ABERDEEN	RENFREW	0816	0915	987				10	
TUES 28	P	"	"		RENFREW	CAMPBELTOWN	1037	1114	974				7	
"	P	"	"		CAMPBELTOWN	ISLAY	1120	1141	"				6	
"	P	"	"		ISLAY	CAMPBELTOWN	1202	1226	975		6·30	2·57	23	
"	P	"	"		CAMPBELTOWN	RENFREW	1233	1309	(13)				28	
THURS 30	P	GBKJH	JAMES %MASON		RENFREW	BELFAST	0834	0931	928				24	
"	P	"	"		BELFAST	RENFREW	1019	1133	929		4·30	2·11	31	END OF RENFREW
									(3)					
										104·45	47·18		1102	

Totals Carried Forward.

EXTRACTS FROM MY LOGBOOK NO.1

Page 6

Totals Brought Forward: 2324.00 | 80.31 | 1747

Date	Type	Aircraft Markings	Captain	Handler's Operating Capacity	From	To	Departure	Arrival	Flying Times Day F/F In-Charge / Second	Duty Never-Flying In-Charge / Second	Instrument Flying PRPS	Remarks
Mon 1 July 1957	V.701	GAMOF	McEnery	X	LAP	Birmingham	0618	0642	570		NIL	
" "	V.701	"	"		Birmingham	LAP	0748	0824	571	12.20 1.00	14	
Wed 3	P	GAKNB	L-White S/Lt Abbott		LAP	JSY	1123	1259	666		30	V-HOT DAY
" "	P	"	"	L	JSY	LAP	1404	1532	667	6.00 2.54	21	
Fri 5	P/Leopard	GALTT	Capt Brierley Capt Appleby	D	LAP	Guernsey	1721	1855	728		32	
Sat 6	ELIZ	GALZT	Thain McGoff McConkey	D	Guernsey	LAP	1926	2054	731	13.00 3.02	23	
" "	ELIZ	"	"	D	LAP	JSY	1631	1759	680		49	
" "	ELIZ	"	"	D	JSY	LAP	1845	2013	705		50	
" "	ELIZ	"	"	L/R	LAP	JSY	2139	2259	694		32	
Thurs 11	ELIZ	GALZV	McLanaghan Seymour McDowell	L/R	JSY	DINARD	0101	0217	699	12.30 5.32	42	DELAY ENTRY DUE W/K +2 SH PX's
" "	ELIZ	"	"		DINARD	JSY	1632	1919	680		17	DIVERTED WX JSY AFTER 4 ATTEMPTS
" "	ELIZ	"	"				2027	2054	"		17	4¼ h (COPE)

Totals Carried Forward: 275.50 | 92.59 | 2074

Page 7

Totals Brought Forward: | 275.50 | 92.59 | 2074

Date	Type	Aircraft Markings	Captain	Handler's Operating Capacity	From	To	Departure	Arrival	Flying Times Day F/F In-Charge / Second	Duty Never-Flying In-Charge / Second	Instrument Flying PRPS	Remarks
Thurs 11 July 1957	ELIZ	GALZV	McLanaghan Seymour	D	JSY	L.A.P.	2224	2328	683	14.00 4.29	42	
Fri 12	P	GAIWD	½ Cole ½ March		LAP	Isle of Man	1358	1601	562		9	
" "	P	"	"	D	Isle of Man	Manchester	1650	1756	063		32	DELAY MTR DUE IWD v/s.
" "	P	GAJIA	"	INCID	Manchester	Isle of Man	2018	2118	078	10.15 4.09	15	
Sat 13	P	"	"		Isle of Man	Liverpool	0757	0843	001		27	
" "	P	"	"	L/R	Liverpool	Isle of Man	0906	1004	004		32	
" "	P	"	"		Isle of Man	L.A.P.	1041	1226	555	18.00 3.29	28	INC. ONE BLIND GIRL
Sun 14	V.701	GAMNY	Lowden Capt Priest R/O Adams	L	L.A.P.	JSY	1224	1318	670		34	FIRST SCHEDULED VISCOUNT TO JERSEY.
" "	V.701	"	McTheer		JSY	LAP	1516	1629	671	9.00 2.07	46	
Wed 17	P/Leopard	GAHCV	Abbott ½ Double		LAP	JSY	1224	1258	666		24	
" "	P/Leopard	"	"	L	JSY	LAP	1414	1544	667		19	INC 2 SPCH1
" "	P/Leopard	"	"	D	LAP	JSY	1633	1814	680		28	CONT OVER

Totals Carried Forward: 519.05 | 107.13 | 2410

EXTRACTS FROM MY LOGBOOK NO.1

EXTRACTS FROM MY LOGBOOK NO.1

EXTRACTS FROM MY LOGBOOK NO.1

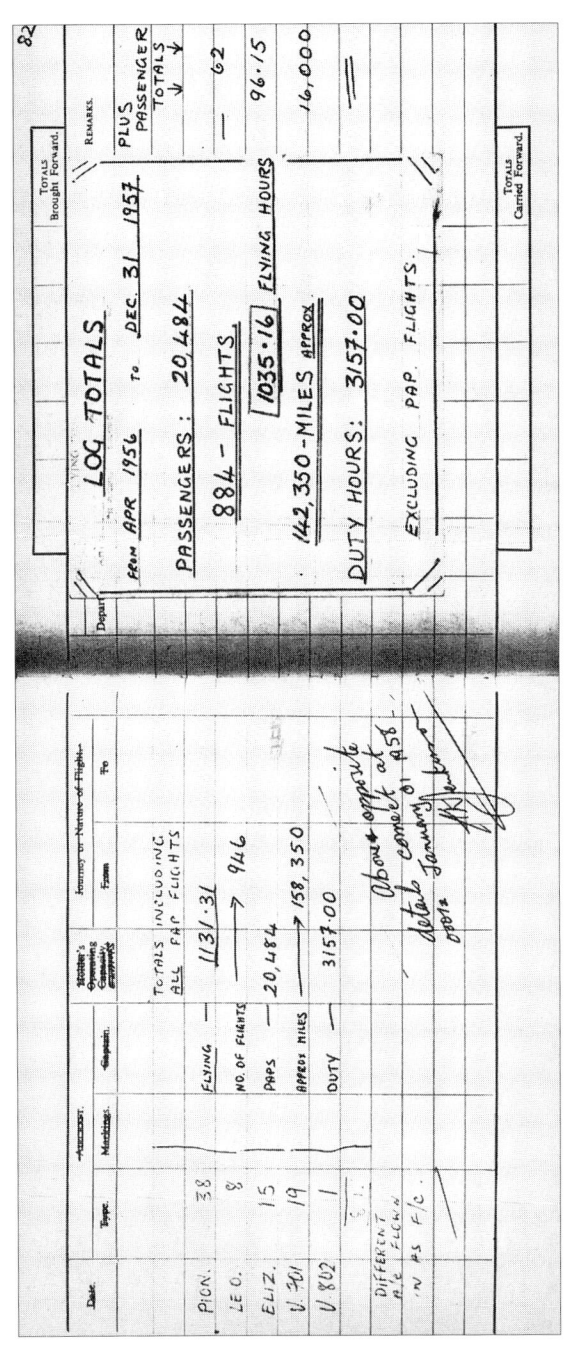

APPENDIX
EXTRACTS FROM MY LOGBOOK NO.2

EXTRACTS FROM MY LOGBOOK NO.2

EXTRACTS FROM MY LOGBOOK NO.2

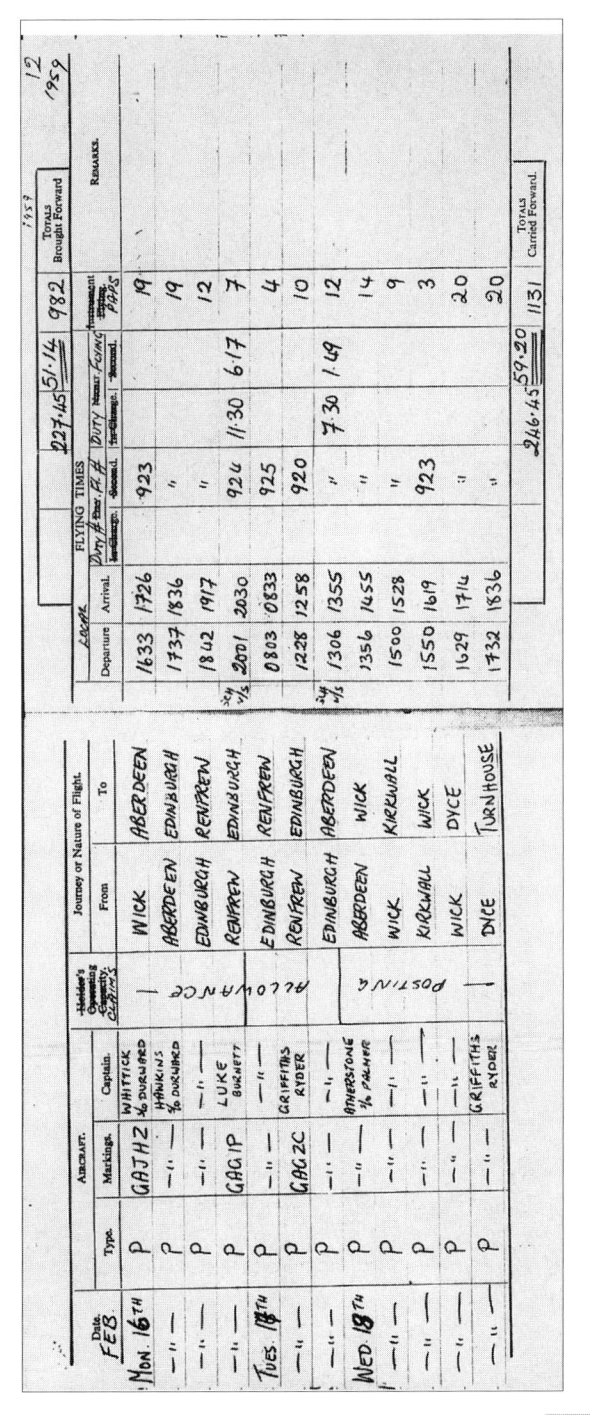

EXTRACTS FROM MY LOGBOOK NO.2

EXTRACTS FROM MY LOGBOOK NO.2

EXTRACTS FROM MY LOGBOOK NO.2

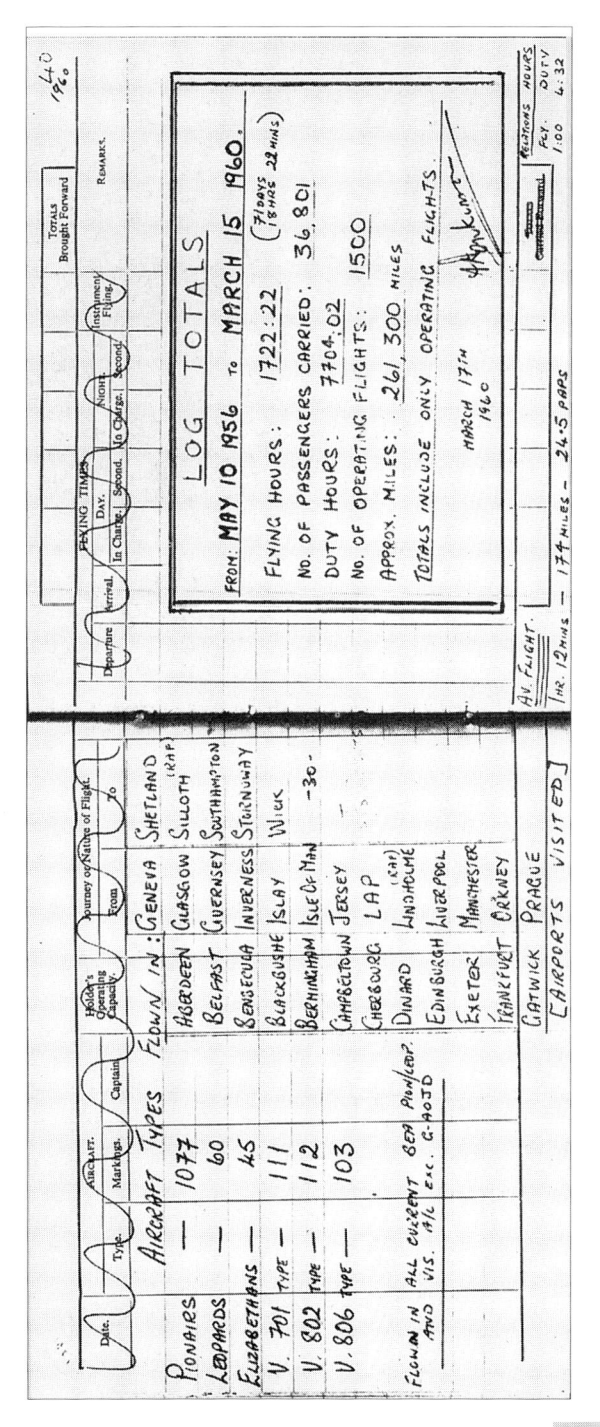

EXTRACTS FROM MY LOGBOOK NO.2

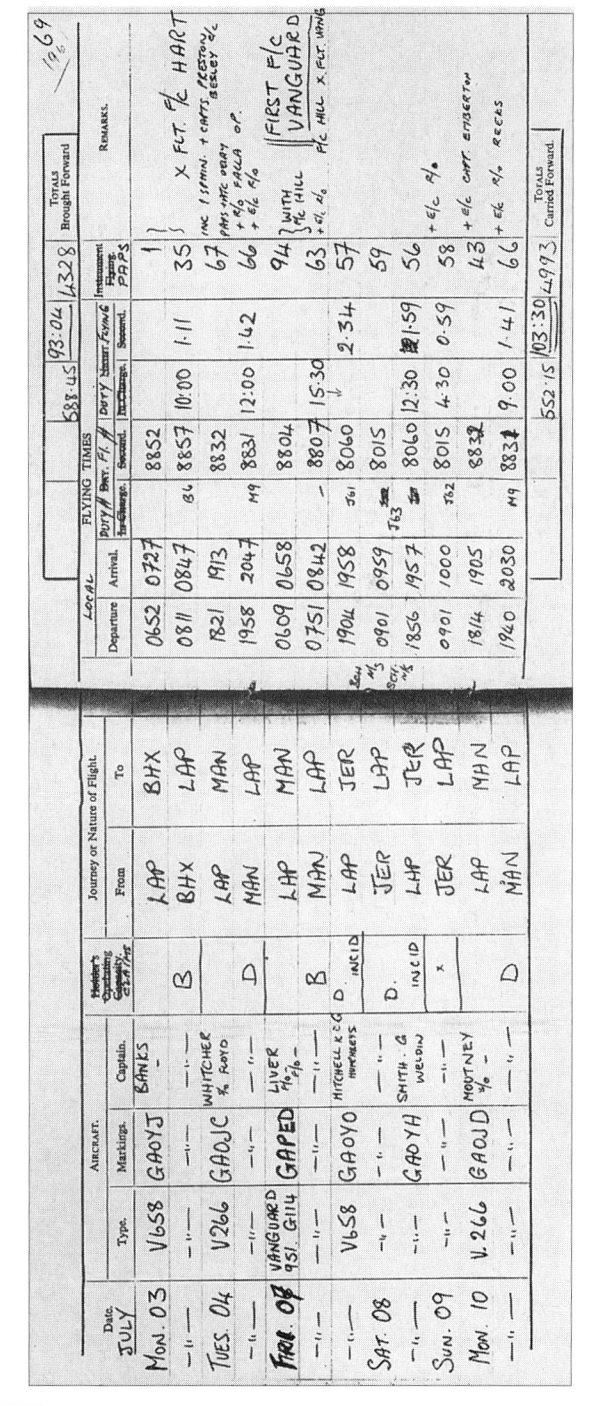

EXTRACTS FROM MY LOGBOOK NO.2

INDEX
BY CHAPTER

A
Abbotsinch Airport 9,10
Adams, Mike 15
Addis Ababa 19
Aer Lingus 6,10
Aero Peru 11
Aerolineas Argentinas 13,19
Aero Mexico 13
Aerostat 16,17,25
Agra 11
Air France 9
Air Malawi 19
Air Uganda 20
Airbus A320 (aircraft) 8
Aisla Craig 7
Akerstedt, Hans 22
Albuquerque 14,15,16
Alderney 8
Alexandria 19
Alitalia 11
Allen, Eddie 15
Allen, Larry 15
Allen, Mike 21
Alsina, Ernie 11
Alton Towers 14
American Airlines 17,20
American National Balloon Championships 15
Anchorage 11
Anderson, Peter 11
Appleyard, Hank 21
Aquitania 2
Arawak Airlines 11
Argosy Freighter (aircraft) 10
Arlanda International Airport 20
Arromanches 17
Ashton Court Park 19,21
Attwood, Neil 11

B
BABS 19,20,21,24
Baker, John 24
Baker, Peter 11,19,20
Balkedal, Janne 14,21
Balloons & Airships 25
Bareford, David 17,21
Barnes, Tracy 15
Barrett, John 25
Barrett, Roger 12,14,16
Bath 12
Battle Creek 21
Bayeux 17
BBAC (British Balloon and Airship Club) 13,14 16,17,20
BBAC Summer Balloon Meet 16

BCAL (B Cal) 12,13,17
BEACON 10
Bealine House 9
Beatrice 13,14
Belgrade 20
Benbecula 7
Bencze, Imre 20
Bermuda 2,13
Bird, John 17
Bish, Pete 13,15,24
Black and White Minstrel Show 2
Blackbushe Airport 8,25
BOADICEA 11
Boesman, Nina 22
Bouteloupt, Bob 22
Boxall, David 25
Bradford-on-Avon 24
Braniff Airlines 16,17
Bridges, Geoff 11,22
Bristol 19
Bristol Freighter (aircraft) 8
Bristol International Balloon Fiesta 19,21,23,25
British Balloon and Airship Club 13,14,16,17
British Balloon Museum and Library 21,22
British National Balloon Championships 19
Brother Tuttle, Cyril 18
Brown, Dick 16
BSAA 2
Buchner, Freddie 20
Buck, Marcus 11
Budapest 20,22
Buenos Aires 19
Burnham Beeches 19
Burgess, Brian 20
Burnell, Roger 12
Bustard, John 11
BWIA (British West Indian Airways) 14

C
CAA (Civil Aviation Authority) 13,17,20
Cabel, Harry 11
Cairngorms 10
Cairo Road 11
Calcutta 11
Camancho, Eric 16
Cameron Balloons 12,23
Cameron, Don 12,13,14,15,19,20,25
Cameron, Hannah 22
Cameron, James 22,25
Cameron, Kim 22,25
Campbell, Don 7
Campbeltown 7
Campion House 4
Canary Islands 10

Cancun 19
Cannandine, Brian 19
Cape Town 11,18
Captain Angus 10
Captain Baker 6
Captain Barker 8
Captain Barrow 12
Captain Brown 10
Captain Carter 10
Captain Childs, George 7
Captain Coleman 9
Captain Cunningham, 'Cats Eyes' 10
Captain Dunford 8
Captain Gray 9
Captain Greenhaugh 8
Captain Griffin 8
Captain Jack, David 10
Captain Joel 23
Captain Kirkland 8
Captain Law 9
Captain Liver 9
Captain Lowden 8
Captain McDowell 7
Captain Mitchell 9
Captain Morley, Eric 17
Captain Openshaw 8
Captain Owens 8
Captain Priest 8
Captain Sandison 8
Captain Scott 8
Captain Sledge 11
Captain Starling, Eric 7
Captain Swain 20
Captain Taylor 7
Captain Thom 9
Captain Ward, Paddy 11
Captain Watts 8
Caravelle (aircraft) 9,15
Cariacou 14
Castle Ashby 16
Castle Bourscheid 22
Castle Howard 17
Chambers, Nat 20
Channel Islands 8
Charing Cross Hospital 16,17
Chaston, Gwen 9
Chichicastanango 15
Chingola 11
Chisica 13
Chong, Rene 25
Christopher, John 25
Cirencester Balloon Meet 14,15
Cirencester Park 14,15,16

Cliquot, Veuve 15,16
Club World 8
Cobbold, Roland 13
Collier, Alan 22
Collier, John 14
Comair 11
Comet (aircraft) 8,9,10,11
Comstock, Bruce 17,21,24
Comstock, Tucker 21
Continental Airlines 15,16
Coombes, Karen 25
Copenhagen 20
Cork Harbour 2
Costa de Beauregard, Jean 22
Cote d'Azur 8
Cowley, Jack 15
Creedy, David 15
Crown Point Airport 11
Cruikshank, Tony 20
Culley, Ian 20,24
Cutter, Sid 14,16
Cuzco 17

D
D'Souza, Tony 11
Dakota (aircraft) 4,6,7,10,11
Dalcross 7
Dan-Air 21
Dante 12,13,14
Dante Balloon Group 12,13,14,17,18,19,25
Darnell, Ted 24
Daventry 8
Davis, Clive 23
DC3 (aircraft) 4,6,7,8,10,11
DC4 (aircraft) 2
De Marque, Noel 22
Deauville Airport 25
Delhi 4
Delta Airlines 15
Denver 10
Des Moines 15
Dinard 6
Donnelly, Tom 14
Dr Perkin, G.D. 17,22
Dulles Airport 10,17
Dunfermline 14
Dunfermline Hospital 3,4
Dunlop Street 3
Dunnington, Phil 12,14,15
Duntisbourne Abbotts 14

E
Eagan, John 22
East African Airways 11,13
Eastern Airlines 12,19
Edinburgh 8
Editor Cheeseman 8
Eeva 10
Ehrler, Chuck 15
Eldorado Airport 13

Elizabethan (aircraft) 5,6
Entebbe Airport 11,13
Ethiopian Airlines 11
European Balloon Championships 22

F
FAI 22
Fair Isle 7
Fareham 4,10
Farnfield, Anthony 11
Father Hollings, Michael 17
Father McPherson, Donald 2
Father Murphy-O'Connor, Patrick 4
Father Tigar, Clement 4
Fayre Road 10
Fidani, Jaques 22
Fieldhouse, Peter 22
Finnair 10
First Officer Hind 6
First Officer Laver 8
First Women Pilots Balloon Meet 16
Fisher, Paul 20
Flamingo Lake 11
Flight Manager Greenhalgh 8
Flight Manager McLannahan 8
Flight Manager Preston 8
Floden, Dennis 14
Folies Bergere 4
Forbes, Malcolm 17
Formby 16
French Balloon Meet 15

G
Gabra, Adib 18,19
Gatwick Airport 8
Geddes, Bob 11
George, Bill 15
Georgetown 11
Gillespie, Ian 13,17
Glasgow 8
Gloster Airship Society 16
Godfrey, Tim 23
Gordon 1,2,3
Gourock 3
Grandmother 3,10,11,12,13,14,16
Great Shefford 25
Green, Geoff 13
Green, John 14,18,23
Greenock 1
Grimmond, Joe 7
Grubb, Shirley 23
Guadeloupe 23
Guatemala City 15
Guernsey 4
Guyana 14

H
Hadeed, Myrna 11
Halifax 2
Hall, Celia 20
Hall, Dr Teddy 14

Hamilton 2
Hanby, Ross 16
Hanlon, John 18
Hannover 21
Hannu 10
Harper, Roger 22
Harris, Jonathan 24,25
Harrison, Dave 11
Hart, Kay 8
Harte, Peter 10
Hatton, Kevin 19,20
Hayes, Olive 13
Hebrides 7
Heineken International Balloon Meeting 13
Helsinki 10,17
Hervieu, John 8,22
Hibbert, Stuart 1
Hill, Maurice 9
Hillman, Alan 11
Hines, Terry 22
Hoare, Rod 11
Hockley, Bernard 16
Hodd, Peter 11
Holton, Geoff 15
Honfleur 25
Horder, Peter 23
Hornfeck, Pete 19
Horrack, Larry 14
Hughes, Alan 25
Hughes, Graham 10,11
Humphries, Graham 18
Hutchins, Phil 22
Hyde Park 4
Hyland, Martin 15

I
Iberia Airlines 10
ICAO (International Civil Aviation Organisation) 6
Icicle Meet 14,15,16,17,18,19,20,21,23,24
Indian Airlines 11
Indianola 15
Inetrnational Air Tattoo, Fairford 14,15,16
International Albuquerque Balloon Fiesta 14,15,16
Isak, Michael 20
Iserlohn 14
Isle of Arran 1,7

J
Jones, Jean 18
Joseph, Leslie 11
Juarez, John 20

K
Kaieteur Waterfall 11
Kalamazoo 24
Kariba Dam 11
Kasterlee 14
Kathmandu 11
Kelly, Tim 16

Kemble Airfield 14
Kenya Airways 11
Kew Gardens 17
Khartoum 18
Kilmorie 1,10
Kindley Field 2
King, Len 23
Kingdom of Libya Airlines 11
Kirk, John 18
Kunert, Roger 25
Kutas, Jim 18,22

L
Lagos 11
Lake Ontario 14
Lan Chile Airlines 19
Lang, Andrew 16
Langford, Peter 13,14
Lawrence, Kathy 14
Le Bourget 9
Le Feuvre, Gerry 6
Le Geyt, Reggie 10
Leeward Island Air Transport (LIAT) 11,14
Levin, David 24
Lewis, Roy 6
Lewis-Smith, Anne 16,20,24
Lewis-Smith, Peter 21
Leys, Vincent 24
Liddiard, David 13,17,18,19,20,24
Liddiard, James 13,20,25
Liddiard, Jo 20,24
Liddiard, Richard 13
Lilongwe 19
Linden Hall Hydro Hotel 4
Linkenholt 13
Linz, Dietrich 20,21
Lisbon 10
Liverpool 8
Livingstone (Zambia) 11
Lloyd, Andrew 15
Lochboisdale 7
Lome 11
Lord Bathurst 14
Los Rodeos Airport 10
Lourdes 20,25
Lovell, Gary 23
Lubbe, Ken 11
Lubumbashi 11
Lufthansa 20
Lusaka 11
Lusby, Sandra 17

M
MacGaul, Keith 14
MacGilvray, Gerry 11
Machrihanish 7
Machupicchu 17
MacRae, Ian 17
Malmesbury 23,24
Mangrove Bay 2

Markham 14
Marsh Benham 13,19,20
Maso, Jack 19
Mason, Stan 23
May, Chris 23
MCA (Ministry of Civil Aviation) 10
McCabe, Gervase 25
McDonald, Mike 14,19
McGuire, Mike 11
McKewan, Dave 11
McKie, Willie 13,20
Meehan, Kevin 13
Melborne, Maria 25
Mexicana Airlines 19
Millward, Anthony 8
Montbard 15
Monte Carlo 8
Moscow 8,21
Mount Everest 11
Muir, Dick 18
Mulaney, Eamonn 23
Mull of Kintyre 7
Mumbai 11
Munson, Dave 13,14,23
Munster 13
Murcott 21
Murtoff, Bill 15
My father 1,2,3,6
My mother 1,3,9,10,11,16,18,25

N
Nairobi 11,16,18
Nassau 15,16
Navarro, Carlos 13
Ndola 11,17
New Delhi 11
New York 11
Newbury 13
Newcastle Emlyn 16
Niagra Falls 14
Nice 8
Nicola 10,15
Nicosia Airport 8
Noirclerc, Robbie 15
Nuneham Park 23
Nutts Corner 7

O
O'Connor, Paddy 8
O'Toole, Laurie 18,21
Ocho Rios 19
Ogilvie, Andy 11
Orkney Islands 7
Orrel 11
Osterley 4
Outer Hebrides 7
Oxford 8

P
Paisley 7
PanAm 15

Panama City 15,20
Paris Air Show 9
Patuxent Air Base 10
Paul Tissandier Diploma 23
Payne, Diane 21,22
Pearls Airport 14
Phelp, Joe 13,25
Philadelphia 10,19
Piarco 11
Pickering, Jenny 11
Pionair (aircraft) 5,6,7,8,9,25
Pleece, George 18,23
Port of Spain 11
Potsa, Charlie 20
Prague 22
Preece, Chris 11,21
Prestwick 7,11
Pretoria 18
Priest, Jane 9
Prinair 16
Prince Andrew 22
Pritchard, Norman 15
PSNC (Pacific Steam Navigation Company) 13
Puerto Rico 14

Q
Qantas 11

R
Ramos, Eduardo 13
Ramshaw, Mike 11
Rand City Airport 11
Rapide (aircraft) 8
Raven Balloons 16
Raymond, Clive 23
Reading 19
Recife 19
Redhead, Celia 13,18
Reims 15
Renfrew Airport 6,7
Reykjavik 12
Rhoades, Martin 20
Rio de Janeiro 19
River Clyde 7
Robertson, Neil 17,18
Robertson, Stuart 18
Robinson, Anthony 25
Rocky Mountains 10
Root, Alan 13
Roseau 14
Rosyth 3,4,16,23
Rotorura 18
Royal Aero Club 22
Royal Nepal Airlines 11
Rugby 13
Ruislip 5
Rutherford, Linda 16
Rutherford, Tom 16
Ryan Air 25
Ryan, Ann 25

Ryan, Laurie 13

S
Sabrata 11
Sadler, James 11,23
Saftarjong Airport 11
Salisbury, Rhodesia 11
Salt Lake City 10
Saltus Grammer School 2
San Francisco 10
San Jose 15
San Juan 17
San Remo 8
Santiago 19
Santo Domingo 17
Sao Paulo 19
Sargeant, Peter 18
Saunders, David 25
Savernake Forest 16,25
Scaur Lodge 2
Schade, Monika 13,21
Scot's Poor 25
Scottish Highlands 6
Second Officer Moore 7
Seiger, Arno 13
Sekki 17
Shand, Tina 15
Shannon 10
Shaw, Justin 25
Sheppard, Tom 24
Shetlands 7
Silloth Airfield 8
Simmonds, Kenneth 14
Singapore 11
Sloper, David 17,20
Smith, Angela 16,23,24
Smith, Anthony 16,23,24
Smith, Clare 16
Smith, David 21
Smith, Martin 25
Smith, Natalie 25
Smith, Phillip 24
Smithhills Street 7
Snook, Allan 14
South African Airways (SAA) 11,18
Southampton 18
Southsea Pier 1
Southport Hospital 3,16
Spaeth, Debbie 24
Sparks, Mike 15
Speakers Corner 4
Spellward, Paul 25
Spencer, Pete 11
St Brelades Bay Hotel 4
St Lo 17
St. Helier 6
St. Kilda 7
St. Lucia 11,13,17
St. Ouen's Bay 8
St. Peter Port 6
Stafford, Tim 14
Staines 12
Stanford Hall Meet 13,17
Stansted Airport 25
Starkbaum, Joe 14
Stavanger 23
Stellenbosch 11
Stoors, Pierre 22
Stornoway 7
Stott, Norman 8
Stratfield Saye 13
Sudeley Castle 19
Suez Canal 11
Sumburgh Airport 7
Swissair 11

T
Table Mountain 11
Taj Mahal 11
Tasker, Nigel 13
Tegel Airport 20,23
Tempelhof Airport 20
Tenerife 10
Thai Airways 11
Thatcham 11
Thibo, Pit 22
Thompson, Garland 18
Thompsons Falls 11
Thorne, Mike 18,19
Thorne, Vic 19
Thorpe, Hazel 8
Thunder Balloons 14,18
Tiree 7
Torremolinos 9
Tortola 14
Trans Texas International Airlines 15
Trident (aircraft) 10,11,14,15,16
Trinidad and Tobago 11
Tripoli 11
Tristani, J.P. 10,14
Tristani, Reggie 14
Troy, Denis 4
Truffi, Victorio 19
Tulum 19
Tunis 13
Turnbull, Andrew 25
Turnbull, Gerry 20,24
Turner, Ian 7

U
Uganda 13
Ungermark, Seve 16
United Airlines 10,15
Upper Bucklebury 13

V
Van de Velde, Francis 5
Van Zyl, Tertius 11,18
Vanguard (aircraft) 9
Victoria Air Terminal 9,15
Victoria Falls 11
Vigie Airport 13
Viking (aircraft) 5
Viking Centre 5
Virgo, Ken 21
Viscount (aircraft) 5,6,7,8,10,25
Voortrekker Monument 18

W
Ward, John 18
Warsaw 21
Washington 10,17,21
Watford 10,11
Watkins, David 14
Webb, Beth 11
Webb, John 11
Welek, Peter 13,18
Welkom (Orange Free State) 11
Western Airlines 15
Western Balloons 14
Westonburt 25
Westwood, Mark 13
Weymouth 4
Whiting, Gill 8
Wick 7
Wickins, Mike 23
Wigan 3
Wilkinson, John 25
Williams, Crispin 11
Williams, Dave 11
Wills, Linda 25
Windsor 9,17
Wingham, Harold 15
Wirth, Dick 14,15,21,22
Woburn Balloon Meet 20
Woessner, Paul 17
Wolstenholme, Colin 25
Wood, Joan 10
Wood, John 10,23
Woof, Roger 22
Woolaton Park 19
Woosnam, Max 15
World Gas Balloon Championships 20
World Hot Air Balloon Championships 14,16,17
Wothe, Eugene 14

Y
Yateley 19
York 17
Yost, Ed 14,17

Z
Zagreb 18,20
Zambia Airways 11,17
Zeebrugge 13,14
Zurich 8,11